THE INDUSTRIAL REVOLUTION IN COMPARATIVE PERSPECTIVE

Edited by

Christine Rider
and
Mícheál Thompson

KRIEGER PUBLISHING COMPANY
MALABAR, FLORIDA
2000

Original Edition 2000

Printed and Published by
KRIEGER PUBLISHING COMPANY
KRIEGER DRIVE
MALABAR, FLORIDA 32950

Copyright © 2000 by Christine Rider and Mícheál Thompson

All rights reserved. No part of this book may be reproduced in any form or by any means, electronic or mechanical, including information storage and retrieval systems without permission in writing from the publisher.
No liability is assumed with respect to the use of the information contained herein.
Printed in the United States of America.

FROM A DECLARATION OF PRINCIPLES JOINTLY ADOPTED BY A COMMITTEE OF THE AMERICAN BAR ASSOCIATION AND A COMMITTEE OF PUBLISHERS:

This publication is designed to provide accurate and authoritative information in regard to the subject matter covered. It is sold with the understanding that the publisher is not engaged in rendering legal, accounting, or other professional service. If legal advice or other expert assistance is required, the services of a competent professional person should be sought.

Library of Congress Cataloging-In-Publication Data

The industrial revolution in comparative perspective / edited by
  Christine Rider and Mícheál Thompson.
    p. cm. —(Open forum series)
  Includes bibliographical references and index.
  ISBN 0-89464-990-6 (pbk. : alk. paper)
  1. Industrial revolution. 2. Economic history. I. Rider,
Christine. II. Thompson, Mícheál J., 1953- . III. Series.
HC51.I553 2000
330.9′034—dc21   99-15418
                                                  CIP

10 9 8 7 6 5 4 3 2

CONTENTS

Editors' Preface v
Acknowledgments vii
About the Contributors ix

Introduction 1

Part I: Preconditions 13

Chapter 1. Literacy and Industrialization in Modern Germany 17
John E. Murray

Chapter 2. "Populationism" and the Social Policy of Austrian Absolutism in the Eighteenth Century 33
Philip Pajakowski

Chapter 3. Preparing for the Industrial Revolution: Sociocultural Changes and the Formation of "Britain" 49
Mícheál Thompson

Chapter 4. No Longer an Island: Exploring the Significance of Atlantic Trade to the Industrial Revolution 69
Robert T. Schultz

Part II: Processes 85

Chapter 5. Science, Technology, and the Industrial Revolution 89
Paul Lucier

Chapter 6. The Contribution of Technological Diffusion Patterns to British Economic Growth, 1750–1850 109
Harry Kitsikopoulos

Chapter 7.	Tradition and Modernization: State, Society, and the Development of Industry in Eighteenth-Century Russia *Gennady Shkliarevsky*	129
Chapter 8.	Beyond the "National Consensus": Recent Research on the Origins and Trajectory of Germany's Industrial Revolution *George S. Vascik*	147

Part III: Consequences   **161**

Chapter 9.	The Standard of Living of English and French Workers, 1750–1850 *Casey Harison*	165
Chapter 10.	The Debate on the Condition of the Working Class in France circa 1840: A Study in Ideology *James B. Briscoe*	179
Chapter 11.	Technological Change, Unemployment, and the Late Industrializing Countries: The Example of Japan *Christine Rider*	203

Part IV: Conclusion   **229**

Chapter 12.	The Industrial Revolution in Comparative Perspective *John Komlos*	233

Bibliography   249
Index   265

EDITORS' PREFACE

In the summer of 1995, a dozen scholars representing twelve different orientations in economics and history arrived in Munich, Germany, to begin a process of discovery that ultimately gave birth to this book. All of them had responded to the call for applicants for a National Endowment for the Humanities (NEH) summer seminar on the Industrial Revolution, organized and capably directed by John Komlos, the noted anthropometrician at the University of Munich. After a competitive selection process, these twelve were finally accepted, made their travel plans, and embarked on two months of intensive study of one of the most significant socioeconomic processes in the history of modern civilization.

Strangers to each other at first, by the end of their stay they had shared their views and ideas on the developments known as the Industrial Revolution (IR), and learned much from each other. Each contributed a different insight on a particular aspect of the IR; these insights complemented one another. The result is this book, made up of a set of distinctive yet complementary chapters that were the products of this seminar, and which describe different aspects of the Industrial Revolution in comparative perspective. It is comparative, not only because the experiences of more than one country and one continent are included, but also because of the time frame, which spans several centuries to the present day.

The papers divided into three logical categories. The first grouping, **Preconditions**, focuses on issues which are traditionally considered as contributions to the start or the speed of the IR in any particular country. These four chapters look at the connections between literacy and industrialization, social policies (which could only have been introduced by *national* governments), the importance of trade and colonization for putting European industrialization into an international context, and the process of creating a single "nation," which was a precondition for the creation of a nation-state and modern political developments. In the seventeenth and eighteenth centuries, the role of the state was actively discussed, and very often, of crucial importance in encouraging the activity that in some way, encouraged the jump to a higher growth path.

The second section, **Processes**, examines activities and events which were concurrent with, or part of, the IR. These chapters investigate the role of technological diffusion, the dissemination of scientific and technological knowledge in Britain, the leading role of the state in early Russian industrialization, and the differences and similarities between Germany's industrialization and that of other countries. For example, the IR is often defined only in terms of the adoption of new technologies, but it is also important to consider exactly how new technologies were accepted, and how the spread of scientific knowledge took place; again, this consideration has implications for modern societies, even though many of the mechanisms are different today.

The third section, **Consequences**, covers issues that are often thought to be initiated by the structural changes associated with industrialization, especially the impact on ordinary people and their standard of living. One chapter here also shifts focus from Europe (and its colonies) to consider the case of Japan, the first Asian country to industrialize.

Finally, John Komlos provides a concluding chapter which gives a fitting, thoughtful summary of the Industrial Revolution in comparative perspective.

ACKNOWLEDGMENTS

One of the most rewarding tasks for anyone writing or compiling a book is to thank all those who have helped to bring the book to publication. Our most heartfelt thanks go, first and foremost, to the National Endowment for the Humanities, whose far-sighted program to make funding available to college teachers to attend research seminars made this particular seminar with this particular group of scholars possible. It is true to say that without the NEH, this book would not have existed. We also thank John Komlos, who initially worked with NEH to organize the seminar, who established the framework for our research, and whose expertise in economic history combined with his graciousness as a host made our summer in Munich such a productive one. Many thanks also to his staff who worked tirelessly to make the seminar a success, and who definitely eased the process of living in Munich.

We also greatly appreciate the efforts of Cathy Rizzo, who was responsible for typing most of the draft manuscripts into the computer, and Zavi Baynes, who shared in typing many of the revisions. We thank Reza Eftekharzadeh and Farough Vakil who assisted with the graphs. We thank Gordon Patterson and Krieger Publishing for their assistance with all the editorial phases of the book's production, with special thanks to Elaine Rudd.

Last but definitely not least, the editors have their own thank yous to make. We are grateful to the authors for making our task that much easier; this book is a truly cooperative effort. Christine Rider is, as always, thankful for the support and encouragement of Gary Mongiovi. Mícheál Thompson thanks Heide Thompson who supported him in going to Munich—and encouraged him to come back! Thanks also to Gerti Bartke whose advice and strength were only a phone call away; and Frau Kniha who welcomed Mícheál into her home and to Munich. *Diolch yn fawr!*

Christine Rider
St. John's University
Mícheál Thompson
Miyazaki International University

ABOUT THE CONTRIBUTORS

James B. Briscoe is program head of computer studies at the University of Maryland, European Division, and is currently teaching history and computer science in England, France and Germany. He received his Ph.D. from Columbia University. His research interests focus on the Saint Simonian movement.

Casey Harison is assistant professor of history at the University of Southern Indiana, Evansville, Indiana. He received his Ph.D. from the University of Iowa. His particular interest is nineteenth-century French social and working class history.

Harry Kitsikopoulos is clinical professor of economics at New York University, New York. He received his Ph.D. from the New School for Social Research. His research covers the diffusion of agrarian and industrial technologies from the late feudal period until the Industrial Revolution.

John Komlos is professor of economics and chair of economic history at the University of Munich. He received his Ph.D. from the University of Chicago. His main interests are the conceptualization of the Industrial Revolution, and the study of the relationship between nutrition and modern economic growth, particularly by using anthropometric indicators of the biological standard of living, and he has published extensively in these areas.

Paul Lucier is visiting assistant professor of Science and Technology Studies at Rensselaer Polytechnic University, Troy, New York. He received his Ph.D. from Princeton University. As well as his research into the history of technology, he is also interested in the history of medicine.

John E. Murray is assistant professor of economics at the University of Toledo, Ohio. He received his Ph.D. in economics from Ohio State University. His research on Shaker communal societies has appeared in *Explorations in Economic History, Bulletin of the History of Medicine,* and *Journal of Interdisciplinary History;* he is also researching historical anthropometric studies of America and Germany.

Philip Pajakowski is associate professor and chair of the Department of History at Saint Anselm College, Manchester, New Hampshire. He received a Ph.D. from the University of Pennsylvania. His primary interest is in the political, social and cultural history of the Habsburg Empire in the eighteenth and nineteenth centuries, with special emphasis on issues of social conflict and state authority.

Christine Rider is professor of economics in the College of Business Administration, St. John's University, New York. Her first degree is from the London School of Economics, and her Ph.D. was received from the New School for Social Research. Her areas of research include economic history, the post-communist economies in transition, and social policy issues. She is the author of *An Introduction to Economic History* (Southwestern, 1995) and editor of *Socialist Economies in Transition: Appraisals of the Market Mechanism* (Elgar, 1992).

Robert T. Schultz is assistant professor of history at Illinois Wesleyan University, Bloomington, Illinois. He holds a Ph.D. in history from the University of Minnesota. His research interests cover various topics in labor history, cultural history and class issues in American films, and he has published articles in these areas.

Gennady Shkliarevsky is associate professor of Russian history at Bard College, Annandale-on-Hudson, New York. He received his Ph.D. from the University of Virginia. He has published in *Journal of International Studies in Management and Organization, Russian History/Histoire Russe, Journal of Modern History,* and is the author of "Labor in the Russian Revolution: Factory Committees and Trade Unions 1917–1918." His current research is on Russian working-class writers.

Mícheál Thompson is a faculty member in the Humanities Department at Miyazaki International College, Japan. He holds various graduate degrees, including a Ph.D. in history from Carnegie-Mellon University. He is the author of several articles on history, education, and culture, and is also the editor of *Welsh Studies* (University of Rio Grande, 1996).

George S. Vascik is assistant professor of history at Miami University, Oxford, Ohio. He holds a Ph.D. from the University of Michigan. He has written broadly on the political economy of the German countryside in the Imperial era, and is currently completing a biography of the agrarian politician, Diederich Hahn.

INTRODUCTION

The changes that occurred in regional and national economies, and in the global economy as a whole, during the period called the "Industrial Revolution" (traditionally dated as beginning in the middle of the eighteenth century) were profound, perhaps more profound than any which had taken place before. Although many economic historians, especially those who were among the first to look at this period as a time when something unique and revolutionary occurred, focus on the economic changes, change in reality involved the complete range of cultural, political and social life. Later economic historians viewed these changes as less revolutionary, and pointed out that there had been many such periods of expansion in the past.

But these other periods of expansion eventually came to an end. This is what makes the Industrial Revolution of such continuing interest to historians of all stripes. The entire international economy is irrevocably different today as a result of these changes; the period of long-term, secular expansion did not reverse itself, and the Malthusian ceiling was broken through. In other words, what prevented previous periods of expansion from continuing was that population growth came up against the constraint of limited resources; the Industrial Revolution made it possible for human societies to overcome these constraints. Once material limits were overcome, changes in other areas of life could be imagined: human societies were no longer limited to what had always been done in the past.

Perhaps it is easier to think of the Industrial Revolution as being composed of a large number of smaller events dispersed widely over time and over many regions—and which in fact are still going on today. The "Industrial Revolution" is then a composite term used to reflect the efforts of historians to make sense of this diversity by highlighting the features and achievements which events in different countries and at different times have in common, and which also separate them. There is no consensus among historians about what happened, when, how, and why. The very diversity of the historical record encourages debate among economic historians in particular and all historians in general about how to interpret the Industrial Revolution, what features were indispensable to it, what its significance was (and still is), and—for some at least—whether calling it the Industrial *Revolution* conveys a meaning which subsequent research has proved to be inaccurate.

The contributions to this collection examine various aspects of what is called the Industrial Revolution. The purpose of this collection is not to resolve the question of whether it was *revolutionary* or *evolutionary;* whether the Eurocentric bias of the first generation of historians of the IR was justified; or any of the other issues that have occupied the pages of academic journals and books. Rather we attempt to present a combination of country-specific discussions and more synthetic articles, designed to allow the reader not only to appreciate the various interests of the contributors (whose varied backgrounds and research interests give an eclectic flavor to this collection), but also to begin to form their own opinions on the central questions raised in any analysis of the Industrial Revolution. It is probably true that the Industrial Revolution represents the major historical watershed out of which the modern world emerged. Its "evolutionary" or "revolutionary," universal or specific nature, are what is open to debate and discussion among historians. What is less open to debate is the reality that the modern global economy and polity would not exist in anything like its current form without the developments of the past two hundred years; the Industrial Revolution is in some measure a key to understanding not only the immediate past, but also the present and the future. We hope that the views presented here will make a contribution to the discussion.

What is unarguably the central debate among historians about the Industrial Revolution is whether it was actually *revolutionary* at all. This is not a debate merely about words. Few would doubt that the world (or at least the western world) was *not* markedly different by the end of the Industrial Revolution as compared to its beginning. Key changes centered around the pattern of economic and social relations throughout society, and in each society considered individually. The differences, for good or ill, were dramatic and few areas remained untouched. These changes were sufficiently rapid to be noticed very generally; the lives (and lifestyles) of grandchildren were markedly different from those of their living grandparents. The effects of the Industrial Revolution were then sensed as being revolutionary, giving birth to a whole new range of opportunities and of dissatisfactions, and to the virtual birth of nostalgia for something lost, a sentiment which rarely, if ever, had affected individuals in the past. *The fact of change, and the pace of change were tangible and thus the revolutionary consequences of the Industrial Revolution were abundantly clear.* The expectation of change and innovation, and of continued improvement from one generation to another in terms of living conditions and economic well-being is an abiding legacy of the Industrial Revolution.

Even the most revisionist historian does not question this interpretation of the Industrial Revolution as being "revolutionary." What is questioned is the idea that the underlying "forces of growth" which provided the engine of growth in the Industrial Revolution were somehow new. What makes the Industrial Revolution unique for these historians is that a combination of economic and historical circumstances allowed what had always been preexisting forces to come together in ways that had not been possible before. Some of the results may have been "revolutionary," but historians holding this view maintain that the underlying facts of the Industrial Revolution exhibit a continuity with what went before (and perhaps with the essential underlying structures of economies), which indicate that the Industrial Revolution was in essence evolutionary in its causes. Implicit in the assumptions of many who adopt this view are ideas about the universality of "laws" of economics, psychology and society which favor an "evolutionary" interpretation of the Industrial Revolution. This implies that this particular period was simply an accelerated phase of what had been "natural" all along, and which is, therefore, by extension also natural for all other societies.

The contribution by John Komlos, organizer of the seminar, represents this viewpoint, and provides a useful synthesis of the arguments in favor of the evolutionary interpretation of the Industrial Revolution. He examines the research which shows how earlier efforts of the "forces of growth" to overcome the obstacles confronting them had been perennially stymied by a demographic (Malthusian) cycle. The true victory of the Industrial Revolution was to break out of this Malthusian trap and thus allow the "forces of growth" to achieve what had always been latent in them. The mechanism by which this was achieved varied from one country to another and from one decade to another but, while not strictly speaking inevitable, the pattern was enabling rather than artificial or coercive.

Although this view of the Industrial Revolution has gained much currency among economists and historians in recent years, it really is a radical break from most of the interpretations which previously dominated the field. The Industrial Revolution has been critiqued from two principal positions as being anything but "natural" or evolutionary. On the one hand, the Industrial Revolution has been assailed as inherently destructive of all that went before it, and as inimicable to all that is best in human nature and community. On the other it has been regarded as representing the final, nearly fatal aberration which, while perhaps inevitable, can serve only to underline the need for humankind to seek more viable futures. Though the former is largely associated with "conservatives" and the latter with the more Marxist Left, it is apparent that they share much common ground—though the psychology behind the two positions differs substantially. The standpoint adopted by Komlos, and by other "revisionists," can thus be seen as a radical point of departure in the debate over the Industrial Revolution.

ORGANIZING PRINCIPLES

It is possible to identify three main areas of concern to historians when dealing with the Industrial Revolution: What *caused* it? What happened and why? What were its effects? These areas provide the organizing principle for this collection.

In the **Preconditions** section, four chapters analyzing some of the developments that traditionally preceded the Industrial Revolution are presented. When economic historians attempt to understand why events happen when they do, they investigate the environment in which they occur; if this environment is not favorable to a particular development, either it does not occur or it occurs much later than it otherwise would have done. Some characteristic features of the Industrial Revolution are the widespread adoption of steampower, mechanization of industry (using metal machines), expansion of productivity and output, globalization of markets, and so on. Added to these are some already-existing features of economic life which were dramatically expanded as a result of these changes: globalization of the economy, use of the corporate form of business organization, paper money, banking, and so on. None of these changes could have become incorporated into everyday life unless there was a willingness (or at least no serious opposition) to do things differently, so sociocultural changes also become part of this "favorable environment." Looking only at European experience, the formation of this favorable environment had been occurring for centuries, coexisting with all the developments associated with the erosion of feudal relationships.

There were, of course, geographical and temporal variations which account for the differences in the industrialization (or as some historians would put it, modernization) experience. One of the key elements in the spread of the Industrial Revolution has always been assumed to be literacy. In this view, to be able to read and write allowed not only for the dissemination of information but also for the creation of a literate workforce which could make the Industrial Revolution happen. The assumption that the link between literacy and "modernization" is automatic is still a largely untested one, and John Murray tests this at the local level, the basic building block of any generalization, and by reviewing previous studies. As this chapter indicates, although the period of the Industrial Revolution did see some expansion in literacy, there is no apparent *automatic* link between industrial employment and literacy. What he does find is that the availability of schooling is a better explanation of literacy, which subsequently improves a society's economic development potential. Indeed his study goes some way to reinforce the idea that industrialization was not a major factor in increased European literacy; rather the relationship is reversed. This finding perhaps has some relevance in today's world, where many countries at the beginning of an industrialization effort are also grappling with problems concerning the provision of various social services, including education.

The next two chapters are concerned with the emergence of the nation-state (the traditional unit of analysis for many historical studies), and the ability of effective government action to influence social outcomes. In the centuries leading up to the Industrial Revolution, most European societies, after having shed their feudal political forms, began creating the modern nation-state and government. Phil Pajakowski and Mícheál Thompson both investigate the impact of these political changes; Austria, the subject of Pajakowski's chapter, attempted to establish a coherent economic and social policy based on a fundamental principle, while Great Britain lacked this unifying idea.

Austria in the late eighteenth century is an example of absolutism combined with a systematically organized central government, in contrast to the movement to a wider dispersion of power in Great Britain, where many different groups were successful in asserting their interests, but without eliminating the power of the central government. The policy program of the Austrian government can be seen as a last fling of the old idea that a larger population means greater wealth and power for a country; "populationism," although presented as an example of the rulers' compassion, really was an example of social manipulation. However, as Pajakowski makes clear, despite extensive state intervention in the Habsburg Empire, the Industrial Revolution did not "take off" there except in parts of Bohemia and Hungary, although many reforms did help the emergence of a modern state by limiting the exercise of traditional privileges, for example. State intervention, though in favor when the Industrial Revolution was beginning to spread, could not itself *cause* the Industrial Revolution; it was the result of a preexisting philosophy which had little to do with industrialization. One can draw similar parallels with the environment today: what is needed for effective development is a "favorable environment," and government action may or may not contribute to it.

Thompson focuses more on those sociocultural changes that paralleled the Industrial Revolution, and which can be viewed as examples of noneconomic changes which were necessary for the acceptance of economic ones. He notes that there were few dramatic changes in social life before 1750, but the beginnings of change—for example, in the structure of the family and household, status of women and children, role of religion—did influence how people reacted to change and assimilated it. The movement away from the particularism associated with traditional structures and toward the creation of a unified state in Britain is detailed in the way that most of the various nationalities in Britain internalized the ideology of "Britishness." Interestingly enough, the components of this ideology—Protestantism, individualism, respect for property rights—have traditionally been associated with the timing of the Industrial Revolution in Britain. The gradual process by which a populist ideology of the state was propagated in Britain provided the basis on which the Industrial Revolution could take place, and on which it could spread, not only in Britain but to all the parts of the world which were influenced by Britain in one way or another.

Robert Schultz tackles a problem which has been frequently neglected by European scholars of the Industrial Revolution, namely, the role of the New World. His primary contention is that the New World, and most especially North America, was indispensable to the progress of the Industrial Revolution both as a source of raw materials and of markets for finished products. Schultz cogently and persuasively argues the centrality of this Atlantic economy to the success of the Industrial Revolution in the United Kingdom, and therefore to the industrialization process as whole. Europe's escape from the Malthusian trap was not due to any conjunction of solely European circumstances, but can be attributed, at least in significant measure, to the widening of European horizons (especially the economic ones) by the positive role of North America. He makes a forceful case for the wider coverage of the emergence, growth and impact of such transatlantic activity in studies of the Industrial Revolution.

Schultz surveys the different positions taken in the literature, and concludes that it is important to take a broader approach to this subject for three reasons. First, the existence of North American markets helped provide outlets for expanding output in Europe. Second, the existence of the North American colonies helped the process of capital accumulation in Europe by providing nutrients, a safety valve for expanding populations, and tax revenues which were used to finance the construction of infrastructure. Third, there is a two-way relationship between industrialization and colonization, not a one-way link as is often assumed.

If we summarize the contributions in this section, the main conclusion would be that state intervention in and of itself was separate from the process of industrialization per se, but could accelerate or retard that process.

The next section, **Processes**, considers some of the actual developments that took place, focusing on Britain, Russia and Germany. The Industrial Revolution may well have entailed a varying range of political and societal circumstances in order for it to become the leading force in many societies, but one which few would ignore is the effect of technological change, the focus of the next two chapters. These chapters link the ideas and practices that for many make the Industrial Revolution so "revolutionary" in its impact.

Paul Lucier links the eighteenth century's scientific revolution and the thirst for knowledge it established to the industrial changes that it encouraged, by looking at the people who were thinking the new thoughts and putting them into practice. New ideas were discussed, and new practices put to work, through the medium of the connections among the scientists, industrialists, engineers and artisans. In Britain, unlike continental Europe, private enterprise rather than the state took the lead in popularizing these new technologies. The thirst for knowledge that was the outgrowth of the scientific revolution resulted in a widespread acceptance of what was then called natural philosophy as *useful* knowledge; the popularity of scientific societies and lecture series meant that these ideas became disseminated quickly through all levels of society. Hence many industrialists and artisans were actively involved in the process of testing and adapting new technologies; this inventiveness contrasts with the French experience in which the state established "model industries."

While Lucier's chapter focuses on the people involved in spreading the new technologies, the focus for Harry Kitsikopolous's chapter is on the patterns of this dissemination. The rate at which technology diffused has a lot to teach us about how the Industrial Revolution affected different parts of the economy, about what sorts of technology spread most quickly, and about what the obstacles were to such diffusion (whether cultural, economic, or merely pragmatic). The advantages of a given innovation were not always obvious at the time of its discovery and initial application, and its diffusion was far from automatic. This frequent lack of swift diffusion indicates not only caution on the part of investors and other interested parties, but also certain societal limitations and parameters restricting the rate of technological diffusion. Technological diffusion patterns can teach us a lot about what made the Industrial Revolution happen when and how it did.

At this time, and much more so later, ideas spread fast, and both theoretical concepts and technological applications became known both within Britain and in other areas of western Europe. However, the extent to which they had an impact on a society depends very much on whether they fell on fertile ground. The last two chapters of this section give two contrasting examples: Russia, which failed in its initial experiments to introduce modern industry, and Germany, which succeeded.

In the chapter on Russia, which describes how Peter the Great was at the forefront of efforts to modernize industry, Gennady Shkliarevsky delineates the ways in which Russia participated (or at least tried to do so) in these eighteenth-century developments, and the often striking differences between what happened there and what happened farther west. As in the Habsburg realms as described elsewhere by Pajakowski, governmental action attempted to shape the course of the Industrial Revolution. However, in Russia the nature of government and society made for a very different process with very different results. The highly personalized nature of the Czarist state rested on the idea that (in theory at least) the Czar was not only at the center and apex of society but was also directly involved in all aspects of Russian life. Decisions rested entirely with him and his will was quite literally law. Implementing this will, or even understanding it, was a challenging task, and penalties for misunderstanding were severe. Shkliarevsky gives a detailed overview of how this worked, with some startling examples. His analysis of the role of Peter the Great's modernizing efforts in Russia, what it changed and what it did not, provides a fundamental explanation of this period in Russian history, and it serves as a good basis for an understanding of much that was to come after it in Russia.

Russia failed at this time because modern industry was incompatible with the traditional society, where forced labor was common, private property rights were not protected, individual rights could be arbitrarily ignored by the Czar and his agents, and where, in general, there were few incentives for change. Russia's experience reinforces the importance of noneconomic changes, and shows that top-down decision making cannot make a difference in a society resisting modernization.

Germany was different yet again and George Vascik provides an overview of these differences, and of the similarities between Germany and the rest of northern and western Europe. He surveys the recent literature on German development available in English, which can be divided into two basic groups. The first includes researchers working in the *Sonderweg* tradition, which maintains that Germany's Industrial Revolution was unique and special. Although all nations' economic development is unique, this Germanic tradition puts special emphasis on the relevance of political developments for Germany's industrialization: the continuation of the control of the "premodern elites" over economic life undermined democratic movements, discredited economic and political liberalism, and to a large extent, was responsible for Germany's aggression in the twentieth century. The second group of research focuses on the importance of regional differences, and emphasizes the regional nature of development.

The way in which the Industrial Revolution was implemented in Germany was complex, not the least of these complexities stemming from the fact that before 1870 Germany did not exist as an entity, and after this date much regional variation of culture, economy, society, and policy persisted. Vascik makes clear that the Industrial Revolution was central to Germany, however varied its forms may have been and however contested it was at the time and for subsequent generations of historians. The main debate is between the "social-critical orthodoxy" which describes Germany's industrialization as unique, especially given its political linkages, and those who emphasize the essentially regional nature of German economic development. Germany as a unified, industrialized state was of key importance to Europe and the world in the nineteenth century and later, and Vascik gives us an appreciation of the diversity which underlay this importance, and the variety of interpretations to which this has given rise.

As is apparent, the Industrial Revolution involved changes in all aspects of life and was dependent at least to some extent on many preexisting changes. In addition, its implementation and impact were diverse rather than uniform. These issues form the focus of the

Consequences section. The Industrial Revolution was not regarded at the time as unambiguously "good" and certainly has not been so regarded since. James Briscoe and Casey Harison address these issues.

For economists, one of the main results of the Industrial Revolution has been its impact on material life. Because the technological changes increased productivity and output, rises in the material standard of living should be the logical outcome of the Industrial Revolution. This concept is the focus of Casey Harison's chapter, which surveys the evidence on living standards in Britain and France. Two factors are important here: the eighteenth-century belief in the inevitability of progress, and the promise that rising output levels in the nineteenth century would benefit all members of society. However, the evidence is mixed, and can be interpreted to justify either the pessimistic view (living standards did not rise) or the optimistic view (living standards did rise). Harison discusses different measures that are available and shows their advantages and disadvantages; at best, the short-run costs tended to offset the benefits, but this situation reversed in the long run. He also notes that French observers tended to be much more skeptical about the rewards of industrialization than the British, which underscores the need to be careful with interpretations of statistical evidence.

This skepticism is one theme in James Briscoe's chapter. He looks at how the evolution of the Industrial Revolution, and particularly its social ramifications, shaped competing ideologies at the time, many of which are still with us. He covers the development of the public debate in France, where the legacy of the political and social transformations of the Revolutionary period may have made commentators more socially conscious of the revolutionary nature of the changes occurring as a result of industrialization. The extremes of poverty which the Industrial Revolution caused, or at least made manifest, led commentators not only to describe conditions as they saw them but also prompted them to suggest "solutions." Social criticism was inevitable, living conditions being so manifestly awful. Critics tended to fall into one of three main categories: those who believed that the Industrial Revolution was being achieved at the cost of traditional standards and values which had been dominant before; those who accepted the "inevitability" of the Industrial Revolution but raged against it while believing that it was a transitional stage to something better; and those who acknowledged the inevitability of reality, but sought both to make others aware of it and to ameliorate its worst features. The Conservative, Marxist, and Liberal traditions can all be seen to have their origins here and Briscoe provides an invaluable starting point to understanding these traditions. In particular, the development of the individualist-utilitarian philosophy, that individuals were free to exploit their own power, within the context of an industrializing France where impoverishment was widespread, led to official reports which tried to shed light on the causes of poverty. These studies were also examples of the same reality being interpreted in different ways: thus, industry could be seen as either representing inevitable progress (good), or impoverishment (bad).

The final chapter in this section, by Christine Rider, widens the perspective beyond that of Europe by looking at the process and consequences of the Industrial Revolution in Japan. Schultze and Thompson both examined the extra-European dimension of the Industrial Revolution to some extent, but Rider specifically concentrates on a non-European country and, by extension, on the results of the Industrial Revolution on other non-European countries and globally. The very differences between the progress of the Industrial Revolution in Japan and in Europe, both chronologically and culturally, make it an interesting contrast, and they also make it potentially instructive for the study of other countries. As Rider makes clear, the late arrival of the Industrial Revolution in Japan, combined with the various factors of cultural and social isolation which had contributed to this delay, made the Japanese experience unique. However, this uniqueness was in the way that Japan integrated the Industrial Revolution into its society while maintaining much that had been characteristic of pre-Industrial Revolution Japan. Japanese society had many features which facilitated the incorporation of the Industrial Revolution, and though the social costs were often very high, the social fabric and the customs which held it together were both sufficiently resilient and flexible to allow it to stretch without breaking. Japan's proximity to the vast markets of mainland Asia and the fortuitous trading conditions following the globalization of the world economy in the last decades of the nineteenth century significantly enhanced Japan's ability to industrialize. In reviewing all of this, Rider enables us to see both the costs and benefits of Japanese industrialization, what made it unique, and what (at least potentially) can be carried over from the "Japanese model" to other countries facing the consequences of the Industrial Revolution.

The chapters in this collection address some of the central questions raised by the Industrial Revolution: its origins; what made or allowed it to happen; the differences between countries, especially the role of preexisting societal differences in shaping the distinct path of the Industrial Revolution in given countries; the impact of state formation and ideology; the roles of literacy, technological diffusion, and the dissemination of technical knowledge; its social costs and benefits; its spread beyond Europe; and some of its implications for today. The study of the Industrial Revolution is a particularly rich one, involving as it does an analysis of all the key features that distinguish the modern and contemporary world from what went before it. To repeat the important point made by John Komlos, this period is the one in which human societies begin to break out of the Malthusian trap, and harness the forces of growth.

The Industrial Revolution was a key watershed in modern history, and the modern world cannot be understood without some appreciation of the causes and consequences of industrialization in the nineteenth century. It was (and is) a global phenomenon which expressed itself in specific and varied ways around what might be called a "universal core" of permanently enhanced productivity. Its uniqueness and revolutionary character are part of a broader evolutionary process; the balance between these two aspects rests on the specific national and regional contexts of any particular episode of industrialization. This collection offers some keys to understanding this watershed and raises questions for further research. The interpretations presented in this book illustrate the diversity of views on the Industrial Revolution. There is still much work to be done on the Industrial Revolution, and we hope that this collection will stimulate such additional research.

Part I
Preconditions

INTRODUCTION

The four chapters in this section are concerned with developments that help to set the stage for a country's industrialization. Comparing preindustrial countries with those that have industrialized reveals several differences. The latter have higher per capita incomes and productivity levels, a smaller percentage of the labor force in agriculture, a larger percentage of Gross Domestic Product (GDP) originating from nonagricultural sectors, generally improved social statistics (for example, literacy, life expectancy, health care and so on), and a more effective, more centralized government.

In Europe, the period from the sixteenth century on is usually regarded as a period during which institutional changes helpful to, or concurrent with subsequent industrialization began to occur. Among these were the development of nation-states as more effective political units—which also had the economic effect of enlarging markets and thus stimulating the development of larger production units. Also important were improved transportation facilities which lowered the costs of acquiring resources and of moving finished products; the defining of property rights and the reduction of risk, to improve the chances for successful individual enterprise, the creation of a free labor force by removing the last vestiges of feudal relationships, and the acquisition of skills by a workforce that would contribute to expanded productive activity.

Different aspects of these processes come under scrutiny in this section. John Murray's chapter looks at the links between literacy and industrialization as one factor contributing to skill acquisition. He finds that while education, literacy and industrialization are linked, causality does not run from improved literacy to industrialization; the association is more complex. Philip Pajakowski investigates one example of the widespread European trend towards centralized government, and the attempts of the Austrian government to adopt policies to encourage the increase of wealth, specifically with a policy of "populationism," which tried to encourage population growth. Using this example, he shows that these policies had very specific social goals as well. The chapter by Mícheál Thompson analyzes some of the sociocultural changes that have traditionally been associated with the economic changes of the Industrial Revolution in Britain, and which helped to get these changes accepted; he also considers the development of an ideology of Britain as a nation-state.

The chapter by Robert Schultze reevaluates the importance of New World resources and trade to British industrialization.

It is likely that when considering the timing of any country's "Industrial Revolution," the creation of what may be termed a favorable environment is the key variable. This environment must include both elements that encourage industrialization and the removal of elements that would block it. Although it is possible to think of a multitude of elements that could be part of either group, these chapters will help to identify some of them.

1
LITERACY AND INDUSTRIALIZATION IN MODERN GERMANY
John E. Murray

INTRODUCTION

Many factors contribute to economic development, and today we know too much to attribute growth and diversification in an economy, including that of Germany, to any single factor. Historians and economists often identify certain factors as more important than others. For example, many quantitative studies indicate that rising education levels can be a powerful stimulant to long-term economic growth. Fortunately for historical studies, when people in the past bought or bequeathed property, or were married, or joined the military, they left evidence of the simplest possible level of education: whether they could sign their names. Frequencies of such "signature literacy" have been estimated for many populations of the past. Economic development, it is not surprising to learn, has been associated with higher literacy rates. In the case we will be concerned with here, the effects of literacy on making the modern German economy are subtle and varied. Although the research described in this chapter finds no significant linkage from literacy directly to the level of industrial activity in modern Germany, mid-nineteenth century literacy did have an effect on the growth of the entire German economy, effects which extended to the turn of the twentieth century.

The measurement of literacy in the past presents fewer problems than one might think. We rarely know if a common person in the past could read, but many people did leave evidence of their writing skills: either in the form of their signed name, or a mark such as an "X" if they were unable to sign for themselves. Marriage certificates, wills, deeds, military records, and petitions to legislatures, all offered common people opportunities to give their assent to written statements.

Many of these documents are held in archives, and are accessible to qualified researchers. People who could sign their name to these documents did so, and those who could not generally marked an X in place of a signature, which was then attested to by a witness. Signature literacy, then, measures a special kind of literacy. Some who signed could not write anything else, or perhaps were unable to read at all. Some who marked may have been able to read even the Bible, which was widely used as a primer.

Signature literacy *rates* are given by dividing the number of signatures by the total number of people signing or marking. It is possible to make some generalizations from a knowledge of signature literacy rates: "Scholars agree that signature literacy rates are an intermediate measure of literacy, higher than writing rates but probably lower than reading rates" (Lockridge 1974). Lockridge also noted that, at the very least, comparing the signature literacy rates of various groups allows reliable comparisons of their relative levels of overall literacy.

The virtues of education for an industrial workforce center on issues of productivity and labor mobility (Schultz 1975). Intuitively, a more educated worker should be a more productive worker, but the causal mechanism behind this relation may have been more obvious in the past than it is today. An employee who could read a set of instructions or blueprints could work with less supervision. By possibly enabling a worker to understand a production process better, education made it easier to learn new production techniques. A more educated worker should be better able to deal with changing market conditions; an example of this type of adaptation could be a decision to migrate to take a higher paid job somewhere else. One consequence of such migration was a more productive economy, since the migrants were presumably more productive in their new, better paying jobs. The tendency of the literate to be overrepresented in migration flows is well established in the historical literature (Nicholas and Shergold 1987). There are many reasons for this, including differential returns to literacy in the source and destination (literates could earn higher incomes where they were going than where they came from), and most obviously, that literates would have easier access to written information about the prospective destination.

The conventional wisdom regarding the history of German literacy and the role of literacy in industrialization is the subject of this chapter. Traditionally, the rise of German literacy was associated with the Reformation, as the Protestant emphasis on the *Word* (God's truths as revealed in the Bible) replaced Catholic emphasis on *objects* (Gawthrop and Strauss 1984). Schools to teach basic scriptural literacy appeared in the wake of Luther (circa 1527), resulting in literacy rates in Germany that were higher than anywhere else in Europe outside Scandinavia. Several centuries later, high levels of literacy enabled the Prussian system of technical education to produce a highly skilled workforce. German industrialization followed in the nineteenth century, and the economy grew rapidly to displace Britain as Europe's greatest economic power.

But the conventional story is misleading in some essential respects. Although the rise in German literacy dates from the time of the Reformation, to be sure, more widespread access to elementary schooling may be due less to Lutheran activity than to the seventeenth- and eighteenth-century activities of the Pietists, a Lutheran sect that stressed *individual* scriptural reading and understanding. Differences in literacy between Germany and France before the mid-nineteenth century may be due less to demand factors, such as religion, than to basic differences in the method of financing schools, which is more a supply issue. And exactly what kind of economy does literacy tend to produce? Rather than connecting literacy with German achievements in heavy industry, it may be more accurate to relate literacy to economic growth in general, especially in the nonmanufacturing parts of the economy. In short, it may be that in the German case, literacy is related to the growth of the larger economy, suggesting that the Industrial Revolution expressed itself in many different ways in the various countries that have industrialized.

PAST DEMAND AND SUPPLY OF LITERACY

It is helpful to separate the influences on the growth of literacy in Germany into two components, demand and supply. The demand for literacy consisted of parents' intentions to have their children learn to read, as well as adult illiterates' efforts to become lettered. There were many motivations for learning to read: reading and writing were pleasurable, could lead to better paying jobs, or could aid an individual's efforts to attain eternal salvation through the study of Holy Scripture. But this education was not free: the time spent learning how to read or write could have been spent working in the field, factory, or home. This is the economic dimension of the decision to become literate. What I will now attempt to do is to assess the role of the Reformation in increasing the demand for literacy.

The Demand for Literacy

Traditionally, the increase in literacy in Europe has been seen as a direct outgrowth of the Protestant Reformation. Protestantism emphasized the individual's reading of the Bible, in contrast to the Catholic tradition of communal worship centered on the Sacraments, objects consecrated through priestly intermediation. Martin Luther's Bible (New Testament, 1522; Old Testament, 1534) was not only a landmark in the development of a unified German language that transcended the many Germanic dialects, it was also a symbol of Protestant efforts to bring scriptural reading to the common folk. The most successful creation of a literate nation was Lutheran Sweden, where required reading lessons resulted in near universal literacy as early as the late eighteenth century. In contrast, conventional wisdom maintained that the reason for lagging literacy rates in countries such as France was the continuing influence of Catholic efforts to minimize such individual reading.

A recent strand of revisionist literature indicated that this picture has been drawn too sharply, and lacks appropriate nuance (Graff 1987; Gawthrop and Strauss 1984). The value of a written tradition may be more appropriately seen as a *Christian* one: traditionally, the Bible was accessible to anyone who knew Latin, a common second language in premodern Europe. In fact, the Catholic Church had taken advantage of Gutenberg's invention of the printing press in the late fifteenth and early sixteenth centuries to promote the use of published prayer books and catechisms.

The Lutheran achievement consisted of not just the emphasis on the role of Scripture in the practice of Christianity (i.e., *sola Scriptura,* the belief in salvation through Scripture without reference to Tradition), but also the creation of a network of schools that resulted in increased reading literacy. Exactly what that type of literacy meant, however, is a controversial issue. Luther himself, especially after the Peasant Revolts of 1524–25, began to retreat from his earlier faith in the ability of the masses to understand scripture correctly. In order to guide learners, Luther wrote catechisms, or manuals that contained the doctrine that was thought to be essential to the faith, and oral drills and recitations were used to teach from the catechism. Only minimal literacy skills were needed to get through such lessons, which were similar in spirit to methods used in the formerly Catholic institutions. Teaching through catechism resulted in doctrinal clarity, but at the cost of failing to instill in students creativity in problem solving or the ability to answer their own questions. What this means is that imposing present day connotations of literacy, such as creativity, for example, when evaluating the past is not always helpful.

According to Gawthrop and Strauss (1984), the wider spread of more effective schooling that led to universal literacy awaited the Pietist movement of the late seventeenth and eighteenth centuries. Beginning as a reform movement within the Lutheran church, Pietism emphasized personal interpretation of scripture, and its adherents provided schools that taught scriptural reading literacy. Teachers in Pietist schools, using an example from Halle in 1702, directed students to recite from the Bible and then retell the story in their own words. Pietist publishers produced unprecedented numbers of Bibles at unprecedentedly low prices. In the eighteenth century, one Pietist publisher sold two million complete Bibles, more than ten times the number of Bibles sold in Germany in the first century after publication of Luther's Bible of 1534. When accompanied by compulsory school attendance laws, the first in Prussia in 1717, German literacy steadily grew at a much faster rate than after the Lutheran Reformation. Gawthrop and Strauss conclude:

> ... the Pietist demand for universal religious literacy was instrumental in creating the institutions through which German society achieved a high rate of literacy in the course of the eighteenth century. (op. cit., p. 54)

The Supply of Literacy

The north-south differential in European literacy rates has been well established (Sandberg 1982). Northern European countries had higher literacy rates than southern European countries up to the early twentieth century. Because a map of confessional (i.e., religious) differences looked rather similar to a map of literacy differences, many commentators (at least in northern Europe) were quick to assert a causal role for religion in determining literacy rates. But again, this explanation may obscure as much as it explains. Some Protestant countries, such as England, did not attain particularly high literacy rates, while some Catholic countries, such as Belgium, did. That is, variations in literacy rates are not explained solely by religious differences.

For example, Maynes (1979) examined the cases of confessionally mixed regions in both France and Germany. The Vaucluse, in southern France, was a predominantly Catholic region with low levels of literacy, while Baden, in western Germany, was a predominantly Protestant region with high literacy rates. Overall, in the eighteenth and nineteenth centuries, literacy rates in Baden tended to be higher than in the Vaucluse. However, in Baden itself, Maynes found no relation between religion and literacy, while in the Vaucluse, Catholics tended to be more literate than Protestants. This was in fact typical of many regions in Europe: there were high literacy rates in Protestant areas and wide variations in Catholic areas (Graff 1987, pp. 187, 206, 286–90). Rather than associate literacy differences with religious variations, a better explanation may be differences in school attendance, which was much higher in Baden than in the Vaucluse.

This is what Maynes suggests: that the supply of schooling was the critical factor in literacy differences, and that this is essentially unrelated to religion. In the first third of the nineteenth century, schooling in Baden was less expensive for each pupil, and so more prospective pupils could afford to go to school. The lower cost was, in her view, due to the retention of communal sources of school funding that allowed for lower tuition charges. It is highly likely that such cost considerations played a much greater role in the growth of literacy in Germany than compulsory schooling laws (1717 in Prussia, 1772 in Saxony, and 1802 in Bavaria), which proved impossible to enforce. Because these laws had virtually no impact on actual student attendance (Graff 1987), it seems prudent to look for explanations of German literacy in other areas.

In addition, it seems that cost considerations were important not just in Baden, but elsewhere in southern Germany. Table 1.1 shows the percentage of teacher income that came from student fees in two regions of southern Germany, Baden and Bavaria, and in the Vaucluse, in the first third of the nineteenth century. Typically, students paid, directly, much less of their teachers' salaries in Germany (no more than about a third), than in France, where they paid half or more. The sim-

Table 1.1
French and German School Finance: Percentage
of Teacher Salaries from Student Fees

	Vaucluse	Baden	Bavaria
1800	89	25	NA
1836	49	37	34*

*1833
Sources: Maynes (1979); Lee (1977).

ilarity of the Bavarian data (Lee 1977) to the data from Baden implies that this result may be generalizable at least to other areas in southern Germany. It may even be typical of most of Germany: Lamberti noted that about 25 percent of teacher income in Prussia in the early nineteenth century came from tuition fees (1989, p. 18).

Historically, French and German schools got their funding from different sources. In the Vaucluse, public funds to pay teachers had been limited in the Ancien Régime, and teachers depended heavily on tuition fees for their income. The Revolution temporarily brought about free public schools paid for entirely from government funds, but these vanished in the post-Revolution chaos. French schools in the early nineteenth century, therefore, had virtually no government support, and, as noted above, mostly relied on tuition fees for their income. In contrast, German schools regularly supplied their teachers with certain communal rights provided by all in the community. These included the right to moonlight as the parish organist; to act as paid witness at baptisms, weddings, and burials; to receive food from each member of the village; and to work a small amount of village-held land. As a result, German schools depended less heavily on tuition, and more students could afford to attend. In fact, German attendance rates were much higher than those in France or Britain (Maynes 1979; Lamberti 1988). In summary, the inference that *regional* differences in literacy rates resulted from *individual* differences in religious belief is a textbook example of the *ecological fallacy* (applying inferences drawn from aggregate, or ecological, data to individual behavior), since it seems more likely that literacy differences followed from region-wide variations in school financing.

LITERACY AND INDUSTRIALIZATION IN NINETEENTH-CENTURY BAVARIA

It is an anachronism to speak of "Germany" before the late nineteenth century. Until then, German-speaking Europe was a collection of autonomous states, mostly under the domination of either Prussia or the Habsburg Empire at any given time. The various Prussian-led confederations were often at loggerheads with the Austrian Habsburgs over domination of the smaller Germanic states. One of these states with a tradition of independence up to the twentieth century was Bavaria. It will be useful to examine the literacy-industrialization relationship in Bavaria and greater Prussia separately, as two case studies, because in each case, the relation is quite different from the picture presented by the conventional wisdom.

The Context of Bavarian Literacy

Paradoxically, high literacy rates in Bavaria did not lead to industrialization, which occurred much later in Bavaria than elsewhere in Germany, and for most of the nineteenth century, the Bavarian economy was predominantly agricultural. Holborn described Saxony and Bavaria at this time as "peasant economies," to emphasize the presence of many small landholders in these areas which were so different from the vast estates of the Prussian Junkers (Holborn 1969, p. 373). Certainly Bavaria was one of the least industrial members of the Zollverein, the German customs union which Bavaria joined in 1834 (Pollard 1981, p. 225). Bavaria was anxious to protect its small industries with higher tariffs. Typical examples of such industries in Munich, the Bavarian capital, were royally chartered gold and silver, woolen, and leather manufactories (Pollard 1981, p. 82); in other words, traditional crafts writ large in a semifactory setting. Since Bavaria's population was predominantly Catholic, this example provides another instance of the limited usefulness of the religion-literacy relationship.

Court documents provide evidence of Bavarian literacy rates. The Bavarian government, along with other southern and central German states, experimented with stricter marriage requirements beginning in the 1820s, in part to diminish the numbers of the poor in their midst. Relying on the population theories of Thomas Malthus, it was thought that if marriage (and hence procreation) was restricted to those who could afford it, the proportion of the population too poor to marry would fall (Knodel 1967). The result was not a decline in poverty, but an increase in illegitimacy. In order to determine wealth at marriage, a couple, and their parents if they were living, had to testify before a justice of the peace as to the size of the dowry and the couple's occupational status. It is these records that provide measures of wealth and of signature literacy for a substantial proportion of the Bavarian population.

Records from two Bavarian areas (*Hofmark*) in the 1840s show consistent patterns (see Tables 1.2 and 1.3). Lee (1977) examined records from Massenhausen, and I studied records from Egmating.[1] As far as I know, these are the only published data on Bavarian literacy in English or German. Lee grouped signers by size of landholding, a full holding down to small holders of one-sixteenth of a holding. I grouped signers according to the value of their wealth: less than 200 Gilders, 200–500 Gilders, 500–1500 Gilders, 1500–2500 Gilders, and above 2500 Gilders. Both areas show similar literacy rates by wealth cate-

Literacy and Industrialization in Modern Germany

Table 1.2
Percentage Literate and Wealth in Bavaria, 1840s

	Wealth Category: I = Poorest; V = Richest				
Bavarian Hofmark	I	II	III	IV	V
Massenhausen, 1840–47	54	72	72	76	78
Egmating, 1843–48	65	79	76	78	76

Wealth category refers to landholdings in Massenhausen and wealth at marriage in Egmating, see text for details. Massenhausen data from Lee (1977); Egmating data from *Brief Protokoll 1432, Nr, 239*, Stadtarchiv München

Table 1.3
Percentage Literate in Bavaria, by Sex, 1840s

Hofmark	Male	Female	Combined
Massenhausen	72	72	72
Thalhausen	64	45	57
Egmating	86	50	71

Source: Same as Table 1.2

gory: in the poorest group, one-half to two-thirds were literate, and about three-fourths were literate in the four wealthier groups.

To the extent that signers could be identified by sex, Table 1.3 shows some similarities in men's and women's literacy rates. Literacy in Egmating was similar to Massenhausen's overall, but Massenhausen had surprisingly equal rates for men and women. Egmating and the region of Thalhausen, which consisted mostly of small holders, had similar male-female literacy differentials. Large differentials such as these were more typical of the rest of Europe than the similar literacy rates in Massenhausen. To make a comparison, in the 1840s, male literacy in Britain and France was about 65 percent, and female literacy was about half in Britain, and one-third in France, much lower rates than in Bavaria. Bavaria, thus, had quite high literacy (Cipolla 1969, p. 72).

Bavarian Literacy and the Bavarian Economy

However, these figures were misinterpreted in an important survey, and it is important to set the record straight if we are to make sense of the literacy-economic growth relationship in Bavaria. Rondo Cameron's 1985 *Economic History Review* survey of European economic growth stressed the role of natural resources (primarily coal) in accounting for industrialization. He utilized Alexander Gerschenkron's theory of relative backwardness (1962). Gerschenkron maintained that those European economies that lacked certain necessary sectors, such as a financial system, for example, could substitute other mechanisms in place of the missing sector to induce growth. For instance, if finance markets were undeveloped, the state could force capital accumulation through taxation of surpluses. Similarly, in Cameron's view, economies could substitute human capital for natural resources in the right circumstances, and the result would eventually be similar levels of heavy industry in both coal-rich and literacy-rich economies.

Cameron correctly identified Bavaria as an agricultural economy, but he also claimed that Bavaria suffered from low literacy rates, which was not correct. He claimed that in the 1840s, Bavaria had an illiteracy rate of about 60 percent, but it would be more accurate, as noted above, to say that the literacy rate was about that high in the poorest sectors, and higher in wealthier sectors. Cameron's difficulty stemmed as much from a faulty theory as from a simple misreading of the data. Once he committed himself to the Gerschenkron model of literacy leading to heavy industry, the Bavarian pattern of high literacy plus agriculture would be an anomaly standing in the way of a consistent explanation of industrialization.

The paradox can be resolved by broadening the literacy-economic growth relationship. That is, literacy may be more accurately described as one factor in economic growth, through its influence on the service, financial, and transportation sectors, rather than having an influence only on manufacturing. One possible way that literacy can affect the larger economy was through a literacy-finance nexus, as proposed by Sandberg initially for Sweden, and then for the rest of western Europe (Sandberg 1979, 1982). According to this line of reasoning, high literacy rates induced a greater willingness to use paper money and financial instruments, with the consequence that the economy as a whole became more efficient. Hence it should not be surprising to learn that high-literacy Bavaria was also the home of the first note-issuing bank in the German states, the Bayerisch Hypotheken und Wechselbank in 1835 (Kindleberger 1993). Literacy was a necessity for railway workers, who had to read printed timetables and instructions, as Mitch noted in the case of English workers (1992). The first railroad in the German states was built between

Nuremberg and Fürth in Bavaria in 1835, and Bavaria was also in the mainstream of German state-organized rail systems, constructing one in 1844 (Pollard 1981, p. 133). Literacy influenced Bavarian economic development along several paths, and economic development in Bavaria was not solely the result of industrialization.

LITERACY AND INDUSTRIALIZATION IN NINETEENTH-CENTURY PRUSSIA

The role of literacy in the economic development of the Prussian Empire was similarly diffuse. It is common to attribute the growth of heavy industry in late nineteenth-century Prussia (by then, the unified Prussian Empire) in large measure to a workforce that had received an excellent technical education (Landes 1969, pp. 342 ff; Cameron 1993, pp. 221, 246), which in turn was made possible by mass literacy (Graff 1987, pp. 292–293). Certain stylized facts regarding this linkage can be established, even if causation is doubtful. Across the entire empire in 1871, literacy rates of 90 percent for men and 85 percent for women placed it among the most literate nations of the world. It is also true that Prussian technical education was thought to be so thorough that it became the model for reformers of engineering education in the United States, Britain, and France. Growth of heavy industry was also impressive, with output of steel and chemicals, for example, growing over 6 percent annually between 1870 and 1913 (Cameron 1993, p. 247).

The Context of Prussian literacy

At this point, it will be useful to distinguish between Prussian technical education and Prussian literacy. High Prussian literacy rates can be related to economic growth in more general terms than to industrial growth in particular. As noted previously, Sandberg (1982) asserted that the most important consequence of mass literacy was the widespread acceptance of the financial system as a place to store economic surpluses. A banking system characterized by universal banks that were closely related to the industrial enterprises which they financed has long been considered a particularly strong advantage of the German economy in the late nineteenth century. Schooling that leads to literacy may induce, as a by-product, certain characteristics useful in large-scale industrial enterprises, such as orderliness, punctuality, responsibility, and so on. But Mitch (1992) has shown that there was only a weak relationship between literacy in the English workforce and the English Industrial Revolution; similarly in Germany, the relation between literacy and economic growth may go through paths other than just heavy industry.

It has been hard to quantify the effects of Prussian technical education on economic growth. Although Prussia instituted compulsory school attendance in 1717, enforcement was uneven until the nineteenth century, but by the 1830s, school attendance approached 100 percent of school-aged children. From the 1840s on, industrialists in the Rhineland began to push for the inclusion of useful subjects such as geometry and drafting in secondary education (Schluenes 1979). After mid-century, the provision of more scholarships enabled more students to attend technical schools in Berlin and the provinces, where they could study engineering and design (Lundgreen 1975). It is difficult to be precise about the effects of such education on the economy as a whole. Techniques developed by Denison have estimated that the proportion of twentieth-century American economic growth that was due to increases in the educational level of the work force was about 20 percent. Lundgreen used Denison's models to estimate that only about 2 to 6 percent of growth in the Prussian economy of the late nineteenth century could be similarly attributed. He concluded: "The development of a modern sector of the economy is quite different and far more complicated than the simple production of technical manpower" (1977, p. 77).

Prussian Literacy and Economic Growth

Sandberg (1982) adapted the Gerschenkronian model of growth along the same lines as the quotation from Lundgreen. Where Gerschenkron found relative levels of poverty ("backwardness") to be related to different rates of industrialization, Sandberg proposed that differentiating poverty (low per capita Gross National Product [GNP]) from ignorance (low levels of human capital as measured by education or literacy) provided a better illustration of what drove industrialization. In this view, human capital can be a substitute for physical capital, in much the same way that human capital and natural resources were substitutes for Cameron. This implies that the relation between education and industrialization may be very different from the link between low income levels and industrialization. In fact, what Sandberg found was that the full effect of education on per capita income was not immediate, but took two generations to be noticeable.

I would like to specify Sandberg's thesis a little differently. I suggest that in the Prussia of the Second Empire, literacy was the outcome of

Literacy and Industrialization in Modern Germany   29

schooling, and literacy in turn was related to per capita income levels with a one generation lag. I further propose that industrialization was also related to per capita income, but that literacy and industrialization were not related to each other in a direct causal way.

These relationships can be tested using Sandberg's technique (1982). Where information of the exact levels of literacy and income were unavailable, he estimated rankings of several European nations for literacy and income, and compared these rankings. Data are available for a variety of economic measures for the various Prussian provinces, but coverage is not uniform over time and place; furthermore, cardinal data are not available for some categories, although ordinal data are. Thus, using a variety of sources, Table 1.4 presents rankings of the eight Prussian states for which data could be found on schooling levels in 1841, literacy rates in 1871, per capita income in 1900, and a synthetic ranking of industrialization around 1900.

In a slight variation of Sandberg's method, I also estimated Spearman rank correlation coefficients.[2] This is a statistical test to see whether two rankings of the same entities are essentially the same or different. For example, consider three rankings of Olympic figure skaters, and recall the tendency of East-bloc judges to grade their own skaters more favorably than other skaters. A Spearman test would show rankings of the same skaters given by an American and a Canadian judge to be basically the same, while the rankings

Table 1.4
Rankings of Prussian States

Schooling, 1841	Literacy, 1871	Per capita Income, 1900	Industrialization, 1900
Saxony	Saxony	Brandenburg	Westphalia
Pomerania	Brandenburg	Rhineland	Rhineland
Westphalia	Westphalia	Westphalia	Silesia
Brandenburg	Rhineland	Saxony	Saxony
Rhineland	Pomerania	Silesia	Brandenburg
Silesia	Silesia	Pomerania	Pomerania
Prussia	Posnania	Posnania	Prussia
Posnania	Prussia	Prussia	Prussia
Posnania	Prussia	Prussia	Posnania

Sources: Schooling rates in Engelsing (1973); Literacy rates in Graff (1987), d. 285, which is taken from Cipolla (1969); per capita income in Borchardt (1991); Industrialization from Borchardt (1991) and Landes (1969).

given by a judge from the former East Germany would be significantly different from either of the first two judges' rankings. What I am testing here is whether rankings of Prussian states by schooling, literacy, per capita income, and industrialization (a notoriously difficult concept to define) were essentially the same or different. The closer the Spearman coefficient is to 1, the more similar the rankings. The significance level is the probability of incorrectly claiming that two rankings are similar, hence the lower the significance level, the better.

Table 1.5 presents the results of the statistical tests and a diagram (Figure 1.1) indicating links of causation. Here, causation is asserted if, first, a significant Spearman correlation is established; second, if chronologically, the cause precedes the effect; and third, if there is some economic reason for supposing that the causal (independent) variable influences the effect (dependent) variable and not vice versa.

Three relations fit this definition of causality. First, schooling levels in 1841, as determined from army records, "caused" literacy levels in 1871 as estimated by census records; this would be expected, if Prussian schooling in mid-century was at all effective. Second, literacy in 1871 "caused" per capita income in 1900. This is an extremely interesting relationship, with strong similarities to Sandberg's claims of a literacy-income relationship throughout Europe as a whole from the mid-nineteenth to the mid-twentieth centuries. In both cases, a long-term effect of literacy on per capita income can be seen. Finally, industrialization and per capita income around 1900

Table 1.5
Spearman Rank Correlation Coefficients
for Measures of the Prussian Economy

	Literacy, 1871	Per capita income, 1900	Industrialization, 1900
Schooling, 1841	0.78**	0.46	0.43
Literacy, 1871		0.91**	0.54
Per capita income, 1900			0.69*

* = correlation significantly different from zero at significance level between 0.025 and 0.05
** = correlation significantly different from zero at significance level between 0.01 and 0.025

```
Schooling, 1841 ──────────▶ Literacy, 1871
                                    │
                                    │
                                    ▼
Industrialization, 1900 ◀────────── Per capita income, 1900
```

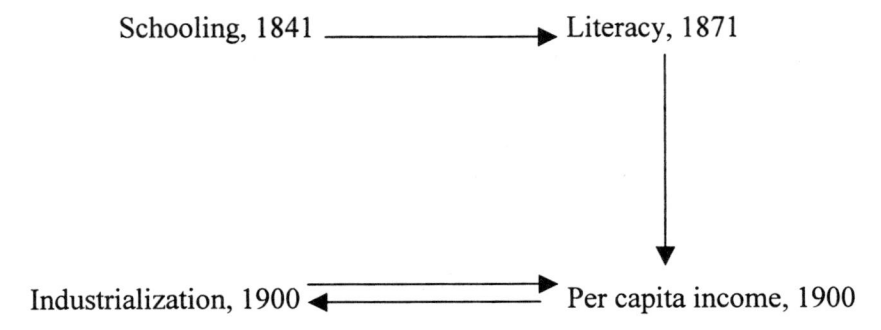

Figure 1.1 Model of Estimated Relationships in Nineteenth-Century Prussian Economy

are strongly related. This is not surprising. What is interesting is the lack of a significant causal relation between literacy in 1871 and industrialization in 1900. Thus, while literacy may have induced higher incomes, it had no significant effects on industrialization over the same time period. I would conclude from this that the effects of more literacy were not confined to a single sector of the economy such as heavy industry, but were in fact diffused throughout the entire economy.

CONCLUSION

The role of literacy in economic growth is an issue at the heart of this chapter. The idea of an Industrial Revolution is an analytic construct. The European economy, of which Germany would later constitute the single largest component, did not undergo a discontinuous economic shock analogous to the storming of the Bastille, but rather evolved into the complex system we are familiar with today. We may find it convenient to identify certain years as a time of especially eventful change, somehow defined. But confining any one nation's Industrial Revolution to events that occurred in the mining, metallurgical, or manufacturing industries reflects activity in only a part of the economy. The German economy as a whole changed significantly over the course of the eighteenth and nineteenth centuries, and it has continued to change since that time.

One factor in this change was the level of education, in this case as expressed by basic literacy. Widespread German literacy resulted from a web of interrelated factors, including religion and school funding. The path from education to development was complex, and did not go directly through heavy industry; rather education was associated with a wide range of other economic activities that themselves led to economic growth. Viewing the Industrial Revolution as the sum of development in all these sectors—manufacturing, finance, transportation, and so on—offers a finer, more complete perspective.

NOTES

1. *Brief Protokoll 1432,* in the Stadtarchiv München.
2. I thank Christine Rider for suggesting this test. Details can be found in Mendenhall (1983, pp. 632–633).

ACKNOWLEDGMENT

I thank Phil Pajakowski and George Vascik for helpful comments, and Dr. Alfred Tausenpfund, Director of the Munich City Archives, for enabling me to use the Egmating manuscript volume. This essay is dedicated to my teacher Lars Sandberg, on the occasion of his retirement from Ohio State University.

2
"POPULATIONISM" AND THE SOCIAL POLICY OF AUSTRIAN ABSOLUTISM IN THE EIGHTEENTH CENTURY
Philip Pajakowski

> In every man and woman there is a stronger desire and potential to procreate than is commonly carried out. The hindrances that block this drive arise only from difficult human conditions, which an enlightened government must carefully study and eliminate. A mild and just government that creates secure and comfortable conditions for its citizens will always be the most populous. (Sonnenfels 1777, p. 232)

These words of Joseph Von Sonnenfels, a professor at the University of Vienna and advisor to Austrian rulers in the last years of the eighteenth century, capture one of the guiding concepts of European states of that time: the need to increase population. Indeed, the Austrian emperor Joseph II maintained that the increase of the population of his empire was the primary responsibility of his government. Austrian rulers' concern for the quantity, and by implication for the well-being, of their subjects contributed to attempts to develop comprehensive measures to augment and manage the population and thus led to the state taking on extensive responsibilities of overseeing the welfare of society. These efforts were a part of a general tendency of European governments to extend their authority in the seventeenth and eighteenth centuries.

The development of absolutism, the concentration of power in the hands of a ruler overseeing a systematically organized central government, was a prominent aspect of the rise of the modern state and has been cited by scholars as an important ingredient in the social transformation of Europe that became known as the Industrial Revolution. The increasing efficiency of European states and their concern to manage their population to enhance their wealth, and thus augment state power, have been seen as contributing to European society's potential to overcome crises and natural disasters and to amass material goods. It has been argued that eighteenth-century European states, influenced by the desire to maximize their power as well as by Enlightened notions regarding the innate dignity of human beings, undertook unique innovations to promote the health, intellectual potential, and economic productivity of their subjects (Jones 1987, p. 130–49). Further scholars have maintained that the increase of population acted to encourage ingenuity, innovation, and, thus, economic growth (Komlos 1989a, p. 120–22). The emphasis Austrian rulers placed on increasing the population of their empires may thus be regarded as an aspect of the emergence of the political and social preconditions of the industrial revolution.

An examination of the formulation and application of policies aimed at managing population growth and productivity will illuminate the workings of enlightened absolutism. By discussing the assumptions behind measures taken to augment the productive populace as well as the measures taken to implement population policies, this chapter will shed light on the extension of the competence and authority of states that was a prime feature of the changes in European society that accompanied the transformation of economic activity in the late eighteenth century. This chapter will thus address the motivations and aims of Austrian Enlightened reformers, their ideas regarding population growth, measures undertaken to regulate the populace of the empire, and the limitations of these policies.

EIGHTEENTH-CENTURY REFORMS

During the reigns of Maria Theresa (1717–1780) and her son Joseph II (1741–1790), the Austrian empire underwent a series of reform efforts that constituted one of the most prominent examples of Enlightened Absolutism. The aims of these measures were to improve the efficiency of the government, increase state power, and raise the standard of living of the empire's subjects. The assumption behind these efforts, one held by many of Maria Theresa's advisors and especially by Joseph II, was that the concentration of state power in the hands of a wisely ruled central government would result in the greatest possible social tranquillity and political strength. The reforms began in the 1740s, after the empire had narrowly escaped dismemberment when it was attacked following Maria Theresa's succession to the throne in 1740, and the process of reform continued to the death of Joseph II in 1790. In the measures undertaken in these years, Austrian officials streamlined the central government and established the authority of central officials at all levels of government; sought to regulate and eventually to abolish the bonds of serfdom that still prevailed in relations between noble landowners and peasants; acted to limit the authority of the Roman Catholic hierarchy, simplify church services, and restrict monasticism; worked to extend primary schooling and reshape the curriculum of secondary and university education; and, especially under Joseph II, implemented a series of ordinances intended to rationalize Austrian society. By limiting the privileges of the nobility and the church hierarchy and rationalizing the system of government, the reform effort laid the basis for a modern state and for dynamic social development.

Motives for Reform

Historians have stressed three sets of motivation in evaluating the origins and purpose of the reform efforts. Some have concentrated on the importance of needs of state in the minds of the reformers. These historians have pointed out that the reform efforts began with a military defeat and focused largely on the requirements of a strong defense. The reform efforts reflected the influence of cameralism, a central European variant of mercantilism that urged rulers to encourage the economic activity of their subjects to increase the state treasury and thereby strengthen their state in competition with other countries. Much of the reform efforts aimed at establishing an army capable of defeating rival Prussia, against which the empire warred from 1740 to 1748 and again from 1756 to 1763.

Other historians have emphasized the primacy of Enlightened sentiments, particularly in regard to the motivations behind the later efforts of Maria Theresa, her chief advisor Wenzel von Kaunitz, and Joseph II. The empress often expressed her motherly concern for her subjects, and Joseph referred to himself as the first servant of the state and his people. In seeking to break down traditional centers of social privilege and cultural restriction, the Austrian reformers appear to have been responding to the ideal of human dignity and commitment to unrestrained intellectual inquiry that were put forward by the rationalist *philosophes* in the mid to late eighteenth century.

More recently, scholars have presented a third possible explanation of the reforms: the need to preserve social order in the difficult economic times of the mid 1700s under the pressure of rising population and the resulting threat of food shortages and public unrest. The population of the central, contiguous lands of the empire rose from approximately 10.5 million in the early 1700s to 21.9 million in the 1770s, during which time the empire gained the province of Galicia but lost Silesia. The Austrian government acted to stimulate economic initiative and to confront the gross social inequality and problems of vagabondage, crime, and unemployment that threatened the social peace of the empire. In so doing, the government helped avert a subsistence crisis and enabled a growing population to support itself through innovations in production (Evans 1994, pp. 10–11; Mueller 1994, p. 160).

These three interpretations need not be regarded as mutually contradictory. In the view of reform-minded Austrian officials the welfare of the subject was the basis of state power, which in turn acted to maintain the condition of a well-ordered society that allowed its subjects to thrive. Social tranquillity was the condition for public happiness, and a happy, contented populace could be relied on to pay the taxes and produce the healthy soldiers that would buttress the power of the Austrian state. Central to all these motivations for reform was the need to encourage population growth and to stimulate the economic productivity of the empire's subjects.

ENLIGHTENED CAMERALISM AND POPULATION GROWTH

Official efforts to enhance the empire's population provide a good illustration of the policies of the Austrian reformers, who may be referred to as Enlightened cameralists. Cameralism was an early form of political economy that gained prominence in central Europe in the late seventeenth and eighteenth centuries. Cameralists encouraged their rulers to strengthen the state by carefully managing economic resources. Among the policies they advocated were regulating foreign trade to encourage the export of manufactured goods, regional coordination to maximize economic output, and the grooming of the largest possible base of population endowed with a variety of productive skills. Cameralism became the basis for formal training in state administration in the German states, and the first chair of cameral studies in Austria, held by Sonnenfels, was established at the University of Vienna in 1762. In their efforts to develop comprehensive social policies, the Austrian reformers combined cameralist ideas with the Enlightened humanitarian sentiments of the late eighteenth century.

In seeking to increase the population and maximize its productive efforts, the Austrian authorities undertook a series of measures to protect the welfare of subjects, to ensure public order and security, and to more efficiently distribute the population of the empire by encouraging the settlement of sparsely inhabited regions through efforts at colonization. These measures stemmed from a general theory of "populationism," which provided the underpinnings for attempts to develop a systematic state social policy (Kann 1960, pp. 175–78).

Populationism proceeded from the basic assumption of the cameralists that the welfare of the state required the growth of population. Reasoning from the primary consideration of the interests of state, cameralists posited the simple proposition that the greater the population, the greater the tax revenues and military resources available to the ruler. The Enlightened cameralist Sonnenfels, concerned with the welfare of the individual as well as the state, regarded the increase of population as advantageous to subjects as well as monarchs. He reasoned that the burdens of the state would be lighter if they were divided among a greater populace. Later cameralist thought emphasized the circulation of money as the primary measure of state wealth, and maintained that an increase of population would stimulate trade and thereby intensify the blood flow of the state.

Population and Productive Employment

Of course, according to the reasoning of the cameralists, the increase of population alone would not ensure the strengthening of state power. The rising population must find productive employment to add to the collective wealth of society. To increase its strength and perform its duty to its subjects, the state must promote the welfare of its subjects and thereby secure the common good, which eighteenth-century political theorists defined in a materialistic sense. The German cameralist Johann Heinrich von Justi, who taught briefly in Vienna and strongly influenced Sonnenfels, defined the basis for the attainment of the good life by dividing living standards into three levels. The level of "indispensable necessity" provided the minimum of food and shelter to enable a person to work; "true comfort" offered the subject hot meals, furniture, and the consumption of articles for pleasure such as tea, coffee, and spices; "luxury" afforded the indulgence in consumption for the sake of fashion and involved waste. Justi regarded the attainment of true comfort among a broad segment of the populace as desirable for the state and even regarded luxurious consumption as beneficial as long as luxury goods were produced domestically so that no money flowed out of the state to enrich foreign producers (Engelhardt 1981, pp. 58–60). The more Enlightened, more individualist, Sonnenfels maintained that the attainment of prosperity was a basic right of the subject.

POPULATION GROWTH POLICIES

According to cameralist views, the enhancement of the fertility of its subjects required a systematic social policy implemented by the state. This policy entailed economic measures intended to prevent the flow of money abroad and to encourage the growth of domestic manufactures. Thus, for example, the woolens factory established in Linz in 1671 by an imperial privilege was freed from guild restrictions by a patent of 1707 that allowed it to sell its products throughout the empire. Linz grew to be the largest textile center of the empire by the 1750s, and, when the factory's owners threatened to declare bankruptcy, Maria Theresa took control of the business to maintain this large manufacturing center (Kühnel 1960, pp. 138–39). Further, the empress enacted penalties for papermakers that failed to implement advanced technology, and Joseph II awarded prizes to inventors and machine builders. The central government sought to break down customs barriers between the constituent parts of the empire, and high tariffs were imposed on the import of certain manufactured goods in the 1750s and 1760s. Finally, throughout the century, the government financed the construction of roads to link the lands of the empire (Good 1984, pp. 28–30).

Beyond these efforts to stimulate economic growth the government imposed measures to encourage childbearing and promote the hard work, self-discipline, health, and security of the populace. Both coercive measures and efforts to protect its subjects' welfare were to contribute to these goals. Cameralist reformers believed the state must shape its subjects' thinking to instill them with rational desires as well as the traits necessary to attain them. Eighteenth-century reformers clearly perceived a natural human tendency toward idleness, and devoted much attention to restricting begging, vagrancy, and other nonproductive activities. Consistent with the assumptions of Enlightened absolutism, the Austrian cameralists identified the monarch as the arbiter of the public good who set the definition of socially beneficial work. The cameralists assigned the enforcement of these measures to the newly created local police agencies, whose tasks included oversight over matters of public health and propriety, supervision of the price and quality of food, registration of births and deaths, and control over the registration of foreigners and religious minorities, as well as the apprehension of criminals.

Encouraging Marriage and Childbirth

Efforts to increase population began, obviously, with measures to encourage childbirth; the first requirement of population growth was increased conception. For the Austrian reformers, the main means to this end was marriage. This attitude had its basis both in moral judgment and in practical calculation, for rates of infant mortality were thought to be considerably higher for illegitimate children than for those born to married mothers (Leuchtenmüller-Bolognese 1981, pp. 191–92, 197–99). Under Maria Theresa the government eased traditional restrictions on marriage. In 1765 the prohibition imposed by craft guilds on the marriage of journeymen was abolished as was the traditional requirement that a peasant serf receive his lord's permission to marry. In 1776 the government lifted a ban on the marriage of common soldiers. A law of 1770 forbade men and women to enter religious orders before the age of twenty-five; the intent here was in part to reduce the prominence of monasteries and convents in Austrian society, but the measure also gave young people more time to consider marrying before taking vows of celibacy. Marriage was not, however, desirable for all social groups. To avoid procreation among unproductive people, the government forbade the marriage of vagabonds and vagrants.

Other government initiatives also revealed a more coercive approach to the promotion of childbearing. The revised criminal code issued by Maria Theresa in 1768 prescribed the death penalty for persons convicted of infanticide, abortion, and sterilization. Mothers found guilty of willfully killing their infant children were to have a stake driven through their hearts after being laid in the grave. The text of the code explained that especially severe measures were required for the state to protect its most vulnerable subjects (Leuchtenmüller-Bolognese 1981, pp. 205–6).

In an effort to protect the health and regulate the behavior of their subjects, the Austrian reformers sought to drastically reduce prostitution. Prostitutes were blamed for the spread of venereal disease in the eighteenth century, and cameralists clearly believed that association with prostitutes misdirected young men's energies and distracted them from marriage. Prostitutes were subjected to fines, to humiliating public punishment, including the stocks, having their heads shaved, and sweeping the streets, and even to expulsion from the empire. Further, to rid the capital of undesirables and increase the population of a frontier region, prostitutes were often transported down the Danube River to the Banat of Temesvar, a province on the border of the Ottoman Empire. The treatment of patients suffering from venereal disease further illustrates the mixture of charity and concern for public instruction and moral discipline that characterized the Austrian Enlightened reformers. Venereal disease was traditionally regarded as divine retribution for sin, but Enlightened cameralists viewed the disease rather as a social problem that aroused both sympathy for the afflicted and concern to demonstrate the consequences of improper behavior to the populace. Thus, under Maria Theresa, a hospital was established in Vienna to care for victims of syphilis, but it was also open to general visitors so that the public could observe the effects of the disease on patients (Leuchtenmüller-Bolognese 1981, p. 201).

The attempt to channel and restrict sexual behavior constituted only a part of Austrian population policy. Enlightened cameralism also entailed extensive measures to ensure the health of subjects and to provide care for the indigent. A prominent official concern was the need to protect subjects against infectious disease and unscrupulous merchants by overseeing the quality of drugs and food. Among the duties the cameralists assigned to police officials was the inspection of markets and apothecaries to ensure the purity of their products as well as fair prices. Further, the cameralists advocated the establishment of district medical officials to inspect sanitary conditions and to register births, deaths, accidents, and the incidence of disease. The gathering of such information would clearly aid in efforts to monitor population and identify threats to public health.

POLICY TOWARD THE POOR

The Enlightened reformers' distinctive mixture of compassion, practical calculation, and social manipulation is well illustrated by their approach to care for the poor and for retired or widowed families. Poverty and vagrancy were prominent concerns in the mid to late eighteenth century. The increasing rural population put pressure on existing farmland and drove the younger sons of poor peasants to leave their land and take up begging or crime. Also, the extensive warfare of the mid-1700s required the recruitment of large numbers of soldiers, many of whom were released after the wars ended. Gangs of wandering former peasants and soldiers harassed urban burghers and extorted money from isolated farmers. Poverty and need thus aroused concerns for the maintainance of public order and for the security of productive subjects. Maria Theresa, Joseph II, and their advisors clearly recognized an obligation to care for impoverished subjects. Further, the number of unemployed overwhelmed the resources of communities and churches, which traditionally had provided charity. The assumption of poor relief by the central government was thus an aspect of the centralization of authority that typified Enlightened absolutism.

The Deserving and Undeserving Poor

In their efforts to confront problems of poverty and begging, Austrian officials sought to distinguish between the deserving poor, who required care and relief, and the undeserving, who needed discipline to counteract their laziness. Among the most ambitious efforts at social welfare was the enactment of an empire-wide system of poor relief by Joseph II in 1782. To eliminate begging, the poor were to receive payments of up to one-third of a laborer's wage. The system was to be financed by contributions and by the sale of monastic property confiscated by the state. Parish priests collected and distributed the money, but state officials determined who was eligible to receive the payments (Bernard 1994, pp. 243–46). Joseph's welfare system thus corresponded to his religious reforms aimed at making the Catholic church a socially oriented institution under state supervision.

Further welfare efforts were directed at workers in major manufacturing centers. With four thousand employees in its central complex, the Linz Woolens Factory was the largest industrial enterprise in the empire. When it was temporarily under state control in the 1770s, the factory employed physicians and surgeons to treat its workers. Further, the government provided money and donated buildings to hospitals established by religious orders to care for the people of Linz. Linz workers also took part in a pension plan that was established under Joseph II as an extension of a pension system for workers in state-owned salt mines that had existed since the seventeenth century. The cameralist administrators who introduced these measures justified them by explaining that only employers who provided for their employees' futures could expect to attract good workers to onerous jobs that often undermined their health at an early age (Kühnel 1960, pp. 142–63).

In the 1770s the Austrian government responded to a disastrous famine by undertaking traditional measures but implementing them on a scale that illustrated the growing resources and efficiency of the state. Bad harvests in 1770 and 1771 resulted in a food shortage in much of central Europe with particularly serious consequences in Bohemia. Reports of starvation and the threat of mob violence led the government to undertake a series of relief measures that escalated in scale and intensity. Having forbidden the export of grain first from Bohemia, then from the entire monarchy in the fall of 1770, Maria Theresa next established price controls for grain and sent officials to confiscate hoarded grain supplies. To prevent the illicit export of food for higher prices, she established military patrols over border crossings and imposed the death penalty for smuggling. Grain supplies from military storehouses were distributed by the Bohemian authorities, and finally, in fall 1771, the central government purchased sufficient grain to feed Bohemia's population in Hungary and transported the food to the stricken province. The response to the Bohemia famine typified the cameralist approach to crisis management, a mixture of palliative measures and social controls, and dramatically demonstrates the ability of the Austrian government to mobilize resources to prevent a serious problem from becoming a human and social catastrophe. Moreover, the clear poverty of much of Bohemia's peasantry led the empress and her son to consider more drastic means of alleviating their exploitation by the province's aristocracy, including the abolition of serfdom.

POLICY LIMITATIONS

Nonetheless, Austrian social welfare initiatives were limited in their intended purpose and in their effectiveness. The intention behind many of the measures was to provide sufficient income to the poor to sustain life and to prevent the outbreak of riots that could threaten public safety. Further, a shortage of resources at the state's disposal hampered the undertaking of extensive commitments to public welfare. The pensions made available to Linz workers or their widows amounted to at most one-third of their previous wages, and the imperial poor relief payments reached only about one-half the rate set by Joseph II (Bernard 1994, pp. 246–48; Kühnel 1960, p. 153). Problems of vagrancy, begging, and the general unruliness of the poor perhaps abated but were by no means eliminated by these measures. Moreover, the government did not intend to eliminate social distress by welfare measures, since the root of these problems was seen to lie not only in misfortune or natural calamity but also in the weaknesses of character of the impoverished. The imposition of discipline on the idle thus also belonged to the Austrian cameralists' methods of population management.

Moral Weakness of Beggars

Enlightened cameralism thus further entailed attempts to eradicate the bad habits of the idle, both to instill better traits in the indigent and to protect productive subjects from molestation by the poor. A central concern was begging, clearly a common phenomenon in the eighteenth century. The oversight over public begging belonged to the responsibilities of the police, who were charged with certifying legitimate beggars and punishing the illegitimate. The police ascertained whether beggars were truly unfit for work and issued certificates attesting to their disabilities. Further, the legitimate beggars were to abide by Christian moral strictures; they were required to attend mass regularly and to partake in the sacraments as prescribed by church teaching. Thus, legitimate beggars had to prove that their poverty resulted from misfortune rather than immorality. Harsh treatment awaited vagabonds and beggars who were found to lack clear disabilities and thus to fall outside the begging statutes. Uncertified beggars and vagabonds were regularly rounded up and driven out of their locality. Repeated statutes of the 1700s banned vagabonds from entering Vienna, and the authorities expelled vagrants from the empire by simply shoving them across the Turkish border (Bernard 1994, pp. 238–43; Melton 1994, pp. 229–32).

Official policy toward the indigent extended from regulation and expulsion to attempts to reform their behavior by improving their characters. The Enlightened cameralist Sonnenfels identified the cause of vagrancy and petty crime in a psychological unwillingness to work that could be corrected by the imposition of strict discipline. Thus, he recommended that idlers and petty criminals be submitted to a strictly regimented daily schedule including hard labor. He advocated the establishment of prisons and workhouses to break down the character defects of criminals and accustom them to an orderly life and hard work. In typically rationalist fashion, Sonnenfels advocated the abolition of the existing practice of torturing suspected criminals, because he thought torture was an ineffective means of proving guilt. He also recommended the abolition of the death penalty, because he believed the prospect of a life sentence at hard labor would more likely deter prospective criminals than would the threat of execution. Moreover, the heavy work performed by convicts would benefit society and could lead to their rehabilitation. Although Sonnenfels helped convince Maria Theresa to abolish torture, his scheme for a two-tiered system of correctional institutions was not implemented. Nonetheless, the Austrian authorities began to establish workhouses and prisons in the late seventeenth century, a process which continued throughout the eighteenth century. In accordance with cameralist doctrines, inmates were forced to perform heavy labor to pay for their upkeep and to contribute to the imperial economy.

COLONIZATION AS ECONOMIC OPPORTUNITY

In attempting to control poverty, the Austrian reformers also recognized the need to provide economic opportunity to poor peasants, discharged soldiers, and other marginal groups. Recently conquered lands on the eastern frontiers of the empire were regarded as underpopulated and therefore became the subject of major plans for colonization and settlement. The economic development of these regions, Galicia and the Banat of Temesvar, could thus serve both to relieve population pressure in the central Habsburg lands and to increase the economic potential of the monarchy. Colonization became an important component of populationist efforts to exploit the empire's resources to the fullest and to rationalize patterns of settlement.

The primary location of efforts at colonization was the Banat of Temesvar, a province on the southeastern border of the empire. Annexed from the Ottoman Empire in 1718, the Banat was administered as a cameral province under the direct jurisdiction of the imperial Treasury (*Hofkammer*). Economic policy in the province came under the control of Aegid von Borié, a member of the Council of State (*Staatstrat*), an enthusiastic populationist who furthered the career of Sonnenfels. The region thus became a center for populationist efforts to manage settlement and economic development (Jordan 1967, pp. 76–77; Osterloh 1970, p. 31). Cameralist officials had long regarded the province as underpopulated and as a field for economic experimentation, and sporadic efforts to attract settlers began in the 1720s. Under Maria Theresa officials tried to develop the production of rice, dye crops, and silk by attracting skilled immigrants from Italy, but large-scale colonization began in the 1760s, in part to resettle soldiers discharged from the army at the end of the Seven Years' War. Under the direction of the Population Commission in Vienna, settlers were recruited in the western provinces of the empire, their travel costs were paid, and they were provided with farms, animals, and implements, primarily on lands belonging to the crown. The settlers held their lands as heritable property and were freed from taxation for six years, but they were required to begin to repay the state for their resettlement after five years. The state established new villages for the settlers and provided them with training as farmers, as well as with doctors, teachers, and pastors. Nonetheless, the effort to introduce settled agriculture faced the resistance of native pastoralists, and the difficult work of draining marshes for farmland exhausted and even killed the settlers. In 1773, after over forty thousand Germans and a great number of Serbs and Romanians had settled in the province, the effort was suspended, and in 1778 the Banat was merged with Hungary.

Galicia, a northeastern province annexed from Poland in 1772, provided a second field for populationist immigration. On a visit to the new province in 1773, Joseph II determined that it was underpopulated and henceforth consistently advocated concerted measures at colonization. Austrian economic planners viewed Galicia as a land suited primarily for agriculture and hoped German settlers would improve the level of farming of the country both by introducing new methods and by providing an example of hard work and efficiency to the supposedly more backward Polish and Ruthenian natives. Thus, here, as in the Banat, the government paid transportation costs for German colonists and provided them with housing, farmland, implements, and animals in carefully laid out, newly constructed villages. Because they were to provide an example to the Slavic population, the German colonists were to be placed under the strict supervision of district officials. Idle or sloppy peasants were subject to fines or even forfeit of their land. Approximately eighteen thousand colonists settled in Galicia, mostly in the 1780s.

Failure of Resettlement Policy

Although the efforts at colonization brought tens of thousands of new settlers to the eastern provinces, the ultimate success of the enterprise is questionable. The government abandoned efforts to colonize the Banat after Joseph II visited the region and pronounced the project a failure. By the standards of the Enlightened rulers, Balkan lands were thought to be too backward for the government to provide the basis for the pleasant, ordered life appropriate for the subjects of a civilized state. In the late 1700s the Habsburg Empire avoided efforts to annex new lands to the southeast, perhaps because the rulers judged Balkan peoples and terrain to be unsuitable for incorporation into the empire (Roider 1994, pp. 317–21). Similarly, efforts to advance Galician agriculture through colonization also achieved doubtful results. The government failed to provide new housing quickly enough for the arriving settlers, who therefore lodged for long periods with Polish and Ruthenian peasants. Because farm implements and animals were also slow to arrive, the colonists appear to have drained rather than advanced the province's resources, at least in the short term. The empire appears to have lacked the material capacity to implement vast resettlement schemes involving the migration of people, the construction of new housing, and the draining and clearing of extensive farmland.

In general, Austrian populationist measures suffered from insufficient state resources. As we have seen, imperial efforts at poor relief and pension plans were seriously underfunded. A further problem was that state officials were charged with a wide variety of responsibilities and were overburdened (Bernard 1991, pp. 119–21). For example, newly annexed Galicia was divided into eighteen districts, each with a staff of a district captain, a few administrative assistants and soldiers, one physician, one surgeon, and one midwife. In a province with roughly 2,700,000 inhabitants scattered over 83,000 square kilometers, such a small administrative force was unable to effectively perform its assigned tasks of overseeing the order, security, health, sanitation, births, deaths, and economic activities of the populace (Glassl 1975, p. 83).

CONCLUSION

Despite these limitations, the significance of Austrian populationism lay in the attempt of cameralist officials to establish a coherent economic and social policy based on a fundamental principle. In their efforts to further the increase of population, Austrian reformers extended the boundaries of state activity and redefined the nature of the state's responsibilities. Efforts at managing the empire's population entailed extensive new operations for the central government, including registering subjects' movements, monitoring their health, and conducting the first imperial censuses. The cameralists thereby established an expanded state administration that systematically gathered information on its subjects and sought to apply this knowledge to direct social change. In accepting the need to care for the welfare of the public, Enlightened cameralists brought state action into areas previously reserved to the oversight of the church, the nobility, and town councils, and thus challenged traditional social structures that often resisted economic innovation. By breaking the power of guilds to restrict the production and sales of goods, for example, the central government encouraged the growth of capitalist business practices aimed at broad markets and employing new techniques.

Further, efforts to promote the health and education of the populace enhanced the level of skill and productive potential of the empire's subjects. Attempts to transfer settlers to new regions corresponded to a widening of the scope of economic policy from a local to a national level.

The efforts of the Enlightened cameralists thus laid the basis for the transformation of Austrian economy from a localized, feudal system of production to one based on broader regional concerns and employing innovative methods. These were essential prerequisites for the industrial growth of the coming century. By expanding the capabilities of the state, the Austrian reformers contributed to the development of the preconditions of dynamic economic growth.

3

PREPARING FOR THE INDUSTRIAL REVOLUTION: SOCIOCULTURAL CHANGES AND THE FORMATION OF "BRITAIN"

Mícheál Thompson

INTRODUCTION

Whether viewed as an example of revolutionary or evolutionary change, few historians question the fact that "something" happened in Britain in about 1750, conventionally called the "Industrial Revolution." However, like all historical events and processes, the Industrial Revolution began when and where it did for a number of very specific reasons. While the Industrial Revolution is often viewed as a primarily economic process involving changes in employment patterns or production techniques, for example, it also involved and was the result of, far-reaching sociocultural changes. It is the historian's job to try to make clear the events and trends which shaped a major event like the Industrial Revolution and to highlight their particular significance. In this chapter, the focus is on noneconomic issues, partly to complement the bulk of work on the Industrial Revolution which tends to abstract the economic from the political and the social. However, the economic and the noneconomic are entwined in the Industrial Revolution, as indeed they are today, and economic issues form a constant backdrop to the discussion.

The question as to why the Industrial Revolution happened when and where it did has long challenged historians and especially economic historians. By and large, a consensus has been reached concerning the primary issues to be explored. Joel Mokyr provided a classic summary of this consensus in 1985:

More changed in Britain than just the way in which goods and services were produced. The nature of the family and household, the status of women and children, the role of the church, how people chose their rulers and supported their poor, what they knew about the world and what they wanted to know—all of these were transformed. (Mokyr, 1985, p. 1) [Emphasis added]

The initial concern of this chapter is to explore the relevance of these issues to explain why the Industrial Revolution occurred when it did. Following this, an additional explanatory factor is explored, namely, the creation of "Great Britain," and the ideology that justified the creation of this state. I have made a deliberate effort to discuss Ireland, Scotland, and Wales as their inclusion in practical terms during this period was an essential component in the complex of processes leading to the Industrial Revolution in the British Isles. The creation of Britain involved not only a set of decisions and actions at the political level, and an even more fundamental implementation of them at the economic and social levels, but also the formation of an ideology of "Britishness" which supported, facilitated, and justified this creation.

FAMILY AND HOUSEHOLD

The family and household form the basic unit of the society and economy. Families respond to, and in turn help to shape, changes at a wider level. The period prior to the Industrial Revolution saw a range of such changes, and family and household structures in part reflect these changes. In looking at families, the first question must be *which* families? Britain was characterized by pronounced regional variations and by even more pronounced social ones. The progressive triumph of a system of wage labor and proletarianization, and the rise of rural industries (sometimes called "proto-industrialization")[1] which was in some measure a response to it, created and entrenched a system of class differentiation which further served to distinguish attitudes to families and households. Lawrence Stone has characterized this period as one of transition from the "Open Lineage Family" through the "Restricted Patriarchal Family" to the "Closed Domesticated Nuclear Family" (Stone 1979). In essence the transition was one from families in which the interests of the wider kinship network or community took precedence to one in which privacy, affective individualism, and personal autonomy were dominant. This change to nuclear families was reflected in areas as diverse as domestic architecture (to provide more rooms and more privacy) to an emphasis on greater autonomy for women (or at least wives) and the assumption that education for both sexes was a desirable norm. Clearly, some of these changes did indeed take place; they began in the middle and upper classes, and were generally dictated by the possession of significant amounts of disposable property. But for the vast majority of people in Britain, this latter condition did not apply. While a weakening of kin and village structures did occur, it was often perceived as a loss rather than a gain, and in many areas the earlier pattern of families and households was maintained as long as possible, even being re-created in new settings whether in Britain or in the colonies. Changing economic conditions allowed for earlier marriages in some areas, but there is little evidence that such marriages were contracted with a view to disrupting existing extended kin and community contacts. Marriage and the establishment of households had traditionally been regulated by economic conditions; an expansion of economic opportunity allowed for more households but not necessarily different types of households. The "Closed Domesticated Nuclear Family" subsequently provided a cultural model for the lower levels of society throughout the nineteenth century, but by 1750 few outside of London and its provincial satellites had yet adopted it.

WOMEN AND CHILDREN

In terms of the status of women and children, the model presented by Lawrence Stone and others is one in which the women and children of the property-owning classes were progressively liberated from constraints imposed upon them socially, and in which women gained a greater degree of autonomy within the household. In addition, childhood began to be "created" as a distinct phase of life with its own rules and with a stress on educational and moral learning. Once again, though this development was increasingly true for property owners, it was not yet the case for the majority of people. Traditionally, women and children were part of a family (and kin) economic unit in which they were expected to play a full part. Women were active economically to at least as great an extent as were men. Agricultural work was shared, and while a sexual division of labor did exist, in some areas, task flexibility was the norm.

Childhood was less a distinct period in and of itself than a time of "insufficient adulthood" in which tasks were restricted largely on the basis of physical capacity. This was not, however, a "rural idyll" in which subsequent "bourgeois" norms had yet to be enforced; rather it was a society which quite literally could not afford to lose potential labor for any reason. Putting children to work as soon as possible may have been justified as an encouragement to honest labor and the avoidance of idleness, but it was in most cases both economically necessary and sanctioned by immemorial custom. The onset of rural industrialization (proto-industrialization), enclosure of agricultural land, and changes in agricultural specializations did little to change the role of children in most areas. People could marry and start families earlier, but work was still required from all family members. The effects of rural industrialization varied, such that in some areas women achieved a small measure of financial independence while in other areas it merely allowed for an earlier replication of existing roles; it certainly did not lead to substantial innovation in the lives of women or children (Kussmaul 1990). Even in the 1850s, over 25 percent of women were listed as fulltime workers and it is likely that the real number was far higher. Farm work for women declined after 1750, but it was replaced by industrial and paid domestic work. The extent to which both women and children were involved in this work can be indicated by the legislation which was passed to regulate it, even though the time taken to pass this legislation sometimes meant that it reflected a situation which had already changed.

RELIEF OF THE POOR

Though women and children contributed much to the early workforce of the Industrial Revolution, their social roles evolved slowly, largely as a result of economic change rather than as its cause. In many ways, the role of the poor was similar: initially they provided a source of available labor, while later their work was regulated to make their contribution more effective. Poverty, though it was a semipermanent condition for a few continually, was a possibility for most at various times. The Poor Law, which was developed in the last years of the reign of Queen Elizabeth I in the 1580s and 1590s and which remained in force until the 1830s (largely unchanged until the "Speenhamland Reforms" of the 1790s), was designed to address this problem.

The "Old" Poor Law was nationally mandated (within England and Wales) but administered locally. It functioned to provide relief, enforce discipline, express communal responsibility, and serve as a "potent reminder of social distance" (Wrightson 1986, p. 201). It differed from most other European systems by its uniformity and comprehensiveness, coupled with effective enforcement, its reliance on local taxation and its "relative certainty and generosity" amounting to between 1 percent and 2 percent of national income (Slack 1990, p. 30). Awards were restricted to a person's home parish or parish settlement, so it proved an effective means either to maintain people at home or to allow them to move in response to relative labor scarcity.

In addition, the measure of insurance and security that it provided effectively gave protection from destitution, thus "permitting" smaller families by removing the need to have large numbers of children to provide for parents in their old age. It probably also had some effect in restricting the opposition to the progressive enclosure of common land which was taking place. Subsistence migration (when people had to move because of crop failure or the lack of food in their own regions), as opposed to migration to areas of greater opportunity, thus declined at this time, and at the end, was virtually restricted to subsistence migration into England from Ireland where the Poor Law had little practical effect. Subsistence famines also disappeared in England and Wales in the 1640s (though not in Scotland and above all not in Ireland) as a result of both the poor law and the tendency for regional variations in the prices of agricultural products (especially grains) to be eliminated following improvements in transportation.

As the "Old" Poor Law was financed by local taxation and managed by local notables, there was often a subtle calculus involved by both recipients and contributors to it. Recipients had to decide whether to take Poor Law payments or to migrate in search of work; contributors had to decide whether to pay for the Poor Law, through taxes, or whether to hire additional labor and thus complete larger projects at the same time, that is, paying wages and reducing their Poor Law contributions. The latter incentive undoubtedly led to many large-scale agricultural projects (such as the draining of the Fens in the east of England) at the same time as it increased the pace of land enclosure. At other times, economic migration was encouraged because enforcement of Poor Law settlement policy was flexible. As a result of this combination of factors, the Old Poor Law "underpinned the growth of an economically mobile wage force; encouraged the consolidation of farms and facilitated the separation of smallholders from the land; provided local incentives for agricultural capital formation and industrial development; and kept population growth under control" (Solar 1995, p. 16).

Although the motivation for the Old Poor Law may have been to prevent civil unrest and the uncontrolled movement of "sturdy beggars" (an Elizabethan legal term denoting adults who were physically able to work but did not do so), it actually gave a measure of security to the laboring poor which was largely lacking in other parts of Europe. But the reliance on local taxation on land proved unworkable as the process of industrialization progressed, and the Old Poor Law was replaced with a new and more punitive one in the 1830s, just in time for Charles Dickens to chronicle its harshness and inhumanity in his novels. However, the Old Poor Law undoubtedly helped the initial stages of the Industrial Revolution by making possible a mobile workforce, even if it was an often unwilling and badly treated one.

This was true only in England. The Old Poor Law was ineffective in Ireland, and largely avoided in most of Wales where the extended kin and the village community still opted to look after "their own." In Lowland Scotland a poor law comparable (though less generous) to that in England developed. North of the "Highland Line" the ideal, which was still adhered to in Wales, gradually slid into something closer to the Irish model where an ineffective poor law was accompanied by a weakening of traditional structures leading to either emigration out of Britain or subsistence migration within it.

KNOWLEDGE OF THE WORLD

Mokyr's sixth category: "what they knew and what they wanted to know" is in many ways the most problematic noneconomic issue in the environment surrounding the Industrial Revolution. Leaving aside issues of religion and politics, to be discussed later, the primary questions are those of literacy (and what was read) and the effect of the "Scientific Revolution" alongside the documented rise in skepticism and "rationality." Of these issues, the former is more easy to assess than the latter although remaining an area requiring further research. Literacy in the Middle Ages was severely restricted largely to priests (and not even to all of them) and to a very slowly increasing number of lay people employed in law, business, or government service. This upward trend in literacy continued through the years leading up to the Industrial Revolution, though it was subject to substantial variations over time, and more specifically, with regard to geography and occupation.

In many cases, most people learned to read and write, sometimes just one and not the other, based less on a desire for learning than on occupational necessity. Illiteracy may have declined from 80 percent to somewhat less than 50 percent for traders and craftsmen during this period, but for laborers and "husbandmen" the level of illiteracy seems always to have fluctuated in the narrow band of 90 percent to 100 percent, even in the more developed areas of the southeast of England (Graff 1987). Less than half of the men and more than half of the women were unable to sign their own names so, even given the inadequacy of signatures as a measure of literacy, the number of functioning illiterates must have been considerable. The fact of such widespread illiteracy does not however tell us much about access to "new" knowledge or access to new jobs. In addition, the progress of literacy was not unilinear. One generation was not necessarily more literate than the one which preceded it; in fact, the contrary could be the case.

It is probably correct to view the acquisition of literacy as part of an overall familial and societal strategy directed at economic survival rather than as the conscious pursuit of a concrete "good" in its own right. If a job market "required" literacy (or at least put a premium on it), then it would be acquired—if not, it would not. The onset of the Industrial Revolution did little at least initially to change this; most "new" jobs did not require literacy, hence the decline in literacy which can be detected in some areas.

"What they knew" was then, as now, often merely dependent on what they were told. Literature could be read aloud and thus influence a wider audience than those who were functionally literate. For the most part this was the age of "Broadsheets" (pamphlets, often illustrated, on a particular subject which was often political or religious) and opinion was shaped by them, hence the importance of the effort to control their production and content. The increase of radical views around the time of the Civil Wars of the 1640s reflected the breakdown of this control; a mistake by the ruling classes which was only infrequently allowed to happen again.

Although this brief outburst of "antiestablishment" literature had a temporarily radicalizing effect on politics and religion, there was no systematic attempt to propagate an understanding of "Science" or indeed anything other than religion and politics. Although the Civil Wars had their profoundly "radical" aspects, they were (for the ideological) fundamentally about the theologically based political "Rights of Man" rather than any claim to base them exclusively in "natural reasoning." There was some technological progress during this period, but with the exception of the role of a few more progressive families and individuals, little was contributed to it by the Scientific Revolution, even after the foundation of its formal institutions in the late seventeenth century. Perhaps the reaction to the Civil Wars may have in some ways impeded the willingness by the authorities to encourage literacy and thus the spread of "new" ideas among the common people.

RELIGION AND POLITICAL THINKING

Religion, and by extension political ideology, was *the* focus throughout this period. It defined what one was, where one stood in relation to one's family and where one stood in relation to others. The whole of politics and most of social life were defined by religion. "Unbelief" became a factor in the eighteenth century, although even then only for the more affluent, and religion was unquestionably dominant as a form of self-definition. In fact the move to unbelief (or some combination of Deism and Agnosticism, a belief in either an impersonal "Divine Principle" or the belief that no certain knowledge about the existence or nonexistence of God was possible) by a very small percentage of the population was accompanied by a move to Methodism and other forms of religious dissent by a far larger number of people. One of the few "truths" which can be maintained about this era is that it was an age of religion, or religions, in which nearly everyone took part.

Religion mattered in a far more self-conscious way (and to all concerned in a far more self-evident way) than it has probably done before or since. Jews had been expelled from England in the late twelfth century, and were allowed back under Oliver Cromwell's Republic only after the execution of Charles I (1649); the various nations of Britain had long been exclusively Christian in their religious allegiance. Following the Reformation (beginning in the 1530s), the Catholic Church had become largely restricted as a popular church to the more remote areas of Britain (Ireland, Lancashire, and western Scotland), though it survived in other areas where the nobility was sympathetic.

In the rest of Britain, the situation was somewhat confused. In nearly all cases the most economically progressive regions (or at least the middle class in them) embraced some form of Protestantism, while the bulk of the population would either reject or embrace it, or continue to practice beliefs which were neither clearly Catholic nor Protestant but rather a reflection of communal ideology. Indicative of this is the continuance of "patterns" or visits to holy wells throughout this period and later in areas as diverse as north Wales and East Anglia. As a result, the population in many areas could either be (re)captured for Catholicism (the case in Ireland and parts of Scotland), converted to some type of Protestantism (as in much of England and Lowland Scotland), or left largely alone until the second wave of the Reformation (as in parts of England and nearly all of Wales). The very virulence with which certain ideas took hold in parts of Britain (including some manifestations of Nonconformity) indicates the degree to which many areas were left "unchurched" for many years. The church settlement under the Tudors (especially Queen Elizabeth I) which created the Church of England was an attempt to include all believers in one national church, but the English Civil War demonstrated its failure to accomplish this. Religion, and religious differences, remained central to British political and social life.

CHOOSING RULERS

The inextricable linkage of religion and politics meant that religion was also involved in the process Mokyr identifies as "choosing rulers." Protest was expressed in religious language and various types of religious movements were the vehicles for expressing discontent. If the twenty-four wars conducted externally at this time were largely fought for commercial and territorial reasons with religion being occasionally invoked, then the twenty-four internal wars of the period often had religion as a central factor, albeit firmly linked to a process of creating a British state. The rebellions in Tudor England all combined religious motives with political action. This was also the case in the Irish wars which stretched from Henry VIII's attempted pacification in the 1540s to the Jacobite Wars of the 1690s. A further clear example can be found in the series of wars in England and Scotland which formed part of the Civil War of the 1640s: Catholics, Episcopalians (or Anglicans), Presbyterians, and a variety of nonconformist and independent sects were mobilized on the basis of religion to contest both religious and political issues. "Choosing rulers" was not infrequently attempted by force of arms.

Part of the reason for this tendency to settle disputes by violence was because the majority of people had little other input into the political process. The Civil War was largely the result of a dispute between one section of the landed gentry and the court versus another section of the landed gentry and the mercantile and commercial interests. Though it unleashed a range of "populist" forces whose attempt to "turn the world upside down" has made them the favorite of generations of historians, the result was not the creation of popular government but rather a compromise settlement between the two contesting parties that restored a system of government much like that which had preceded it.[2] The attempt of James II in the 1680s to subvert this system was defeated militarily.

By 1700, England and Wales were ruled by a Parliament consisting of 220 unelected peers (including 26 bishops) and 489 Members of Parliament (MPs), of whom 80 came from the counties (each with an average of 2500 electors), and 405 from the boroughs or towns (each with an average of just over 200 electors). Most constituencies were virtually controlled by local landholding and commercial interests, and in all nearly 95 percent of the population did not have the vote. The Scottish Parliament was dissolved in 1707 and 45 MPs were added to the English Parliament in Westminster to represent a total of 1.04 million Scots. The Irish Parliament, from which Catholics were banned from participation, was if anything less representative and was abolished in 1801. In sum, "choosing rulers" was not something that British people were expected to do, perhaps accounting in part for the attraction of community-controlled religious movements such as Presbyterianism and later Methodism.

THE MAKING OF THE BRITISH NATION

After exploring the six points that Mokyr believed help explain when and why the Industrial Revolution occurred, there is little to suggest that Britain was on the verge of a great leap forward in 1750. Treatment of the poor was (comparatively) exemplary, but political life, though it could be tumultuous, remained restricted. Only in the religious field had much change happened, and even there the results are somewhat contradictory and highly fragmented both over time and space. It is hard to see any significant transformation in most of Mokyr's list. What then had changed to allow the Industrial Revolution to take place in Britain after 1750? Economic events (such as proto-industrialization) and a concomitant shift in demographic behavior provide some of the answer. Likewise, the unique pattern of English urbanization (with London being so much more internally dominant culturally, demographically, and economically than was the case with any other European city) and the continuing trend toward agricultural enclosure, both contributing to regional changes in agricultural specialization, form a further part of the story.

However, what was just as central was the creation of the economic and political entity of Britain itself and alongside this, the creation of an ideology of "Britishness." It was this ideology which built upon the religious enthusiasms of the population to create an integrated society while at the same time restricting its direct political expression as far as possible. The result was the establishment of a hegemonic consensus which "created" Britain and allowed the Industrial Revolution to prosper.

Britain was created by a long series of political actions which stretched throughout this period. Political differences between regions and nations were progressively eroded; local elites were co-opted, removed or replaced; a British network of transportation and markets was initiated; an ideology was developed to act as the cement for the whole process; and finally Britain (and "Britishness") began to "go global" beginning with the emergence of the Atlantic economy. The result was a composite economic, political, and ideological process of integration. However, the process proceeded unevenly over time and space, developing nuances and variants and ultimately not always succeeding.

Apart from the long drawn out process of integrating the regions of England, the major challenges involved the so-called "Celtic Fringe": Wales, Scotland, Ireland, Cornwall, and the Isle of Man. Cornwall was integrated economically and politically relatively smoothly, despite religiously focused revolts in the sixteenth and seventeenth centuries, and its indigenous language, Cornish, ceased to be spoken in the eighteenth century as the Industrial Revolution took off. It was the first of the Celtic languages to "die," and its demise was an indication of the success of the creation of Britain. Further evidence of the success of this process is given by the experience of the Isle of Man, whose language (Manx) gradually dwindled to extinction only in the twentieth century, with the island itself retaining a tenuous independence to the present. The most conspicuous failure of integration was in Ireland, where the contradiction between economic and political integration on the one hand and ideological integration on the other were never fully resolved and remains unresolved to the present.

Components of "Britishness"

The key elements in the ideology of Britishness were: Protestantism (initially Anglicanism but later extended to include all Protestants); the respect for the property rights of the individual and, by extension, of individualism as such; the Monarchy (when it had been tamed to the purpose); and the creation of a "British" history which, though overtly racist elements were not always excluded, endeavored to unify the nation around common themes concerning such ideas as the pursuit of liberty, which was meant to be primordial to the British soul and to set it apart from those of other (lesser) peoples. The result was an often curious mixture in which King Arthur and Robin Hood rubbed shoulders with the Protestant martyrs executed under Queen Mary in the 1550s and an assortment of military heroes ranging from Richard the Lionheart to Francis Drake. This mixture was eminently flexible, with some elements being stressed more at different times and in different places and with the possibility of new heroes being added to it.

The monarchy became a central part of this ideology under the Tudors (especially Queen Elizabeth I), but the Stuart monarchy was widely challenged, and the Hanoverians (beginning with George I who gained the throne in 1714 as the nearest Protestant heir) received a mixed reception. The monarchy only really gained a large measure of centrality (and popularity) under Queen Victoria (1837–1901) and even then the image of the monarchy was a carefully (re)constructed one (Cannadine 1983).

Likewise, the initial stress on Anglicanism (the Church of England) as the apogee of both Protestantism and the often praised British virtue of tolerance proved to be insufficient, and was replaced by a broad spectrum of Protestantism united by a presumed heritage of liberty and respect for property as opposed to the superstition and absolutist tendencies of the Church of Rome. This ideology was of obvious appeal (and use) to the cohesive property-owning elite who controlled the state but, in its appeal to a history and set of moral characteristics which all British people were presumed to share, it exercised a powerful influence throughout Britain. It even managed to include the descendants of those who had turned the idea of the "Norman Yoke" (the presumed difference between a "Norman" upper class and an "Anglo-Saxon" lower class) into an instrument of rebellion in the 1640s. In addition, this ideology provided sufficient flexibility to enable what was at heart largely an English state to successfully portray itself as a British one, leading not only to the co-opting of local elites, whose self-interest alone would have predisposed them in its favor, but also to the incorporation of the mass of inhabitants of the British Isles whose interests were perhaps less obviously served by it. This applied not only in England but also to other parts of Britain and even further afield.

WALES

Wales lost much of her political independence with the fall of the princely house of Gwynedd in north Wales in the thirteenth century. This loss was reconfirmed with the defeat of the rebellion of Owain

Glyndwr in 1405, and finalized with the accession of Henry Tudor to the English throne as Henry VII in 1485. Wales became an administrative and economic part of the new Britain, although, being on its fringes, its economic role was largely restricted to the supply of agricultural produce to the English markets. The Reformation began in Wales in the 1530s when Henry VIII assumed the title of head of the Church in England (and Wales) and set out on a process of replacing the Catholic Church with the reformed Anglican Church. The Reformation in Wales was then spread through the Welsh language, although much of the country was left relatively unchurched until the "Second Reformation" and the rise of religious dissent. Welsh was used in religious services, but its use elsewhere was discouraged, and literacy in Welsh declined during the seventeenth century. The spread of the English language, including its use by many in the "Old Dissent" (such as Quakers), indicated a gradual decline in the cultural distinctiveness of Wales, and of its becoming a region of Britain (or even of England), as many in England clearly considered it. The rise of Methodism, the Sunday school movement, and the circulating schools initiated by Gruffydd Jones (schools which moved from one area of Wales to another and trained a whole range of individuals in basic literacy) reversed this process, and the coming of the Industrial Revolution led to the increased strength of the Welsh language and its spread to areas which had been partially Anglicized (Thomas 1988).

The continuance of Welsh distinctiveness was not however a challenge to "Britishness"; rather Wales became an integral part of Britain irrespective of the differences between Wales and the other parts of Britain. The acceptance of the British ideology was nearly total, and ordinary Welsh people considered themselves to be Welsh-speaking Britons rather than a separate nationality. The shared ideology allowed for their incorporation on (more or less) equal terms and allowed them to (theoretically at least) participate to the full in the economic and other benefits of Britain and its overseas extensions. It is only in the second half of the twentieth century, as the ideology and achievements of "Britishness" became clearly questionable that alternative ideas about the nature of Wales and of Welshness have been discussed.

SCOTLAND

If language was not an obstacle to Britishness in Wales, the same was not true in Scotland. Scotland was in many respects not one nation, but at least two, and the ideology of "Britishness" proceeded at different speeds on either side of the "Highland Line." Scotland's incorporation into the new Britain began with the joining of the two crowns when James VI of Scotland succeeded to the English crown in 1601. The next hundred years were marked by frequent outbreaks of hostility between elements in the two kingdoms and by civil war in Scotland itself. By the time of the dissolution of the Scottish Parliament in 1707, the differences between the English establishment and the leaders in Lowland Scotland had been resolved. The Reformation had triumphed in the Lowlands of Scotland, although not in the form of Episcopalianism (the version of Protestantism in which the church is administered by bishops) but rather Presbyterianism, thus creating the occasion for the situation whereby the current Queen is head of the Episcopal Anglican Church in England but becomes a Presbyterian when she journeys from Buckingham Palace in London to Balmoral Castle in Scotland. Likewise the English language and the ideology of "Britishness" were also dominant in the Lowlands, though the former had first to defeat the challenge of Lallans (the language in which Robert Burns wrote his poetry) to be the written standard.

In the Highlands, however, the Reformation had been more patchily received, with Catholicism surviving in many areas, and a clan based, Gaelic-speaking society proving resistant to the new ideas. The refusal of Lowland Scotland to use Gaelic to evangelize the Highlands at first allowed the old ways to continue, but eventually prevented Gaelic from surviving as well as Welsh did. Lowland Scotland was firmly integrated into the British market and transportation structures, and thus linked to the wider Atlantic and nascent imperial economies; the Highlands were not. It took the collapse of the Jacobite cause at Culloden in 1745 (the final battle at which the Stuart claimants to the throne, who had been replaced by the Protestant Hanoverians, were defeated), and the Highland Clearances (when the Gaelic-speaking population of the Highlands was evicted and the existing system of mixed agriculture replaced by large estates based on a combination of pastoral farming and hunting) for this area to be finally added to Britain. The Highlands were extensively depopulated, the clans broken, and many highlanders emigrated overseas. Though their society was largely destroyed, Highland heroes (such as Rob Roy) were incorporated into the ideology of Britishness and, alongside tartan and other "authentic" Highland "traditions," added to its popular appeal (Trevor-Roper 1983). The flexible ideology of property-owning Protestant Britons united under the Crown and the legatees of a proud tradition of freedoms had found more adherents.

IRELAND

Only in Ireland was the ideology of "Britishness" to meet with near complete failure. Given the constituents of this ideology and the way in which Ireland was incorporated into Britain, this lack of success is hardly surprising. Ireland was made part of Britain in a concerted way beginning in the 1540s, though there was a long history of earlier sporadic attempts from the eleventh century onward. The process of incorporation included the removal of most of the existing elites (though some accepted the changes) and their replacement with English and Lowland Scots Protestant "planters" (the Anglo-Irish) in much of southern and central Ireland. In Ulster in the north, a more proletarian settlement was encouraged in which mostly Scots settlers took over the lands forfeited by rebellious Irish at the beginning of the seventeenth century. Most noticeably, the native Irish remained largely Catholic and were thus both suspect to the British state authorities and outside of most of the appeal of "Britishness." The Protestant settlers in Ulster, though recalcitrant throughout all of this period, finally acquiesced to the dominant ideology after a rebellion in 1798 and became the exponents of a very unreconstructed ideology of Britishness, the Orangemen, which persists in Northern Ireland.

The de facto exclusion of the Catholic Irish, and its de jure accompaniments in terms of legal restrictions which remained in force until the nineteenth century, led to their ultimate rejection of "Britishness" and their attempt to achieve independence. However, many Catholic Irish in the nineteenth and twentieth centuries maintained an enthusiastic support for "King and Country" which indicates how, while remaining formally outside of "Britishness" they still responded to its appeal. The willingness of the Irish Catholic hierarchy to support the British state, though a constant source of friction to the nationalistically inclined, is further evidence of the ability of the British state to incorporate or at least neutralize potential opposition to Britishness. However, though "Britishness" was a malleable ideology, the existence of an Anglo-Irish community and the Protestants of Ulster precluded its full extension to the Catholic Irish. The nature of the society created in the wake of the integration of Ireland into Britain economically and politically meant that it could never be fully integrated ideologically.

THE FIRST ATLANTIC ECONOMY

Though Ireland may have ended up as an ideological failure for Britain, it remained firmly part of Britain politically from at least

1700 to the First World War (1914–1918). Ireland was also an intrinsic part not only of the British economy but also of the Atlantic one which was forming around Britain throughout this period. This "First Atlantic Economy" was based on the exploitation of trade among the various components of Britain, North America, and the Caribbean. As a source of raw materials, including sugar and its derivatives from the Caribbean, the Atlantic economy contributed substantially to British imports. Of equal significance was the extent to which the export of manufactured goods shifted from being directed to Europe to being channeled into the Atlantic economy; a development that has been labeled the "Westernization effect" (Thomas 1988). The Atlantic economy was, however, not only important as an economic phenomenon, it was also involved in the further extension of the ideology of "Britishness" and the development of its most important offshoot.

The fact that the West Indian colonies had economies exclusively dependent on slave labor was repellent to those British Christian traditions which triumphed in 1833 with the final abolition of slavery in the British Empire. However, the ideology of Britishness, with its foundations in the elaboration of the idea of a freedom loving, Protestant individual with a unique evolutionary history dating back to the mists of Albion—one of the Latin names for Britain, especially the Celtic Britain of King Arthur—had somewhat less difficulty in accommodating itself to racial differentiation and discrimination. This adaptability proved to be an important ideological underpinning for the extension of the British Empire during the nineteenth century. Though racism was part of the ideology of "Britishness" (even if on most occasions only implicitly), it was more flexible than that. The collapse of slavery in the West Indies led eventually to the creation of a new subcategory within Britishness, separated by race but in many respects joined by culture ranging from presumed political inclinations (Westminster style parliamentary democracy) through Methodism to a taste for British leisure activities such as drinking stout (a type of strong, dark beer) and playing cricket. The West Indies was "in" and yet not "of" Britishness in different ways from Ireland but no less certainly. The basic dilemma created over race and Britishness has still not been resolved in the contemporary United Kingdom.

More promising (and plausible) soil for the ideology of "Britishness" were the North American colonies. Here it did indeed take root, but in a form which was anything but welcome to many of its more zealous exponents. At his coronation in 1760, King George III expressed the sentiment that he "gloried in the name of Britain." The extent to which he understood what this might entail may be questioned; however, his conception and that of at least a certain proportion of his subjects differed markedly. This ideology of "Britishness" depended on the rights of "free-born," property-owning, Protestant Britons: the Monarchy was ancillary to this, included for its willingness to endorse this ideology. The degree to which property ownership was restricted in the United Kingdom meant that, at least after the 1640s or 1688 at the latest in England and Wales, Monarchy and Britishness would not come into major conflict. North America was a different place and here the passage of events made such a conflict perhaps inevitable. The initial American resistance to the Stamp Act was based upon a desire on the part of the colonists to maintain their rights as free-born Britons; only later was independence decided on as a last resort when it seemed that not only their rights as Britons but even the "Rights of Man" were threatened. Paradoxically perhaps, the making of Britain, which was so essential in preparing for the Industrial Revolution, also meant the making of the United States. Until the twentieth century, the rights of free-born, property-owning, Protestant (and white) Americans and their links to the British past would provide a sort of doppelgänger or distorted mirror image to the ideology of Britishness.

CONCLUSION

The Industrial Revolution is in many ways the key to the modern world; in its turn, Britain is the key to the Industrial Revolution. Although the economic developments which first came to fruition in Britain were replicated elsewhere—and it should be stressed that the Industrial Revolution was a global rather than a merely British phenomenon—Britain's role in its initiation was crucial. The nature of this role, in economic or scientific and technical terms, has been explored at length in many of the standard texts dealing with the Industrial Revolution in Britain. The Industrial Revolution was not only economic in its origins or effects, it was the product of a complicated set of circumstances and events in British society as a whole, and its results served in turn to reshape that society into something which was markedly different from the society which preceeded it. The form and timing of these events, and in some respects their character, are what set Britain apart and help explain the origins of the Industrial Revolution in that country. Among the many cultural and social developments in Britain immediately before the Industrial

Revolution, the most central was the creation of a self-consciously British nation with an ideology which explained its "unique" character, its religious and ethical dimensions, and its mission in the world. This ideology not only set out to explain this uniqueness but also to create it. In turn, it served both as the rationale for growth in Britain itself and throughout the world, and also as a model for the new United States.

Similarly, changes in family and household structures, and in the roles of women and children, had only a minor impact in most of the constituent regions and nations of the British Isles before 1750. Times had not been peaceful however, and all of Britain had been subject to periodic upheavals in which the political and religious profile and nature of the nation had been actively (and often violently) contested, with a wide range of ideas that were based on the dissemination of broadsheets and popular tracts being discussed.

In all of these upheavals, the religious and the political were inextricably intermingled. The attempts of Queen Elizabeth and her government to eradicate Catholicism and create a broad-based Protestant Church of England collapsed under the Stuarts due to a variety of pressures—Catholicism in Ireland, Presbyterianism and Catholicism in Scotland, and religious radicalism in England. This was a process which culminated with the English Civil War, the execution of Charles I in 1649, the brief establishment of a Commonwealth (Republic), and the restoration of the Monarchy. The result of all these upheavals (especially after the "Glorious Revolution" of 1688 which brought King William III and Queen Mary to the throne) was the creation of a consensus that Britain should include all of the British Isles, and that it should be ruled by a self-selected, small body of landowners and merchants with the monarchy as its figurehead.

This consensus was one factor in the creation of an ideology of "Britishness": it was necessary to unify the British Isles into one nation. The second factor, which had been underlined by the fratricidal violence and the growth of politico-religious radicalism, was that this one nation had to be based on ideas which the majority of the population could be presumed to have in common. This in turn would lead to the perception that the majority were "partners" in this ideology despite their effective lack of direct participation in the political process and the choosing of leaders. The solution, as discussed above, was the "creation" of Britain and Britishness based on the ideal of free, property-owning, Protestants whose role was to lead the way for other peoples, and who expected to be blessed with material prosperity as a sign of the rightness of their cause. It was a "creation" (or invention) in that it created a history and mythology for itself which was then incorporated as being the "true" history of the nation, and both the explanation of its success and the justification for the continued harassment of those elements in Britain which refused to accept (or were unable to share) the ideology. This ideology was then exported, initially to the Atlantic colonies, and formed the "justification" for the British Empire which carried it around the world. The need to "create" the nation hastened the processes of centralization and urbanization and the creation of administrative and transportation structures which could make the nation a reality. It was on this basis that the Industrial Revolution in Britain could take off.

The success of the creation of Britain was spectacular, as was that of the Industrial Revolution. In its turning inward to create strong internal markets and then its turning outward for external markets, not to Europe which would challenge it (and often support its internal enemies, especially the Catholic ones) but farther afield, the creation of Britain inevitably led to the beginnings of a global economy. Partly in reaction to this process, other nations (notably France and the United States) began to evolve their own ideologies as to what their nations were and what made them distinct. The creation of Britain involved the first tentative efforts to create a recognizably modern nation-state and hence, perhaps, its most enduring legacy (after the impetus which it gave to the Industrial Revolution) is the phenomenon of nationalism. The effects of both these legacies have irrevocably shaped the world in which we live and continue to challenge us with their consequences.

NOTES

1. For a description of "proto-industrialization" see Mendels 1972. For a criticism of the utility of the concept see Coleman 1983.
2. "The World Turned Upside Down" was the title of a broadsheet dealing with some of the radical religious and social ideas being discussed at the time of the Civil War. Its title is symbolic of how much change these ideas threatened. See Hill 1984.

4
NO LONGER AN ISLAND: EXPLORING THE SIGNIFICANCE OF ATLANTIC TRADE TO THE INDUSTRIAL REVOLUTION

Robert T. Schultz

Population growth, capital accumulation, technological change, and the emergence of a wage-earning class constitute the major developments in western European societies, particularly in Britain, that scholars typically associate with the Industrial Revolution. An additional significant development, one often discussed separately, is the revolution that increased agricultural output per capita and supplied a growing, urban population with some of the increased nutrients required for industrial labor. The vast literature on these subjects has contributed significantly to our understanding of the process that changed the course of human history.

To supplement these major areas of attention, this chapter reviews the various ways that colonial trade contributed to the Industrial Revolution. The expanding European powers of the sixteenth, seventeenth and eighteenth centuries became increasingly entwined in a dynamic and growing Atlantic economy of New World colonies and Old World metropolises. New markets in staples, slaves, and manufactured goods affected the course of human history on both sides of the Atlantic. Students of the Industrial Revolution have paid relatively scant attention, however, to the impact of Atlantic trade on European societies and economies during and prior to industrialization. This chapter will review the most significant contributions to the literature that address the impact of New World markets on European developments, and it will expose the deficiencies in this literature and suggest some ideas for future research.

No single cause sparked the "revolution." Indeed, some scholars argue that applying the term "revolution" to the industrialization process hinders our understanding of the multiple factors that developed over centuries and simultaneously pushed Europeans into the New World and the modern world (Cameron 1985). No nation or its people went through the process in isolation from others. Demographic expansion, technological innovation, new wage and labor systems, political reform, New World foodstuffs and the nutrients they provided to European populations all significantly affected specific European societies and particular geographic regions as the West industrialized and stepped into modernity. The industrialization process was a succession of steps, often only gradual ones, not one great leap (Jones 1987; Cameron 1985; Komlos 1995).

Joel Mokyr, whose work focuses on technological developments, recognizes the narrow scope of much of the literature on the Industrial Revolution. "Once the economist ventures outside the safe realm of conventional microeconomics and agrees to consider extra economic factors," Mokyr writes, "he or she often discovers that events are hopelessly over determined, that is, there are many plausible explanations for every phenomenon" (Mokyr 1990, p. 8). In his volume on technological creativity, Mokyr goes on to assert that "Discoveries in the New World and elsewhere had a clear and visible impact on Europe" (Mokyr 1990, p. 69). Douglass North and Eric Jones also recognize the significance of expanding markets to industrialization, noting, for example, that "Smithian" growth—i.e., growth based on trade—eroded government restrictions on entrepreneurs, fostered reorganization in manufacturing, and increased supervision of economic ventures (North 1981, p. 167; Jones 1987, pp. 85–103).

Expanding global trade contributed significantly to the industrialization process, but this fact receives little attention in the literature. Inter-European, Mediterranean and New World trade; bigger, faster commercial sailing ships; expanding cities and construction booms in the Old World (e.g., London) and the New (e.g., Boston); growing and migrating populations; quests for gold, silver and spices; New World sugar and African slaves; the fortunes amassed by the planters and merchants involved in the Atlantic trade: these early modern developments demonstrate the increasing commercial nature of the era. A European merchant's fortune often depended on the success of a Barbadian or North American planter's New World estate, and each man's wealth rested on the forced labor of African slaves ripped from their homes and their culture to toil from sunup to sundown in a North or South American field.

This world of intense, transatlantic economic activity, instigated by Europeans but in large part carried out beyond European borders, exists rather incidentally in the literature on European economic development. Sixteenth-, seventeenth-, and eighteenth-century Europe understandably receive most of the attention (Landes 1969; Mokyr 1990; Komlos 1989a). Technological developments, demographic trends, and the changing nature of European institutions dominate scholars' inquiries. What allowed European populations to break through the Malthusian ceilings—that is, the carrying capacities of their environments—that had previously kept those populations in check? Did these demographic changes foster industrialization and the development of new laws concerning property rights? Why did Europeans rather than Asians industrialize when historical developments in China seemed to be pushing the Chinese in that direction? Such endogenous questions—those concerning what occurred *within* a particular geopolitical body, such as Britain—govern most economists and historians' inquiries, even after European countries had long since become imperial powers (Landes 1969; Mokyr 1993; Komlos 1989a; Cameron 1985). By limiting our attention to developments within a single nation, however, we can miss significant exogenous factors, those influencing development from *outside* a country's geopolitical boundaries.

Militant European expansion and waves of emigration in the seventeenth and eighteenth centuries resulted in a global Europe. England was no longer an island. Consequently, national economic and demographic models do not tell a complete history of Britain's or other countries' industrial development. Historians of the Americas have been more inclined to acknowledge the significance of the international context within which industrialization occurred. Perhaps the most prominent historian of the American economy notes that in the early, crucial period of the nation's economic development (1793–1814), "One need look no further than to events in Europe to account for almost every twist and turn in the fortunes of the American economy during those years" (North 1966, p. 36).

American economic growth did not emerge out of a stagnant, isolated national history. It began when the first Europeans set foot on American soil and stepped into a larger, dynamic historical process. Most Europeans from the start had migrated to the New World for economic reasons. As Captain John Smith said of the Englishmen he led to Chesapeake Bay in 1607, "Our gilded refiners with their golden promises made all men their slaves in hope of recompense. There was no talk, no hope, but dig gold, wash gold, refine gold, load gold" (Boller and Story 1992, p. 2). The "recompense" that the Chesapeake colonists would get for the gold they hoped to find would not come from Chief Powhatan and his approximately 10,000 people who lived in 130 villages in the region. (Within sixty years their numbers fell by approximately 80 percent as the English population expanded on the North-American continent.) For the Powhatan people had no need for the gold that Europeans sought so passionately on American soil (Boller and Story 1992, pp. 2–3; Jennings 1976).

Instead, the demand lay across the Atlantic, as did the demand for colonial New England fish, Virginia tobacco, Carolina rice and indigo, and the whale products, timber, grains, livestock and other commodities shipped to England from the lower South, the upper South, the middle colonies and New England. American colonists also exported timber and other trade goods from Atlantic Canada, and sugar and sugar products (e.g., rum) from the West Indies. As the Atlantic economy developed, New World exports enabled colonial planters to purchase manufactured goods from England and other European metropolises, and to import 10–11 million Africans to work their fields. These Africans supplied the labor to produce the rice, indigo, sugar, tobacco, cotton and other staples for which a demand existed on the other side of the Atlantic (McCusker and Menard 1985; Dunn 1973).

This global trade significantly affected European history as well as the history of the Americas. We still know far too little, however, about the impact of the Atlantic economy on European developments.

Researchers' lack of attention to Atlantic trade is apparent in the scholarship on the causes and consequences of European industrialization, which falls into three schools of thought. For the sake of argument I will refer to these schools as the "Hermetic Europe" perspective, the "colonial wake" perspective, and the "Indianist" or "colonialist" perspective. Scholars whose work falls into the first two categories have contributed significantly to our understanding of the endogenous factors that shaped the course of the Industrial Revolution, while the "colonialists" have shed some light on the contributions of the periphery to European developments. A review of the literature demonstrates, however, that to complete the picture we need additional studies on the multiple exogenous factors that affected European industrialization.

HERMETIC EUROPEANISTS

Most "hermetic Europeanists" assume that colonial resources and the expanding Atlantic trade contributed little or nothing to European industrialization. The Industrial Revolution would have occurred anyway; no relationship exists between the Smithian growth of the Atlantic economy and the Industrial Revolution (O'Brien 1982). A further version of this hermetic perspective is the "isolated country" view. Other European markets, resources and population patterns had little or no impact on any single country's industrialization process. All significant factors in that process were endogenous to the developing nation-state. Overseas trade was insignificant for European economic development, for European capital would have been invested entirely in domestic economies and growth necessarily would have followed (Thomas and McCloskey 1981; Landes 1969).

Under the Hermetic Europe rubric I include all those studies that focus on single European countries and leave readers with the impression that industrialization occurred for entirely or primarily endogenous reasons: it would have occurred without access to colonial raw materials and international markets for various types of imports and exports. Although some of these authors pay cursory attention to the significance of markets, they focus almost exclusively on supply-side factors. As one writer asserts,

> The initiative came from the supply side, from technical change . . . Though a combination of change made up the Industrial Revolution, the principal driving forces came from the nature of the inventions in the textile industry . . . and the efficacy of these inventions, which lifted the market for these inventions, at home and abroad, to an entirely new level . . . (Ralph Davis 1979; quoted in Mokyr 1993, pp. 68–69.)

Consequently, this author concludes, "Overseas trade made little contribution to the advent of the Industrial Revolution itself and was not essential in the early stages of its development" (ibid.). Another author concurs:

> I wish to argue that commerce between core and periphery for three centuries after 1450 proceeded on a small scale, was not a uniquely profitable field of enterprise, and while it generated some externalities, they could in no way be classified as decisive for the economic growth of Western Europe. (O'Brien 1982, p. 3)

These writers discuss a variety of trade figures as percentages of a country's GNP—usually Britain's—and conclude that imports and exports contributed little to the country's economic development.

COLONIAL WAKE PERSPECTIVE

A second group of scholars sees a more direct relationship between the American periphery and the European core. They emphasize the connections between colonization and industrialization, and they view colonization as a result of rather than a contributor to the Industrial Revolution. Colonization emerged as a consequence of industrialization. As the wave of European industrialization swelled, colonization expanded in its wake and became important for Europe's economies as continental manufacturing increasingly demanded colonial resources and influenced colonial economic and social developments. Thus, in this view, the Industrial Revolution *became* the engine of colonization; it drove the process of imperialism. European expansion and the dynamic trade and economic linkages resulting from that expansion did not contribute to the economic "take off" but facilitated growth once the revolution was in place.

Those who support this "colonial wake" perspective have something in common with the hermetic Europeanists, for they focus on endogenous factors influencing economic developments. European nations' industrializing economies accelerated the colonial process rather than the other way around. Proponents of this argument concede, as one author puts it, that "metropolitan industry played no significant part in the original seizure of Bengal," for example (Ward 1994, p. 46). After that, however, domestic manufacturing became the engine at home and abroad.

In essence, these authors argue that industrialization created an increasing population of urban dwellers with rising incomes who could therefore purchase colonial imports. Thus, urban growth in British provincial manufacturing towns increased substantially from 1750–1850. The proportion of the population living in towns of 10,000 inhabitants increased from 15 percent to nearly 40 percent of the population (Ward, 1994, p. 54). The conditions of urban life promoted tea drinking, so industrialization accelerated British colonization.

Although these authors focus on Smithian growth as a consequence of an endogenous industrialization process, they ironically concede that merchant capitalists trading tea, indigo, raw cotton, opium and other commodities for the most part reinvested in the metropolis (Ward 1994, p. 50). By the 1820s, 7 percent of the British government's revenues came from import duties on a single commodity—tea (Ward 1994, p. 51).

COLONIALIST SCHOOL

The "Colonialist" or "Indianist" school sees a process quite different from the Eurocentric one envisioned by those who see manufacturing in European countries driving economic growth at home and abroad, with European expansion and global trade as insignificant to the Industrial Revolution. The colonialists argue that the industrialization process was in large part a *consequence* rather than a *cause* of imperialism, that colonial population growth created necessary markets for European manufactured goods, and that New World commodities provided developing Old World metropolises with much needed foodstuffs, timber and other raw materials. Old, landed wealth—"gentlemanly capitalists"—provided significant financing for the Industrial Revolution with funds sent home from India and the West Indies. The process of Smithian growth associated with the expanding markets of the Atlantic economy led the way. As late as 1820, English fortunes based on land and those associated with the service and financial sectors of the economy still outnumbered those amassed by manufacturing (Cain and Hopkins 1986, p. 512).

The Colonialists argue that, at least in Britain, colonization (imperialism) was a necessary condition for industrialization. They point out that many neoclassical economic historians share with Marxist-oriented historians a set of assumptions about British industrialization, for the neoclassicists "relate empire building to stages in the evolution of industrial capitalism" (Cain and Hopkins 1986, p. 501). These authors see financiers rather than manufacturers as the real agents of industrialization. The landed aristocracy capitalized overseas trade and then invested their trading profits in domestic industry. Not until 1850 had "free trade destroyed the old colonial system and . . . ensured the gradual demise of the landed aristocracy . . . " (Cain and Hopkins 1986, p. 525).

DEFICIENCIES IN THE LITERATURE

Despite the contributions of these schools of thought, the arguments hinder our understanding of European industrialization in three ways. The remainder of this chapter will be devoted to discussing these deficiencies in the literature and to demonstrating the necessity for additional studies that focus on the significance of trade to European economic development.

The first way that current scholarship hinders our understanding of industrialization is that those authors who consider the impact of colonization focus almost exclusively on Britain, the British West Indies and India. Their studies consequently place little or no attention on expanding North American markets. Second, some scholars demonstrate a primary concern with proving cause and effect relationships rather than with contributing to our knowledge of the symbiotic relationship between European industrialization and colonization, between Smithian growth and domestic industrialization. Third, a few scholars tend to use data selectively to prove a priori positions.

The economic histories of Europe, like those of the Americas, for the most part concentrate on endogenous economic developments in particular geographic regions. Although historians of the colonial Americas recognize the significance of international trade, the nature of their work causes them to emphasize the economies of their geographic regions rather than how those economies may have influenced European industrialization. Economic historians of colonial British America, for example, study the Smithian growth of the regional colonial economies of the North American continent and the West Indies (McCusker and Menard 1985; Dunn 1973). For the most part, then, historians of Europe share with historians of the Americas a lack of interest in how transcontinental developments affected the Industrial Revolution. They do not ask, for example, how New World population growth and the subsequent demand it created for European exports contributed to capital accumulation in Old World metropolises, capital that was then invested in manufacturing and other sectors. They also do not study the degree to which New World foodstuffs provided the nutrients necessary to support expanding European populations, to feed the emerging class of industrial workers and other urban dwellers. Moreover, they do not ponder the significance of the colonies as a frontier that acted as a "safety valve" to help European populations escape a new Malthusian crisis—a rising population on a finite resource base. Finally, metropolitan exports and colonial imports clearly generated government revenue. However, scholars have yet to explore thoroughly the significance of this revenue in financing some of the government-sponsored infrastructure necessary for industrialization. We need new studies that explore these issues for other imperial powers as well as for Britain.

The second deficiency in the literature—the focus on proving that either Smithian growth led to industrialization or that industrialization occurred independent of Smithian growth—should be solved by new studies that attempt to answer some of the more manageable questions discussed above. New syntheses incorporating these studies can then be written.

The final major deficiency in the literature—the use of selective data to support an a priori position—is related to the political nature of some of the arguments and to the more widely available data in later years. Those who study the emerging global economy from the perspective of the people at the periphery tend to emphasize the lack of development in what became the "Third World." They also emphasize the expanding Europeans' exploitation of African and Native American peoples. In short, European economic achievements involved costs, both human and material. Africans and indigenous Americans paid the price, as did their economies (Wolfe 1982). Likewise, those who study continental European and British economic developments and the process of expansion from the perspective of the Europeans themselves celebrate European economic achievements. They therefore downplay the demographic catastrophes, slave labor, forced migration, and long-term consequences of imperialism (Wolfe 1982; Landes 1969; McCaa 1995; Jennings 1976).

It is not surprising, then, that the Eurocentric literature emphasizes Latin American backwardness and North American and European achievements, while the literature that begins with the periphery focuses on slavery, the exploitation of indigenous peoples, and the emergence of a new European economic elite in the colonies. From the former perspective, inferior Spanish and Portuguese institutions, cultures and practices are responsible for the different, negative historical paths taken south of the North American continent during the colonial period and for the atrocities of forced Indian and African labor systems in that part of the world. A culture of victimization is responsible for the region's postcolonial problems. This literature pays little attention to the forced migration and near annihilation of native peoples in colonial British America and the United States to create living space for expanding northern European and American populations. American lands were not virgin. Europeans removed indigenous populations through war and disease. Little discussion also exists on the use of slavery to produce wealth for European colonists and for Americans of European descent (Landes 1969, pp. 1–40).

The Eurocentric literature hinders our understanding of the relationships between core and periphery for other reasons as well. For example, Patrick O'Brien argues that the commercial relationships between colony and metropolis between 1450 and 1750 was insignificant to European economic growth. He therefore concludes that "the commerce between western Europe and regions at the periphery of the international economy forms an insignificant part of the explanation for the accelerated rate of economic growth experienced by the core after 1750" (O'Brien 1982, p. 3). In the body of his essay, O'Brien defines the periphery as Latin America, the Caribbean, Africa, and Asia. This periphery, he asserts, "purchased about 14 percent of Europe's exports and in 1830 these same regions supplied some 27 percent of European imports" (ibid., p. 4). He then states that when "the southern colonies of British North America" are included, at the end of the eighteenth century "the flows of commodities transshipped between western Europe and regions at the periphery . . . might amount to 20 percent of exports and 25 percent of imports" (ibid., p. 4).

These numbers are quite significant, even more so when we consider that O'Brien never includes New England and the middle colonies of New York and Pennsylvania, or the contributions of Atlantic Canada (ibid.). Moreover, aggregate figures do not tell us anything about the significance of a single import or class of imports to industrial development. And if a single country—England—led the Industrial Revolution as many scholars claim (Landes 1969), then it is more important to understand the significance of Smithian growth to specific countries at particular stages of the industrialization process. Including in these aggregate numbers nonindustrializing European countries, whose import and export figures were relatively insignificant, dilutes the importance of New World Smithian growth to the British Industrial Revolution.

COLONIAL CONTRIBUTIONS

Despite arguments about the insignificance of the New World and the Atlantic economy to European industrialization, scholars have amassed much evidence over the years demonstrating the contrary. It seems quite clear, for example, that the Americas acted as a frontier, a safety valve for expanding European populations. The significance lies in the ability for emigration, not just in the aggregate over centuries, but at particular times and under specific circumstances for various nations.

Wrigley and Schofield, Nuala Zahedieh and others make it clear that many late seventeenth-century Englishmen worried about "overgreat" and "superfluous" multitudes. They feared that food and employment would not meet the needs of the rising "swarms" of British citizens. One promoter of colonization concluded, "like stalls that are overfill of bees . . . no small number of them should be transplanted into some other soil and removed hence into new hives" (Zahedieh,

1994, p. 239). Zahedieh asserts that seventeenth-century "Englishmen had migrated out of a potential Malthusian trap" (ibid., p. 240). Wrigley and Schofield note that 58 percent of the decline in the English population between 1656 and 1686 resulted from emigration (Wrigley and Schofield 1993, p. 228). Zahedieh concurs,

> During the first century of American colonization Britain (England, Scotland, Wales and Ireland—but principally England alone) sent nearly 400,000 emigrants to America, a ratio of emigrants to domestic population almost twice that of Spain in its first 150 years of colonial rule, and more than 40 times that of France in the seventeenth century (Zahedieh 1994, pp. 239–40)

Other scholars (see Zahedieh's 1994 discussion of Habakkuk and Palliser, for example) have noted the importance of new living space for this expanding population, but have paid little attention to the Americas as part of that space.

It is clear that we should not just applaud the British achievement of being able to feed an expanding population. We must also further investigate how, exactly, the British accomplished that achievement. We need to know more about how specific New World foodstuffs contributed to population growth, and about whether the British population would have reached a new Malthusian ceiling had New World emigration not occurred.

These New World immigrants and their descendants created significant, expanding markets for European manufactured goods, and, together with the 10–11 million Africans in the New World, they provided the labor that extracted raw materials and grew and harvested New World commodities such as sugar, rice, indigo, fish and wheat. Europeans increasingly depended on these commodities and expanding markets. Brinley Thomas, for example, discusses the numerous and significant eighteenth-century economic linkages between the New World and the Old. He sheds light on the linkages between European population growth and construction booms that required New World timber, between expanding Atlantic trade and English ship building, between colonial demand for manufactured goods and British manufacturing, between exogenous wars for colonial territory and energy shortages at home (Thomas 1954). Moreover, John Nef makes it clear that the British had developed a significant dependence on external resources as early as the seventeenth century. He notes that Britain solved its seventeenth-century energy crisis by converting from wood to coal to meet its rising energy needs. A wood shortage continued on the island after 1700, however, for "Great quantities of lumber were required for the growing number of ships and horse-drawn vehicles needed to transport people and goods across water and land" (Nef 1977, p. 148). Timber imports from the American colonies and the Baltic were paid for with coal and textile exports.

New World foodstuffs also contributed significantly to the Industrial Revolution. Recent research on nutrition makes it increasingly evident that American foodstuffs provided essential calories for expanding European populations, and for the manufacturing workers who burned more calories than their rural counterparts. In "The New World's Contribution to Food Consumption During the Industrial Revolution," John Komlos postulates that European populations would have reached a new Malthusian ceiling by 1816 had it not been for European cultivation of New World foodstuffs, particularly the potato with its low rate of spoilage, its bulk, which satiated hunger, and its relatively inexpensive calories. If land had been used for traditional crops rather than for the potato, Englishmen would have had approximately 280 fewer calories a day per capita at their disposal. The absence of these calories, Komlos asserts, "could have lowered GNP by as much as 10 percent, even if only half of the extra calories had been consumed by workers" (Komlos nd, unpublished).

The hermetic Europeanists dismiss such claims about New World contributions to British industrialization. They downplay the significance of demand, both domestic and foreign, on facilitating British manufacturing (Mokyr 1977). They assume, for example, that technological innovation would have occurred even if the demand that resulted from increasing domestic and colonial populations had not existed to stimulate that innovation. Supply would have created its own demand. W. A. Cole challenges this assumption. "Supply may create its own demand," Cole asserts, "but only if there are customers both able and willing to buy; and no amount of demand will generate an increase in supply unless producers are both able and willing to respond" (Cole 1981, p. 63). Foreign trade grew faster than the British economy as a whole in the eighteenth century. Britain became a net importer of grain, for example, and developed an important re-export trade to pay for new colonial commodities (ibid., pp. 38–39, p. 44). Cole concludes, therefore, that demand at home and abroad contributed significantly to British economic growth. "The debate about the relative importance of the two may well continue," he asserts, "but the attempt to determine which was primary could be both fruitless and misleading if it is allowed to distract attention from their mutual interaction" (ibid., p. 45).

No Longer an Island: Significance of Atlantic Trade

Other scholars dismiss such arguments. Muriel Grindrod, for one, asserts that "England waited until after 1840, or some eighty years after the start of her industrial revolution, before she began to import an appreciable part of her foodstuffs. Her real dependence on foreign supplies began only around 1850" (Grindrod in Cipolla 1973, p. 477). Grindrod notes that English wheat imports did not increase dramatically until the nineteenth century, and she provides her readers with some examples to prove it: "Imported wheat represented only 3% of the United Kingdom's consumption in 1811–30, rising to 13% in 1831–51, 30% in 1851–60, and reaching 79% in 1891–95" (ibid., p. 477).

We need better estimates, however, of how much wheat the British imported *before* these dates. Grindrod assumes that the amount was less in the eighteenth century than it was in the nineteenth, for imports increased regularly throughout the nineteenth century. But she does not have the data on the eighteenth century that she has on the nineteenth. What is more important to know, though, is how significant eighteenth-century wheat imports were to the British population at *specific times*. Two percent might be a significant amount at a particular stage in the industrialization process and under specific circumstances. It is important to remember, however, that wheat was only *one* imported commodity. How significant were *all* such commodities in their aggregate? How significant were capital inputs from New World business ventures and from domestic ventures tied directly to the dynamic economic activities of expanding Atlantic trade?

We should also remember that the English government recognized the significance of Atlantic trade to England's prosperity and development, for Parliament increasingly regulated trade activities in the late seventeenth and eighteenth centuries. Beginning with the 1696 Navigation Act, the government started to systematize the mercantilist system for one purpose: "to advance the interests of English merchants, shippers, shipbuilders, and producers and to make England, not the other parts of the Empire, wealthy" (Boller and Story 1992, p. 29).

Grindrod and other scholars who dismiss exogenous contributions to European developments write much needed comprehensive analyses spanning centuries, often 1700–1914. A close reading of their work, however, reveals that they have little or no data on the crucial years prior to 1800. Consequently, their assertions about the most important years of the Industrial Revolution and for the critical developmental period that preceded it are almost entirely conjecture.

One also wonders why they extend their studies to 1914. Extensive data on the years *following* the Industrial Revolution does not demonstrate that the increasing Smithian trade *during* and *prior* to the phenomenon was insignificant and that it did not support, in multiple and necessary ways, the phenomenon itself (Thomas and McCloskey 1981, pp. 87–102).

If we imagine Britain industrializing without colonization, then we have to think of where the country would have turned to replace what its colonies provided: British industrialization with more dependence on inputs from continental Europe and Russia, perhaps. One gets the impression from the hermetic Europeanists, though, that if inputs had come from elsewhere, we would be asked to discount those exogenous factors as well. We can always imagine alternatives, but British subjects in these crucial years of the country's historical development did not have that convenience. They dealt with the reality of their historical situation, and colonial contributions seem to be a significant part of that reality.

The purpose of this chapter is not to argue that historians of European economic development should write histories of the colonies. Rather it is important to remember the limitations of our research areas, and to be open to the very real possibility that exogenous factors significantly impacted domestic developments. Surely a historian of the colonies would never propose that European societies had little or no impact on New World civilizations and their economies. Likewise, however, the periphery has always impacted the core—culturally, politically, socially and economically. Over the centuries, people, commodities, manufactured goods and money have migrated in each direction across the Atlantic. Since the beginning of European expansion, people in the Old World and the New have lived with the economic, social, political and cultural consequences of that dynamic interaction.

CONCLUSIONS

Students of the Industrial Revolution need to understand the significance of exogenous factors that contributed to the phenomenon. We must study how capital from American as well as Indian colonial ventures was subsequently invested in domestic enterprises; how nutrients from New World foodstuffs helped populations break through Malthusian ceilings; how colonial frontiers provided additional living space for expanding European populations; how imported raw materials contributed to manufacturing and construction; how governments channeled revenue generated from mercantilist economies into areas that facilitated manufacturing. We must understand linkages.

Arguments that British industrialization did not depend on imports of wheat, tea or any other single commodity tell us little by themselves. It seems clear, however, that the aggregate of all exogenous factors was crucial. It is easy to imagine a country replacing one input with another. It is not easy to imagine Britain replacing *all* of the economic benefits of the growing, dynamic, mercantilist colonial system that the country fought to maintain. John Stuart Mill recognized these benefits 150 years ago when he wrote:

> Our West India colonies . . . cannot be regarded as countries, with productive capital of their own . . . All the capital employed is English capital; almost all the industry is carried on for English uses . . . The trade with the West Indies is therefore hardly to be considered as external trade, but more resembles the traffic between town and country, and is amenable to the principles of the home trade. (Mill, *Principles of Political Economy with some of their Applications to Social Philosophy,* 1848; quoted in McCusker and Menard 1985, p. 8)

We must expand our notion of "town and country" to "metropolis and colony," and we must understand the consequences of the dynamic economic relationships between the two.

Part II
Processes

INTRODUCTION

Historians writing about the Industrial Revolution have raised many interesting questions in trying to decide if an "Industrial Revolution" is a distinct break with past development or a continuation of it. What we need to know in answering these questions is to understand what actually happened, so that we can make a start at identifying an "Industrial Revolution." Some of the issues that have been raised include the following: is the nation or the region the most appropriate unit of analysis? were the changes widespread or limited to a few industries? was the rate of economic growth fast (therefore emphasizing the "revolutionary" nature of the economic changes) or slower than previously thought (giving rise to a more "evolutionary" concept of the IR)? what elements *must* be present?

There are, however, several areas of common agreement. First, that there were certain technological changes that altered the way things were made and that dramatically increased labor productivity. Second, that eventually the resulting increase in output raised living standards in the affected countries. Third, that the structure of each country's economy became more diversified and complex.

Paul Lucier focuses on the people who came up with the new ideas and put them into practice. He describes the various scientific societies and other institutions that helped to make the new discoveries more widely known. Then Harry Kitsikopoulos discusses the rate at which new technology, specifically the steam engine, was adopted by British industry in the late eighteenth and early nineteenth centuries. This is an important issue in helping determine the overall rate of growth: depending on how easily the steam engine could be used in any specific activity, and the extent to which it was used, will contribute to speeding up the aggregate growth rate.

The final two chapters in this section move away from the "traditional" concern with the British Industrial Revolution to observe the industrialization process in other countries. Gennady Shkliarevsky describes the process of early Russian industrialization, and the dominant role played by the state in this process, especially by Peter I and his successors. Shkliarevsky shows that, despite a handful of "activists," the lack of a "favorable environment" will retard the industrialization process, as happened in Russia. Finally, George Vascik summarizes the different views that have been expressed about Germany's industrialization. The traditional practice has been to assume it as a *national* experience; Vascik's sources, especially German historians, have instead pointed out the importance of *regional* differences.

What should emerge from these chapters is a better appreciation of both the common elements that distinguish industrialized economies, and the specific ones that make each unique.

5
SCIENCE, TECHNOLOGY, AND THE INDUSTRIAL REVOLUTION
Paul Lucier

In analyzing the causes of the Industrial Revolution, the role of science and its relation to technological change and industrial innovation have received sustained, if not always in depth, attention from historians, economists, and other scholars. The relation is complex, and it is by no means clear, even with today's hi-tech industry, what the exact contribution of science to technological development is or ought to be. The purpose of this chapter is to sort through some of the conflicting interpretations of the general as well as the specific role of science in the Industrial Revolution. In an effort to keep the discussion within a reasonable framework, I have chosen to concentrate on Great Britain, arguably the first nation to undergo industrialization, but I will also use examples from France to make comparisons, and to underscore different national styles in science, technology, and industry.

The chapter follows a chronological course. Beginning with the Scientific Revolution of the seventeenth century, it outlines the major developments in scientific knowledge and contrasts the British and French understanding of theory and practice. In a sense, this section discusses the supply of science—here defined broadly to comprise scientific ideas, methods, and mentality. In the second section, entitled "the age of improvement," I trace the diffusion of science among entrepreneurs, and examine the ways in which scientists and industrialists interacted. The final section addresses the emergence of engineering in the late eighteenth and early nineteenth centuries.

The argument is straightforward. Since the seventeenth century, scientists have been interested in practical matters, and through their close personal contacts with entrepreneurs they have had both a direct and indirect influence on industrial development. They promoted the adoption of scientific methods in key manufacturing areas and, on occasion, they helped to develop new manufacturing processes, such as chlorine bleaching. Their most important contribution, however, was their advocacy of a particular mentality, what I have chosen to call "technological forwardness"—the predisposition to encourage, value, and take advantage of small and large changes in technology. By the turn of the nineteenth century this technological forwardness had become embodied in the person of the engineer, an individual who designed, built, and operated increasingly advanced technologies, and who thus represented the successful integration of science and industry.

This argument is a revision of the traditional account which for the last fifty years has insisted on the existence of a gap between science and technology, a gap which was only closed in the late nineteenth century with the rise of the new chemical and electrical industries, the so-called science-based industries (Landes 1969). This gap between science and technology was both social and intellectual. Scientists were elites who concentrated on abstract knowledge, such as theories of nature, while technologists, those principally responsible for the mechanical inventions which drove the Industrial Revolution, were lower-class artisans who relied upon tinkering, rule of thumb, and trial-and-error (Floud and McCloskey 1981). The traditional account minimized the commercial contributions of scientists in large part by focusing on their theoretical discoveries; in other words, defining science very narrowly to mean the search for the abstract laws of nature. By this definition, then, anyone who applied scientific methods or theories was not a scientist (Gillispie 1957b; Hall 1974). As we shall see, even such famous theoreticians as Isaac Newton were not entirely above economic issues.

The traditional account has come under attack recently because it was established, in part, as a political counterargument to Marxist scholars who had maintained that science and capitalism were in fact closely connected (Dennis 1997). To preserve the myth that western nations allowed for freedom of thought, in contrast to the state-dictated science of communist countries, the history of science became a story of the development of pure research, and hence not much attention was given to practical science or engineering. But it was precisely these fields that were valued and encouraged by industrialists. Since the end of the Cold War, the political imperative to defend the purity of western science has been removed, and hence interest in the connection of science and capitalism has been revived.

The revisionist argument, however, is not meant to be interpreted as an assertion that developments in science *caused* the Industrial Revolution. On the contrary, the growing interaction between scientists and manufacturers during the eighteenth century was as much a response to changes in production as it was a factor in furthering the adoption and diffusion of new technologies. Science and industry became interdependent, but it was a slow process that occurred over the course of a century, roughly from 1750 to 1850. Nor is the revisionist argument meant to diminish the role of artisans in the Industrial Revolution. Scientists and engineers were principally responsible for the diffusion and application of scientific ideas, methods, and mentality, but scientific discoveries did not necessarily lead directly or inevitably to technological invention and industrial innovation. This point has been made clear by modern scholarship. The "linear model" of technology, as it has been called, did not hold true for any time in the past or even today for that matter (Staudenmaier 1985). Artisans certainly made many important minor improvements to existing machines and processes, and they may well have followed their own kind of thinking, different from that of engineers and scientists (Tunzelmann 1994). But the initiative to implement those improvements or to change production processes, as well as the decision to invest in major inventions ("macro-inventions," to use Mokyr's term), such as the steam engine, came from entrepreneurs. And they often had close working relationships with scientists and engineers. These personal contacts are the key to understanding the role of science in the Industrial Revolution. Thus we need not speculate about some kind of trickle down theory by which scientific ideas and methods somehow filtered down to the artisans (Cardwell 1971; Mokyr 1994). There may well have been a social and intellectual gap between scientists and artisans, but if this was the case, the bridge was the entrepreneur and engineer.

One last point needs to be made in regard to the revisionist argument concerning the definition of terms. Any historical analysis of the role of science in the Industrial Revolution must be sensitive to the fact that the concepts of science, technology and industry have changed over the last two hundred years (Mayr 1976; Kline 1995). In fact, the terms "science" and "technology" themselves might be considered products of the Industrial Revolution; they are recent nineteenth-century concepts. In the eighteenth century, manufacturing was referred to as the arts, and science was natural philosophy. The word "scientist" was not coined until the 1830s, the point at which science becomes a recognizably modern pursuit.[1] Eighteenth-century natural philosophy was not professionalized; it did not have well-defined disciplines or research programs; nor was it based in universities. Natural philosophers were often dependent for monetary support upon generous patrons, many of whom were industrialists. The relations of natural philosophy and the arts in the eighteenth century were much more informal and episodic than those of science and industry today. It was only after the mid-nineteenth century, and arguably as a consequence of industrialization, that the relations of science and industry were formalized and regularized, hence the neologism "technology." In short, industrialization produced technology, not the other way around.

During the eighteenth century, natural philosophers, manufacturers, and engineers not only shared interests in the new inventions and industrial processes, but they also had close working connections with one another. This chapter surveys those connections in an effort to shed new light on the old question of the role of science in the Industrial Revolution.

THE SCIENTIFIC REVOLUTION

In the late sixteenth and early seventeenth centuries, a handful of Europeans began to advocate new ideas about nature and new methods for its study. Central to the Scientific Revolution was a firm belief in the rational behavior of nature, and in the prospect that humans could understand the principles which guided that behavior. The universe operated like a clock; nature behaved like a machine. These were not just convenient metaphors but rather organizing themes for the study of nature—the mechanical philosophy. Two of the most important proponents of the mechanical philosophy were Francis Bacon and René Descartes.

Francis Bacon (1561–1626), essayist and politician (he was Lord Chancellor of England under James I), proposed a method for studying nature called induction. Bacon suggested that natural philosophers seek new principles and facts of nature primarily through careful collection and categorization of data, and secondarily through systematic experimentation. Once understood, these new facts and principles could then be applied to the arts, and to the betterment of humankind. Bacon thus tried to combine theory and practice, and his emphasis on the application of knowledge has subsequently informed much of British (and later American) science, which has often been characterized as utilitarian or, simply, Baconian.

The practical orientation of the British tradition stands in contrast to the theoretical approach of the French. René Descartes (1596–1650) rather than Bacon inspired continental thinkers. French and to an extent German natural philosophy emphasized theory, mathematics, and the deductive method. In other words, instead of collecting and categorizing facts, natural philosophers were admonished to theorize—expound general laws and then rigorously deduce the facts to support the theory. Descartes nevertheless advocated a role for experimentation (to decide between conflicting theories), and he too believed that the laws of nature, once deduced, could be applied in a rational manner to the arts.

Taken together, Bacon and Descartes outlined a new approach to the study of nature, the scientific method—a systematic inquiry involving experimentation, careful observation and recording of data, mathematical formulation, testing of hypotheses, and generalizing laws of nature—for describing the mechanical universe. In justifying this new method Bacon and Descartes held out the prospect of its application to human needs. Whether it be the amelioration of everyday toil or the exploitation of natural resources, natural philosophy had the potential for improving the conditions of life. In this way, Bacon and Descartes attempted to fashion links between natural philosophy and the arts.

In the course of the seventeenth century, many natural philosophers followed these precepts. Perhaps the most famous was Isaac Newton (1642–1727), who used both Cartesian deduction and Baconian induction. Newton's most famous work, *Mathematical Principles of Natural Philosophy* (1687), commonly known as the *Principia,* established his reputation as a brilliant theorist by presenting the law of gravity and the mathematical laws of motion governing earthly and heavenly bodies. Seventeen years later he published the *Opticks* (1704), a work on light, color and heat which epitomized the experimentalist program. Empirical, wide-ranging, and generally useful, Newton's *Opticks* became the model for eighteenth century British science, not his theoretical *Principia.* Moreover, Newton himself took an active role in commercial affairs when he became Warden of the Mint. Although he had few, if any, specific qualifications for the job, his reputation recommended his services to the British government. In his role as government advisor, Newton was the moving force behind the reorganization of British coinage in the early eighteenth century, a responsibility that was decidedly far more economical than philosophical (Westfall 1980).

Newton's service to the British government was a rare departure in British science, for it was the French government, far more than its British counterpart, which sought the expertise of natural philosophers when implementing economic improvements. Antoine Lavoisier, for instance, the chemist known as the father of the chemical revolution in the 1770s and 1780s, consulted with the Paris Arsenal on ways to increase the production of gunpowder for the French army. Likewise, other French chemists advised the government on the manufacture of iron, pottery, tapestries, and bleaching agents. In contrast, British private enterprise, without encouragement or interference from the government, turned to natural philosophy for help in solving decidedly economic problems.

THE AGE OF IMPROVEMENT

During the eighteenth century, the ideas of Bacon, Descartes, and Newton were introduced and adopted among the literate in Europe. The popularization of the scientific method and the mechanical philosophy provides a means, for historians, to connect the Scientific Revolution and the Industrial Revolution. Science became the foundation on which to build a larger and more rational society than ever before. The exercise of reason, it was assumed, would bring great gains in the material, as well as to the political and social, well-being of society. The belief in improvement characterized the Age of Enlightenment, and natural philosophers were the self-appointed promoters of improvement and progress. They spread the message of technological forwardness through the printed press, public lectures, and philosophical societies.

Britain

In Britain, natural philosophy was popularized by men such as John Theophilus Desaguliers (1683–1744). Although Desaguliers may not be a familiar name to most, he, like many practical philosophers, was key to the diffusion of scientific ideas and methods among British entrepreneurs. A Newtonian disciple and a Fellow of the Royal Society of London (the foremost scientific body in Britain), Desaguliers moved easily between theory and practice. He drew the attention of entrepreneurs to natural philosophy through the exercise of his considerable talents as a lecturer. Speaking in London coffeehouses or provincial gentlemen's clubs, he illustrated the principles of Newtonian mechanics through practical demonstrations of weights, pulleys, levers, and other ordinary devices.[2] He stressed the Baconian theme that natural philosophy could improve machines, and hence a philosophically informed entrepreneur would profit from the knowledge of how a Savery or Newcomen steam engine worked (Stewart 1986, 1992).

This message of technological forwardness was well-received by commercial audiences. By the 1760s itinerant philosophical lecturing was fashionable everywhere in Britain, especially in the expanding manufacturing towns in the Midlands and the North. Listeners were willing to pay £1 to £3 for a six-week course, which usually met two or three times a week. The popularity of the lecturers speaks to a general enthusiasm and widespread acceptance for natural philosophy as useful knowledge. This is important to keep in mind, since many scholars have regarded the lack of formal education among Britain's commercial class as telling evidence against the possibility of natural philosophy contributing to the Industrial Revolution. The point is that entrepreneurs need not have gone to university to receive instruction in the scientific method; they could get it at the local coffeehouse.

British manufacturers were very keen on applying natural philosophy and some even became patrons of the sciences. They subscribed to publications (such as the *Philosophical Transactions* published by the Royal Society of London), contributed funds to individual philosophers, and occasionally purchased books for libraries or equipment for laboratories. For manufacturers, natural philosophy was a pursuit befitting an emerging elite: it was genteel, polite, and perhaps even a bit ornamental. But it was also practical and useful. In short, natural philosophy was the perfect balance of gentility and utility (Musson and Robinson 1969; McKendrick 1973).

The establishment of provincial philosophical societies in the 1780s secured the means for formal, regular exchanges of views and opinions among philosophers and manufacturers. Many prominent manufacturers became members of provincial societies, for example, the Strutts of Derby, the Lloyds, Brandts and Phillips of Manchester, and Thomas Bentley of Liverpool. Likewise, many well-known philosophers were members of such societies including the foremost British chemists of the age, Joseph Priestley of Birmingham and John Dalton of Manchester. The provincial philosophical societies provided a forum for the discussion of manufacturing problems, and it was in such places that experimental methods as well as other attitudes from the scientific laboratory—a belief in measurement, analysis and rationalizing processes—were transferred directly to the business world. In addition, manufacturing techniques were sometimes transferred to scientific practice, as was the case with the physicist James Joule, who adopted skills developed in the brewing industry in his experiments on the conservation of heat (Sibum, 1995).

The most active and successful societies were founded in the rapidly growing towns of the Midlands and North of England, the centers of industrialization. There are numerous examples including the Manchester Literary and Philosophical Society (founded 1781), the Derby Philosophical Society (1783), the Literary and Philosophical Society of Newcastle-on-Tyne (1793), and similar ones in Liverpool, Leeds, and Birmingham. The Manchester Lit & Phil was among the largest with some forty founding members, and it was one of the most stable; it has survived to the present day. Its primary concern was chemistry and the dyeing and bleaching of textiles, and in the nineteenth century it became an important model for Victorian scientific societies. But of all the eighteenth-century provincial societies, the Lunar Society of Birmingham best exemplifies the joining of manufacturing and philosophical interests.

The Lunar Society existed for roughly thirty years (1765–1795) with participation at any time of no more than fourteen men. The Society met at a member's house once a month, on the night of the full moon, hence the name, in order that the others could return home without difficulty. Among its more illustrious commercial members were the iron manufacturer Matthew Boulton (1728–1809), the gun maker Samuel Galton, Jr. (1753–1832), and the pottery manufacturer Josiah Wedgwood (1730–1795). The society also included a number of prominent philosophers—the naturalist Erasmus Darwin (1731–1802, grandfather of Charles Darwin), the chemist and geologist James Kier (1735–1820), the chemist Joseph Priestley (1733–1804), and the physician and botanist William Withering (1741–1799). It was an extraordinary collection of individuals who rank with some of the most important intellectual and industrial leaders of eighteenth-century Britain.

The Lunar Society, like most provincial societies, was dedicated to the promotion of the arts and sciences and to the diffusion of knowledge more extensively among the professional and business classes of Birmingham. To that end, the society excluded general tradesmen and mechanics, which might suggest that its contribution to industrialization was restricted. On the other hand, the Lunar society welcomed successful manufacturers of humble origins (millwrights and machine makers) and prominent engineers, such as the famous inventor and instrument-maker James Watt (1736–1819). Another well-known member was William Murdoch (1754–1839), an engineer at the Boulton-Watt works, who helped to develop gas lighting and steam locomotives. The members took an interest in many activities central to the Industrial Revolution: they discussed improvements in the building of canals, roads, wheels, and carriages, and took special concern with the design and metallurgy of steam-engines. They were also keenly taken with improvements in agriculture and experimented with several types of chemical and natural fertilizers. The list could be extended, as it could for any of the provincial philosophical societies, but all these activities illustrate the same thing: the extensive collaboration among philosophers, manufacturers, and engineers during the Industrial Revolution. Perhaps the best example of the dramatic effects of the application of natural philosophy to manufacturing is to be found in the career of Josiah Wedgwood, the founder of Etruria, the renowned Staffordshire pottery (Schofield 1957, 1963).

Josiah Wedgwood (1730–1795) was born into a family of artisan potters in Staffordshire. He had little formal schooling and at a young age was apprenticed to his brother to learn the craft. After a severe case of smallpox, which left him unable to work, Wedgwood began a program of self-education in natural philosophy. He established an impressive library and an extensive correspondence with other natural philosophers. His dramatic success in using natural philosophy to improve the manufacture of pottery resulted from his numerous and detailed chemical experiments.

Wedgwood's interest in chemistry stemmed from his involvement in the Lunar Society where he met Kier and Priestley and became closely involved with their work. Wedgwood became convinced that systematic experiment was the means to solve problems in pottery production and he set up an extensive program to study different kinds of clays and glazes. In fact, Wedgwood's devotion to the experimental method bordered on pathological—he left some ten thousand trial pieces in his quest to find a durable clay and attractive glaze. He also left innumerable records of various routine investigations which reveal his passion for quantification: he calculated everything from the costs of labor to the exact distance covered in his walking tour of his factories.

Wedgwood's most notable scientific work was his invention of a ceramic pyrometer—an instrument for estimating very high temperatures. Because mercury boils at 600° F, mercury thermometers cannot be used to control the extreme degree of heat needed for firing clay pottery. Wedgwood invented a device which changes color, in a regular fashion, at very high temperatures, and thereby was able to monitor and improve the manufacturing process. The pyrometer was put up for sale and adopted by other potters as well as other natural philosophers. The chemists Priestley and Lavoisier, for example, wanted to use it in their experiments. The recognition of his pyrometer as a scientific instrument along with his research on heat resulted in Wedgwood's election as a Fellow of the Royal Society.

Wedgwood's personal dedication, if not obsession, with the scientific method did not prevent him from relying on others to help solve manufacturing problems. He often called upon Priestley for theoretical explanations of the chemistry of ceramics, and he employed a trained chemist, Peter Woulfe, who had been awarded the prestigious Copley Medal by the Royal Society for his researches on acids and alkalis. Wedgwood consulted Woulfe on the possibility of finding a reliable method for extracting and purifying the mineral cobalt used in coloring the famous blue jasper Wedgwood pottery.

Wedgwood made many important industrial innovations by relying on the methods, if not always the theory, of chemical science. This more than anything characterized his belief in improvement and progress, in other words, his technological forwardness. He was the first potter to use a steam engine, the first to develop a cost accounting system, the first to use a clocking-in device in his factories, the first to produce pottery in large quantities for general consumption, and thus the first English potter to dominate the European and American markets. In 1775, Wedgwood made the unprecedented decision to set up a cooperative research program in the hopes of extending his research on clays and glazes with the help of other Staffordshire potters. They were not very sympathetic to the idea, partly because they did not want to fund such a costly program, but also because they were willing to leave technical superiority to Wedgwood on the assumption that his advances would eventually be transferred through industrial espionage. They were correct; Wedgwood's experimental results were quickly stolen, which meant in effect that his successful application of natural philosophy to manufacturing processes were then diffused among other Staffordshire potters and the results sold to the world market (McKendrick 1973).

Wedgwood epitomized technological forwardness—the scientific attitude and approach of English manufacturers during the Industrial Revolution. He found the knowledge of chemists as well as the methods of science to be economically useful and eminently profitable. He ardently believed in improvement, material and intellectual, and was certain that progress was being made on all fronts. Progress meant adhering to a scientific method of careful experimentation and the application of newly discovered facts and principles. This would not only advance natural philosophy but manufacturing and society as well.

France

The case in France was different from that in Britain. Instead of making science more practical and useful, French *philosophes* tried to make manufacturing more philosophical. Their approach was twofold: first, they tried to gather, systemize, and publish information on the best manufacturing practices of the day, and second, they tried, with government sponsorship, to establish model industries. The first approach was carried out by compiling massive descriptive accounts of craft practices. The two most famous projects were the *Description des arts et métiers* compiled by the Paris Academy of Sciences and the *Encyclopédie,* the definitive compilation of knowledge under the direction of Denis Diderot and the mathematician Jean d'Alembert. Once knowledge was organized, the *philosophes* believed they could improve manufacturing processes by illuminating the underlying principles and thereby enlightening the artisan.(Gillispie 1957b) To their dismay, they discovered that artisans were not especially inclined to divulge their trade secrets to curious *philosophes*—other artisans might easily copy their practices if they appeared in print—nor were artisans disposed to read about scientific improvements; many were in fact illiterate. In the end, the *philosophes* realized that changes in manufacturing could not be effected through the publication and distribution of the printed word; it required personal contact.

Establishing model industries proved to be the best method of uniting science and the arts. French government officials in charge of the economy relied on natural philosophers as commercial advisors in the belief that the latest scientific methods and theories could rationalize manufacturing processes. In the royal manufactories at Sèvres (porcelain) and at the Gobelins (tapestries), the government began assigning chemists (all of whom were distinguished members of the Academy of Sciences in Paris) to the staff in the 1750s. They were responsible for developing new products and procedures as well as controlling the composition of materials. At Sèvres, four distinguished Academicians held the position of chemist between 1751 and 1840: Jean Hellot (1751–1766), Pierre Joseph Macquer (1766–1784), Jean Darcet (1784–1800), and Alexandre Brongniart (1800–1840). Macquer, professor of chemistry at the *Collège de France,* is particularly noteworthy for having conducted over 1000 experiments on different clays and glazes, much as Wedgwood had done. In June 1769, Macquer reported to the Academy of Sciences that he had produced the first true or hard porcelain. In addition to his work on porcelain, Macquer was assigned the post of director of dyeing at the Gobelins, a position that Hellot also had held. In 1784 the distinguished chemist Claude Berthollet succeeded Macquer. Berthollet is best known for his extensive research on dyestuffs and the properties of wool, cotton, and linen, published as *L'Art de la teinture* in 1791. As we shall see, Berthollet made a fundamental contribution to the process for bleaching textiles.

Science also played an important role in the founding of the famous iron manufactory at Le Creusot. The mineralogist Gabriel Jars was responsible for locating the deposits of iron ore, bituminous coal, and limestone. And, more important, he introduced the technique of smelting pig iron with coke instead of coal. The first full-scale experiment was conducted under his direction at Le Creusot in January 1769. As part of his role as inspector of metallurgical factories, Jars designed coking ovens and a new kind of furnace, which, for the first time in France, used a steam engine to create reliable power to blow the blast. Up to that time, dependence on water power had severely limited French iron manufacturing. (Gillispie 1980)

In all three cases, Sèvres, the Gobelins, and Le Creusot, the role of the natural philosopher was critical to industrial innovation. But in a sense, it was the French government rather than individual entrepreneurs that exhibited technological forwardness. Scientific methods were imposed from above upon manufacturing. And while the royal manufactories were intended to be models for private firms, thereby spreading the benefits of science throughout French industry, they became in effect royal monopolies. Scientific manufacturing was technologically innovative, but it was also very costly and not easily adopted by nonsubsidized manufacturers. Thus the role of science in French industrialization was constrained by the very government regulations, inspections, and bureaucracy which paradoxically encouraged technological forwardness.

The difference between French and British uses of science can be best explained by way of an example: chlorine bleaching. The development of chlorine bleaching is also very important to the ongoing debate between traditional scholars and the revisionists because it is one of the very few examples of the direct contribution of scientific theory to industrial innovation. Ironically, to many eighteenth-century commentators, the development of chlorine bleaching was not considered an especially unusual event. Acids, alkalis, salts, bleaches, and fertilizers were all chemical products, and chemistry was thought to be the most practical of all the sciences.

Cotton textiles were traditionally bleached by exposure to sunlight or treatment in sour milk or in dilute sulfuric acid. These methods were expensive and time consuming, and a more efficient one was sought through chemistry. In 1774, the Swedish chemist Karl Scheele (1742–1786) discovered chlorine. When the French chemist Claude Berthollet heard of the discovery, he began a series of experiments to investigate its possibilities as a bleaching agent. Between 1785 and 1790 Berthollet published a number of articles on his research and eventually developed a commercial process for manufacturing a bleaching liquid called "Eau de Jeval." This process was then transferred to Britain by James Watt, no less, whose father-in-law happened to be a textile bleacher in Glasgow. The diffusion of Berthollet's process was initially hindered because the bleaching liquid was bulky and difficult to transport due to the need for special noncorrosive carriers. This problem was overcome in 1798, when the manufacturer Charles Tennant developed a more stable, and hence more profitable, bleaching powder.

The development of chlorine bleach would seem a clear-cut case of chemical theory leading to industrial innovation. But traditional scholars have questioned this interpretation because the science was "wrong." Scheele did not discover chlorine; he discovered what he called "dephlogisticated marine acid," which Berthollet reinterpreted as "oxymuriatic acid" or "oxygenated muriatic acid." The modern element "chlorine" was not identified until 1809 by the British chemist Humphrey Davy. Berthollet was applying the "incorrect" phlogiston theory of chemistry, which explained combustion in terms of the burning of a substance called phlogiston. The modern chemistry of Antoine Lavoisier, which interpreted combustion as a chemical reaction involving oxygen, swept away the old phlogiston theories.(Gillispie 1957a; Musson and Robinson 1969; Olson 1990)

This clearly is a case requiring analytical sensitivity. To judge the past solely by present knowledge would vitiate the historical context. Berthollet, Watt, Tennant and many others of the time thought their phlogiston chemistry was accurate and that it was the basis for their successful bleaching methods. Traditional scholars hold that the chemical science was primitive, but the historical actors themselves judged their new theories and materials as industrial improvements, which was their goal, and in their terms they achieved it.

The case of chlorine bleach also serves to highlight distinct national styles in French and British technological forwardness. Berthollet was a member of the Paris Academy of Sciences and had received a stipend from the French government to support his research. In this way, the French government acted as the intermediary to facilitate the application of chemistry to the art of bleaching. In Britain, the government had no such role. Individual enterprise, as displayed by the practical chemist Charles Tennant and by the engineer James Watt, was responsible for adopting and adapting Berthollet's discovery in order to produce a profitable chemical manufacturing process.

ENGINEERING

Fifty years ago, T. S. Ashton made the observation that the most important new industry of the eighteenth century was engineering (Ashton 1948). At a time of increasing debate about whether and how Britain and Europe underwent an Industrial Revolution, Ashton's remark might be of great analytical use. Engineering resulted from application of science to industry, and engineers were actively involved in those industries which experienced both the greatest growth and the most systematic changes in production. Engineering can be regarded as both a cause and a consequence of industrialization. The rise of engineering thus is one way to mark the beginning of industrialization.

To that end, the emergence of engineering in France is much easier to identify and study than that in Britain. The French state, once again, played the key role in institutionalizing the education and employment of engineers. In Britain, as we have seen, the state was not an active force in industrialization or in fostering relations between science and industry. British engineers were a product of private enterprise, and, as we shall see, they were much more entrepreneurial, and hence difficult to categorize, than their French counterparts.

France

Engineering was conceived by the cross-fertilization of scientific rationality and the needs of the state. Its birthplace was seventeenth-century France, and its midwife was the military. Technical experts were needed to design fortresses to withstand the new artillery and at the same time to conduct sieges against other well-designed fortresses.[3] In 1676, the French minister of war created the *Corps du génie* (Corps of Engineering) within the French army. By 1716 the government had come to realize that it needed a similar technical corps for the location and construction of bridges and roads over which the army and artillery moved, hence the establishment of the *Corps des ponts et chaussées* (Corps of Bridges and Roads). These engineers soon took responsibility for a variety of projects deemed crucial to the nation's economic interests such as the construction of canals, river and harbor improvements, water supply systems, and a large network of roads. The projects required a range of technical skills including surveying, mapping, and coordinating materials and labor. Because of the shortage of technical personnel available for the projects, the French government founded the *École des ponts et chaussées* in 1747 and a year later the school of military engineering, the *École du génie* (1748). The schools proved very successful and the state steadily expanded the use of formal education to train engineers; it founded the *École des mines* in 1783 and, during the French Revolution, the most prestigious of all schools, the *École polytechnique* in 1794.

School engineering meant scientific methods rather than apprenticeship learning, and in France there was a hierarchy of engineering based on education. Students at the *École polytechnique* and the other "Grandes École" (*Génie* and *Ponts et chaussées*) trained in theoretical natural philosophy and mathematics. In fact, some of the most brilliant natural philosophers of the eighteenth and early nineteenth centuries taught at the *École polytechnique*—the physicists François Arago, Pierre Laplace, Joseph Lagrange, André Marie Ampère, and Sadi Carnot; the mathematician Augustin Cauchy; and the chemist Joseph Gay-Lussac. *Polytechniciens* were expected to work for the state. Two other Parisian schools established during the Revolutionary period provided additional technical training. At the *École centrale* (1794), prospective civil (as opposed to military) engineers were instructed in a range of sciences and mathematics to be employed in private industry. Below this was the *École des arts et métiers* (1795), where students received basic instruction in mathematics and technical drawing, skills necessary for shop foremen. (Gillispie 1980) At all levels, the philosophical training of French engineers was very impressive, and it became the model throughout Europe.

German engineers exceeded the French in one field—mining—due to the existence of several excellent mining schools. The most famous was the *Bergakademie* in Freiberg, Saxony, founded in 1765 to train engineers who would direct operations at the state-owned mines. As in France, German state-funded mining schools employed prominent natural philosophers, particularly geologists, chemists, and mineralogists to teach and to conduct research related to the discovery and exploitation of mineral resources. At Freiberg, for example, the world-renown mineralogist Abraham Gottlob Werner (1749–1817) expounded his geological theories on the deposition of rocks and on the formation and identification of minerals (Laudan 1987). Hence German mining engineers were well-grounded (so to speak) in the earth sciences.

By 1800 engineering was a firmly established occupation in France and other parts of Europe, and the state was its primary patron. Engineers built what we would call today the infrastructure of industrialization—the network of roads, canals, and later railroads, necessary for the efficient transportation of goods and individuals. They also assumed managerial and production responsibilities in state-owned mines and, in France, in manufacturing enterprises such as the Gobelins, Sèvres, and Le Creusot, precisely the same places where scientists worked as industrial advisors.

Britain

In eighteenth-century Britain, the free market nurtured several kinds of entrepreneurial experts who served the needs of the growing economy. Not all of them can be classified as engineers. Without a rigid educational system and a hierarchical employment structure imposed by the state, the training, occupation, and even the identity of these technically proficient individuals varied considerably. For convenience here, I have grouped these experts under two broad headings: scientific consultants and engineers.

The practice of scientific consulting goes back to the itinerant lecturers of the eighteenth century. Not only did they popularize science in coffeehouses and join provincial philosophical societies, these practically minded natural philosophers also often advised wealthy landowners on improvements. Desaguliers, for one, was the technical expert to James Brydges, duke of Chandos, one of the most successful entrepreneurs of the eighteenth century. Desaguliers offered practical assistance to Chandos on many projects including irrigation, hydraulics, and the use of steam engines in draining mines. In return he benefitted from Chandos's patronage both financially and intellectually; Desaguliers was encouraged and given the means to conduct his own scientific experiments and research (Stewart 1992). This twofold contribution, to scientific research *and* to economic development, distinguished scientific consultants from engineers.

In many ways, British scientific consultants were akin to the French scientists who acted as advisors to the state-run enterprises. British consultants, however, were not paid by the state, and they did not receive government legitimation as scientists, such as election to a prestigious scientific organization. They often held teaching positions in one of the newly founded provincial schools, such as Owens College in Manchester, and they did their consulting work on the side. One of the most famous scientific consultants was John Dalton (1766–1844) of Manchester. He is best known for his atomic theory of chemistry, but what is often overlooked by traditional historians is the large amount of work that Dalton did on problems germane to industry in Manchester: he consulted on steam engines, chlorine bleaching, gas lighting, water analysis, and pharmaceuticals, among other things. In good Baconian fashion, Dalton managed to combine theory and practice. More important, he was not unique; equally instructive cases could be made for the physicist James Prescott Joule or for the chemist Lyon Playfair. By the mid-nineteenth century, many professional scientists capitalized on the new opportunities made available by industrialization, and many companies hired scientific consultants (Thackray 1970; Kargon 1977; Lucier 1995).

The first engineers also received their early encouragement from wealthy patrons, usually aristocratic landowners intent on improving their lands. The mineral surveyor John Farey, for example, worked for the duke of Bedford, and the mining engineer John Williams worked for the earl of Buchan. Farey and Williams were hired to locate valuable natural resources—mineral fertilizer, coal, and building stones. Other early engineers were prominent in the building of canals, roads, bridges, and harbors, much as in France. With the growth in scale of transportation projects, a small, influential group of civil engineers began to make careers supplying expertise. They also created for themselves a permanent place in manufacturing. Mechanical engineers, although not always readily distinguishable from civil engineers, responded to the need to build and operate steam engines.

Most British engineers learned their skills on the job; there were no schools of engineering in eighteenth-century Britain. Although largely self-trained, they were well-read in mathematics and natural philosophy and they had a good knowledge of design. Some even attended lectures by itinerant natural philosophers such as Desaguliers. They were not the illiterate artisans of legend, and it would be historically inaccurate to think of John Smeaton or James Watt as "basically empirical tinkerers" (Mokyr 1994). Many, in fact, were fellows of the Royal Society, thereby receiving a measure of scientific imprimatur for their expertise. By the late-eighteenth century, the demand for technical personnel grew rapidly as manufacturing and transportation projects became larger and more complex. At the same time, engineers were largely responsible for the expansion of industry. The careers of Smeaton and Watt illustrate this very well.

John Smeaton (1724–1792) came from the northern industrial city of Leeds. His father had intended that he would pursue a career in law, but Smeaton chose instead to apprentice himself to an instrument maker. He established his own business in London where he was highly regarded by natural philosophers for his air-pumps (early vacuum chambers), microscopes, and telescopes. By 1750, he had decided to undertake larger technical projects, and in 1755 he received the commission to build a lighthouse at Eddystone, near Plymouth in the southwest of England. His successful design and construction of the lighthouse became the basis for an extensive career in scientific engineering.

Smeaton's most important work focused on improving existing machines for producing power. One study involved the Newcomen steam engine for which he created a table of specifications for standardizing and rationalizing their construction. His most widespread contribution to British industry was his study of water wheels. Smeaton conducted over one hundred detailed experiments in an effort to determine the most efficient use of water power. He found that both overshot and undershot water wheels lost power because of excessive turbulence, and he recommended the use of breast-wheels. These findings became the basis for the rebuilding of water wheels all over Britain in the second half of the eighteenth century, which provided vital increases in power for the new textile factories.

Smeaton's scientific method of engineering was available to other engineers through his numerous publications. His research on water wheels, for instance, was published in the *Philosophical Transactions* of the Royal Society, and this work was awarded the Society's prestigious Copley Medal in 1759. Smeaton was also active in several societies for the promotion of natural philosophy and the arts, in addition to his fellowship in the Royal Society. He established the first society of civil engineers in 1771, later renamed the Smeatonian Society. He was a founding member of the Leeds Philosophical and Literary Society (1783), and an occasional visitor to the Lunar Society, where he met James Watt (Musson and Robinson 1969).

James Watt (1736–1819) also began his career as an instrument maker, and in 1756 he set up business in Glasgow. Part of his trade involved repairing instruments for the university, including a model Newcomen steam engine. Like Smeaton, Watt undertook a systematic investigation of the Newcomen engine in order to improve it. Unlike Smeaton, Watt came upon the idea of a separate condenser, which radically transformed the Newcomen machine into a new type of steam engine. Although Watt's improvement in the end proved far more significant than Smeaton's, both approached their study of the Newcomen machine in the same systematic and scientific way.

In 1774 Watt entered into a partnership with Matthew Boulton, a Birmingham businessman and fellow member of the Lunar Society. The Boulton-Watt firm built steam engines all over Britain. As part of their business, they supplied trained technicians to set up and operate each machine at its new site, and in this way helped to encourage the field of mechanical engineering as well as the spread of scientific methods in the manufacture and operation of steam engines. Where ever there was a steam engine there had to be at least one engineer to run it and behind him stood a number of engineers who helped to design and build it. The engine and the engineer were symbiotic (Cardwell 1971, 1980).

By the early nineteenth century, both British and French engineers had developed a professional self-identity based on their unique role in the industrializing economy. Engineers were responsible for building infrastructure, rationalizing manufacturing processes, and designing, building, and operating complex machinery. They occupied a wide middle ground between natural philosophers and laborers. They found positions in manufacturing firms as superintendents, managers, or foremen. Prominent engineers, such as Smeaton, even shared many practices with scientific consultants, in that both acted as independent advisors and experts (as opposed to being employees) to commercial enterprises. In short, these new men of the Industrial Revolution embodied the union of science and industry.

CONCLUSION

Modern technology has its roots in the philosophy of the Scientific Revolution and in the Enlightenment faith in improvement and progress. Eighteenth-century contemporaries believed that the changes in manufacturing to which they were witness rested on the foundation and application of natural philosophical principles and methods. The culture of natural philosophy provided social legitimation for improvement, and this attitude did much to boost the prestige of science and all things scientific. Not only was it acceptable but it was in fact desirable to foster technological change. For the natural philosophers, manufacturers, and engineers of the Industrial Revolution, the fact that they were able to work closely together was indisputable evidence that they were most assuredly living in a time of progress. Natural philosophy thus became the message and the messenger of progress, and technological forwardness became the new creed of industrialization.

This is also the dominant message we live with today. Science and technology are inevitably regarded as socially "good" because they are "naturally" associated with progress. To impede the growth and application of science means to retard progress and to suffer technological backwardness. Industrialization, however, has come at a cost, not only to society but also to natural philosophy and the arts. For it must be remembered that industrialization has brought science for profit rather than science for knowledge, and industrial engineering has destroyed the craft skills of the artisan and replaced them with the numbing routine of mechanization. These are caveats to caution us that progress can be defined in many ways—politically, socially, religiously; it is not a one-sided definition meaning only advances in science and technology.

NOTES

1. The British philosopher William Whewell was the first to use the word "scientist" in print in his *History of the Inductive Sciences* (1837). The word "science," from the Latin *scientia,* had been used since the seventeenth century.

2. Desaguliers published his lectures as *A Course of Experimental Philosophy* in London (1734, 1744), and the book became popular.

3. The word "engineer" comes from the Latin *ingenium,* meaning engine, and was originally used to refer to military engines such as catapults and other siege engines.

6
THE CONTRIBUTION OF TECHNOLOGICAL DIFFUSION PATTERNS TO BRITISH ECONOMIC GROWTH, 1750–1850

Harry Kitsikopoulos

The economic and structural changes that mark the emergence of modern industrialized societies occurred first in Britain in the eighteenth century and subsequently elsewhere. How rapidly these changes took place lies at the heart of the debate over the "revolutionary" or "evolutionary" nature of the Industrial Revolution. This chapter examines the role of technology, or more specifically, the dynamics of technological diffusion,[1] in Britain. It will investigate three closely related ideas.

First, I will argue that technological change, as shown by the adoption of new productive technologies, was the main driving force behind the process of capital accumulation and growth in Britain after 1760. But second, I will also argue that technological change had an uneven impact on the economy, so that some industries had more rapid rates of output growth than others (see Table 6.1). Finally, there is substantial evidence to argue that the timing of the industrial takeoff roughly coincides with the period when the diffusion of several critical technologies acquired momentum. Output growth, in fact, accelerated after the Napoleonic Wars, indicating a somewhat later timing of the takeoff period in Britain than is usually considered to be the case. These issues will be investigated using examples of new technologies adopted in the more progressive industries in Britain.

THE CONVENTIONAL LITERATURE ON TECHNOLOGICAL DIFFUSION

Many studies have attempted to plot the diffusion paths of different technologies, most utilizing twentieth century data. They all

Table 6.1
Indices of Output, Selected Industries (1841 = 100)

Industry	1770	1815
Cotton	0.8	19
Wool	46	65
Linen	47	75
Silk	28	40
Clothing	20	43
Leather	41	61
Metals	7	29
Food/Drink	47	69
Paper/Printing	17	47
Mining	15	46
Building	26	50
Other	15–50	40–60

Source: Harley 1993, "Reassessing the Industrial Revolution," in Mokyr, ed.

have something in common: plotting the number of cumulative adoptions against a time path results in a rising sigmoid (S-shaped) curve. Interpreted in economic terms, this means that when a new technique is introduced, potential adopters are hesitant to use it, and only a few risk takers adopt it. This early phase is followed by a second one in which many firms adopt the technique; its diffusion thus accelerates rapidly. The third phase, when nearly all firms have adopted the technique, leads to a saturation point.

Several factors influence the dynamics of this pattern of diffusion. First, the *relative prices of capital and labor:* if real wages are high, there is a greater incentive to replace old equipment with more productive, labor-saving new equipment. Second, if the amount of *existing fixed capital* (buildings and machinery) utilizing the old techniques is large, then there is less incentive to scrap it to adopt a new technique. However, the age distribution of existing capital is also important, because the older it is, the faster it is likely to be replaced. Since the fixed capital in most firms in an industry tends to cluster around the average—because it has been put in place at about the same time—then it is likely that the few firms with the oldest equipment will be the first to replace it. Then they will be followed by the majority of firms, which accounts for the sharp upward segment of the sigmoid curve. Finally, the firms which have the newest fixed capital associated with the old technique, which will be the least likely to want to adopt the new technique quickly, will be the last to adopt it.

But third, if the new technique does not have an obvious cost advantage, then the existence of *substitute techniques* may slow down its adoption. Also adoption of the new technique may be slower if these existing techniques capture niches in the industry due to geographic isolation, for example, or if improvements make them more competitive with the new technique.

Finance is a fourth influence, and it can be especially important in affecting diffusion in economies with underdeveloped capital markets. In these cases, the lack of external finance puts an extra burden on the need for internal financing (from retained earnings, for example), which can be inadequate if the industrial sector has not yet achieved high rates of capital accumulation.

Fifth, *expectations*—about the future state of sales, for example—can also be important, especially if a new technique undergoes a process of continuous improvement (Rosenberg 1982, pp. 114, 117–18). For example, while some firms may decide to adopt the new technique early, others may decide to postpone adoption because they anticipate that later improvements may make earlier versions obsolete. This can result in the seemingly odd scenario of rapid diffusion when the pace of technological improvement is decelerating.

A sixth factor is the *structure of the industry,* but economists disagree about its impact. On the one hand, competitive forces in competitive industries may force quick adoption as earlier innovators can gain a (temporary) advantage, but when firms are small, they lack the financing to make adoption effective, especially if fixed capital needs are large. On the other hand, larger firms in more concentrated industries have the financial ability to innovate, but they lack the incentive if competitive pressures are fewer.

The nature of the *labor market* may also influence the speed of diffusion. For example, the lack of workers with suitable skills to operate the new machinery, or worker resistance to innovation, will both slow down innovation. An eighth factor is *technical applicability.* What this means is that a new technique may be applicable only in some stages of production; fast diffusion will take place only when subsequent improvements make it more generally applicable. Finally, *patenting* a new technique can slow diffusion down by preventing access to the technique by firms in the industry other than the patent-holder. Only when the patent expires can diffusion accelerate.

These factors are the ones most commonly cited in the existing literature explaining technical change. There are others, such as business secrecy, imperfect channels of communication, misconceptions about future profitability, and management attitudes to change, for example, which can play a role, but they are difficult to identify or quantify.

Growth rates in different sectors of the British economy at the end of the eighteenth century and the beginning of the nineteenth century were very uneven, as Table 6.1 shows. On the one hand, growth in some sectors was slow, being determined largely by population growth and demand, and here we see largely traditional techniques continuing to be used in them. On the other hand were what could be called the Schumpeterian sectors, where innovation and fairly rapid rates of technical diffusion produced "gales of creative destruction" which rejuvenated the system. Can different rates of technical diffusion account for these differences in growth rates? To gain some insight into an answer, we will look at the cotton industry, the most Schumpeterian sector, where technical change seemed to follow a "sequence of challenge and response" (Landes 1969, p. 84); where an invention in one stage of the production process generated imbalances which put pressure on other stages which were ultimately relieved by further inventions.

TECHNOLOGICAL CHANGE IN THE COTTON INDUSTRY

To see how these imbalances stimulated new technological breakthroughs, it is useful to recall that textile manufacturing consists of four distinct production processes. The preparation stage includes the cleaning and combing of the raw material; next, spinning pulls out and twists the fibers to form yarn; yarn is then woven into fabric in the weaving stage; and finally, dyeing, printing and other finishing steps turn the fabric into a finished product.

The cotton industry utilized "old" technology that dated back to the Middle Ages. In the spinning stage, the traditional spinning wheel was already recognized to be inefficient at the beginning of the eighteenth century, a problem that worsened following the invention of Kay's fly-shuttle. This became widely used in weaving in the 1750s because it speeded up weaving, but at the same time, it increased demands on spinners for more yarn that they could not meet.

In the space of the next twenty-five years, three inventions, Hargreaves's spinning jenny, Arkwright's water frame, and Crompton's hand mule successfully relieved this pressure by speeding up the production of yarn. The final solution came with the self-acting mule, which became available in 1830, although its diffusion was slow until the 1850s, for various reasons. Its acquisition and operating costs

Technological Diffusion Patterns

were quite high, which deterred those factories already using significant numbers of hand mules, an older-technology fixed capital. Resistance to adopting the new technology was also reinforced by the lack of long-term finance, and resistance by spinners who felt threatened by the self-acting mule which would demote them from being skilled operators to unskilled supervisors of machines. Only after coal prices fell in the 1850s, which reduced its operating costs, did the self-acting mule become profitable.

Though the self-acting mule was adopted only slowly, earlier generations of inventions in spinning, especially the hand mule, were revolutionary enough to stimulate feedback innovations in weaving. This was especially noticeable with the power loom invented by Cartwright in 1787. It was patented in 1803, but was not a real market success until 1813; then its diffusion was rapid, especially after the mid-1830s. As Figure 6.1 suggests, there was a nearly hundredfold increase in power looms installed in less than forty years (see below).

Three factors prevented its diffusion from being even faster. First, power looms had to be faster in order to compete successfully with hand looms, but technical problems, mainly yarn breakage, prevented their operation at high speeds. Several improvements in the

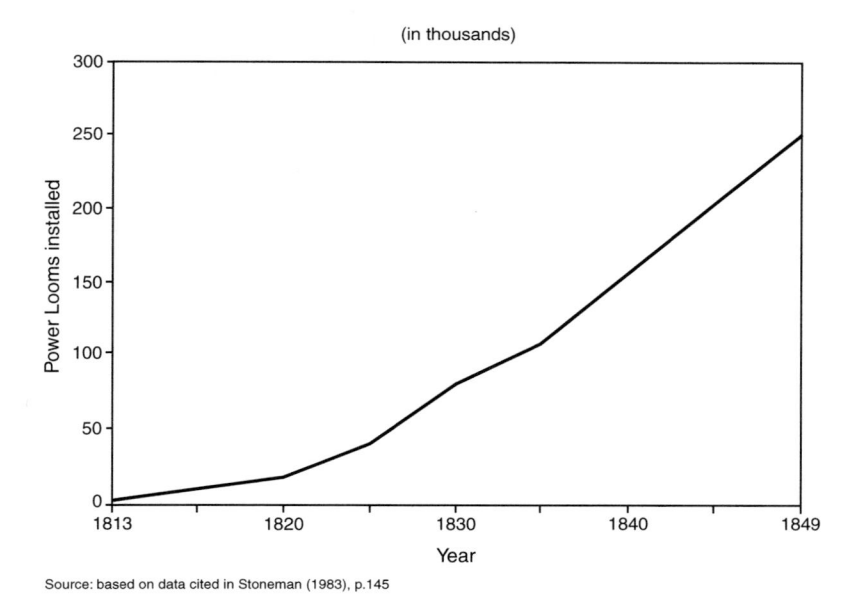

Source: based on data cited in Stoneman (1983), p.145

Figure 6.1 Power looms installed in the U.K., 1813–1849.

1820s and 1830s increased the efficiency ratio between power looms and hand looms to at least 7½ to 1 (Landes 1969, p. 86), and these technical improvements simplified the production process to such an extent that one operative could attend two looms simultaneously. Second, as a result, labor costs were reduced, but because hand loom weavers accepted large wage cuts in the 1820s, the cost advantage of power looms was not very great. The third reason was minor and of only temporary importance: declining demand due to the Napoleonic Wars, and tariff barriers that closed important markets to British cottons during the 1820s.

Technical improvements also occurred in the finishing stages of the cotton industry, stimulated by the increased output of yarn and of fabrics due to mechanization. For example, supplies of bleaching agents increased dramatically (Landes 1969, p. 109–11). Sulphuric acid was very scarce and expensive before the Industrial Revolution, with its price fluctuating around 2s. per ounce. The Bell Process and some other innovations in the mid-eighteenth century improved methods of extraction, and the price of the acid fell to less than one-hundredth of its former level. Improvements then became cumulative. Sulphuric acid mixed with salt is the basis for the extraction of chlorine; chlorine mixed with lime produced a bleaching powder whose production increased from nearly zero at the beginning of the nineteenth century to 13,100 tons by 1850, while its price declined tenfold, from £140 to £14 per ton. Another cleaning and bleaching agent, sodium alkali (extracted from common salt through the Leblanc process invented in France in the 1780s) also became available. Its initial diffusion was slow, but output increased rapidly after the 1820s, reaching 140,000 tons by 1852, while its price fell.

Stimulus from increasing demand played a role in all these developments. Cotton as a fabric had many advantages, so once supply factors reduced its price and made it accessible to the masses, fashion helped keep the momentum going by inducing further innovations. For example, the metal printing cylinder made it possible to print spectacular designs on fabrics that appealed to both the British middle class and to foreign consumers.

TECHNOLOGICAL CHANGE IN THE IRON INDUSTRY

These changes in the cotton industry can be thought of as radical, not so much because they took place within a short period of time, but rather because their cumulative character affected just about every production process in the industry. Similarly, technical advances appeared in iron making at about the same time as those in the cotton industry, and resulted in an impressive growth in output.

Iron production takes place in two main stages. First, ore must be smelted in a furnace to separate the metal from the surrounding rock; this produces pig iron, which is hard and brittle, and suitable only for the production of cast iron. Pig iron is brittle because it contains chemical impurities, which are removed in the second, refining, stage. To get wrought iron, a product that is pure enough to shape, the iron has to be hammered or heated in a hearth using charcoal or coal/coke to remove the impurities. Both hammering and charcoal were costly, while coke and coal added their own impurities.

The challenge, which was met during the Industrial Revolution, was to increase the use of coal, a mineral fuel, which was less expensive than charcoal, and at the same time, prevent any possible chemical contamination resulting from the its use. The start of the solution came with Henry Cort's puddling and rolling method in the 1780s. Puddling required using a reverberatory furnace to heat the metal without it coming into contact with the fuel, in order to separate out the carbon, which has a different melting point than iron. The metal was then rolled in a rolling mill to produce iron in standardized shapes.

Cort's invention permitted the use of both coal and the steam engine, and in turn induced several secondary improvements, or "microinventions," to use Mokyr's term. The most important of these were associated with increases in the size of the furnace. Coal or coke produces hotter temperatures than charcoal, but needs a more powerful blast of air. This was produced by using a blowing cylinder instead of bellows made out of leather, a technique first used in 1760 at the Carron ironworks in South Wales. Iron manufacturers also began to use steam engines instead of water-powered tilt hammers.

Stronger blasts encouraged the construction of taller furnaces with increased output. But the chemical possibilities of combustion could be expanded even further, as was shown by Neilson's invention of the hot blast in 1828. This idea was very simple, but very significant in terms of fuel efficiency: the gases generated by the blast were no longer released into the atmosphere, but recycled back to the furnace, increasing the blast at the same time as it saved fuel.

The diffusion of these innovations was spectacular by any standard. Detailed data about the puddling and rolling processes are lacking, but success can be indirectly deduced from the extent of the use of coal in the iron industry. The use of coke increased gradually, accounting for about half of all iron produced before Cort's invention; then it changed radically so that by the end of the 1790s, virtually all iron was produced using coke (Rosenberg 1982, p. 87; Landes 1969, p. 91).

Both labor and fuel costs fell dramatically due to Cort's invention and subsequent increases in furnace size. Coal needs per ton of pig iron in the smelting plants of South Wales fell from 8 tons in 1791 to 3½ tons in 1830; as a result, the price of pig iron in 1830 had fallen to about one half its price in 1800. Before Cort's invention, a ton of crude iron was produced using three tons of charcoal; afterwards, energy requirements fell to 1½ tons of coke (Landes 1969, pp. 92–93).

Technical improvements in iron production were furthered by the invention of Joseph Hall, who replaced sand in the bed of puddling furnaces with tap cinder; this cut iron wastage from 50 percent of the ore to less than 8 percent. Cumulatively, these improvements resulted in a tremendous expansion of iron output that was supported and further intensified by an increase in demand for military supplies during the war years, the expansion of infrastructure (railways, water and gas piping), and increased demand for agricultural implements and household goods (such as nails, stoves, knives, and so on).

OTHER PROGRESSIVE INDUSTRIES

Several other industries also experienced impressive growth rates at this time, mainly due to technological change. For example, the Frenchman Nicholas Louis Robert revolutionized papermaking by inventing a process that produced paper continuously on a belt of woven wire, rather than individual sheets from a mold, as in the old method. This technique was further improved by an English engineer, and later it was called the Foudrinier process, after the London stationer who brought its first commercial application. The time needed to produce a piece of paper was reduced from three weeks to three minutes. Spin-offs from developments in other sectors also had an impact in papermaking; one example is the use of chlorine bleach which permitted dyed and printed rags to be pulped for paper (Mokyr 1990, pp. 106–7).

Mining, silk and construction also underwent significant, albeit less spectacular, transformation. They experienced simultaneous technological innovations: the widespread use of more efficient steam engines in mining and the adoption of the Jacquard loom in the silk industry. This loom replaced a manual process with an automatic one, consequently eliminating some costly errors that were common on the manual draw loom, and it resulted in lower labor costs. The diffusion of the Jacquard loom speeded up significantly after 1810. The construction industry benefitted from technical improvements in related industries. For example, the supply of bricks increased as a result of improvements in transportation technology which made possible the construction of more durable buildings at lower cost.

SLOWER GROWTH INDUSTRIES

Although there are several other industries with smaller output increases in the 1770–1841 period whose growth seemed more dependent on demand increases; nevertheless, they were still affected by the dynamics of technical change, even if change was slow or took place in marginal areas. The wool industry provides an excellent case study. The preparation of raw wool utilized predominantly traditional techniques, except that the water-driven carding machine was introduced in mills in Yorkshire sometime in the 1770s. Another example shows how slow other parts of the industry were in adapting to new techniques. The condenser, a simple device that removed loose strips of wool from the carder and prepared the roving (fiber strands which constitute the yarn) for the mule, was invented in America around 1830. It was not widely used in Yorkshire mills until 1870, and was unknown in many other regions.

Even though the spinning stage in the cotton industry had been critical in the bottleneck-innovation pattern, the same could not be said of the wool industry. For example, the jenny took at least fifteen years to become widespread in the Leeds area, and the mule was widely diffused only during the second quarter of the nineteenth century. Handloom weaving also survived much longer in wool than in the other textile industries. The power loom was introduced in wool factories in the 1840s, but there were only 14,391 of them in Britain in 1856, most in Yorkshire and Lancashire (Landes 1969, p. 88), while cottage workers continued to use the hand loom.

Many explanations have been offered for the wool industry's slow mechanization, but technical reasons are the most compelling. Wool is weaker than other fibers, making it more likely to break under the pressure of high speeds. Contemporary authorities on textile manufacturing advised running the power looms in wool at one-third the speed of those in the cotton industry; mules were also operated at slower speeds. The result was that mechanization did not offer such significant cost advantages as in cotton.

Another explanation involves the relative importance of labor and raw material costs. In wool, raw materials accounted for about a third of the total value of the finished product in the 1770s, much higher than in the cotton industry, while labor costs were proportionately less (Landes 1969, p. 88). Consequently, there was less incentive to introduce labor-saving machinery.

Technological diffusion in the linen industry was erratic, but overall not very impressive. One problem was the existence of a rubbery substance in flax that had to be removed before the flax could be spun. A French invention to dissolve it was first successfully used in Leeds in 1810, but it took fifteen years for the technique to be used in other parts of the British Isles. Technical problems associated with flax's rigidity, which caused it to break under strain, were mainly responsible for the slow diffusion of power looms: in 1850, only 1,000 were used in the linen industry compared to 250,000 in the cotton industry (Mokyr 1990, p. 103).

THE ISSUE OF TIMING

Technical diffusion is the best explanation, not only in accounting for differences in the growth rates of various sectors, but also for the time it took for the dynamic industries to expand enough to impact the entire economy. Besides the major innovations described in the previous pages, called "macroinventions" by Mokyr, there were many other small improvements which are easy to overlook because of their prolonged and gradual nature. For example, several adjustments in the gearing and shafting mechanism of textile machinery, the replacement of machines made out of wood by those made out of iron, the use of fixed-rail tracks to transport materials, and the use of cranes and elevated platforms to reach the top of furnaces in the iron industry, had small but cumulatively significant effects.

As significant as these developments were, it is the phenomenon of the widespread diffusion of macroinventions that demonstrates the occurrence of an Industrial Revolution and its timing, which I will date as some time in the 1830s.

The diffusion of innovations in the cotton industry in the late eighteenth century, which was described earlier, did not have too much of an impact beyond that industry itself. It was only in the second quarter of the nineteenth century that they became truly widespread; a period, moreover, when some other important indicators of sectoral growth, such as the consumption of raw cotton, also begin to accelerate (Mitchell and Deane 1971, p. 179). A similar pattern is observable in iron. The output of pig iron increased to a level significant enough to make an impact on the entire economy only after

Cort's inventions permitted an increase in the size of furnaces (Mitchell and Dean 1971, p. 131).

But more important, I will argue that the main reason why the British economy did not "take off" before the second quarter of the nineteenth century is the slow diffusion of the steam engine, the invention that came to define the core of the technological paradigm of the period. Detailed data are lacking, but what is available shows that the total horsepower of steam engines became statistically significant only when the railroad age was well underway (see Figure 6.2). Several explanations have been offered for its slow diffusion.

First, *technical considerations* are probably the single most important factor, in spite of the many improvements that took place in the development of an efficient engine. The first workable engine was built by Thomas Savery in 1698. It consisted of two parts, a boiler to heat water, and a cylinder to hold steam. Air pressure caused the water to rise into the receiver; as steam built up, it expelled the water, and the cycle would repeat. The Savery engine was very inefficient in its use of fuel because it had no piston, so cold water came into contact with the steam and there was a considerable loss of energy.

Newcomen's atmospheric engine, available in 1705, was the next generation. It solved some of the inefficiency problems by using a pis-

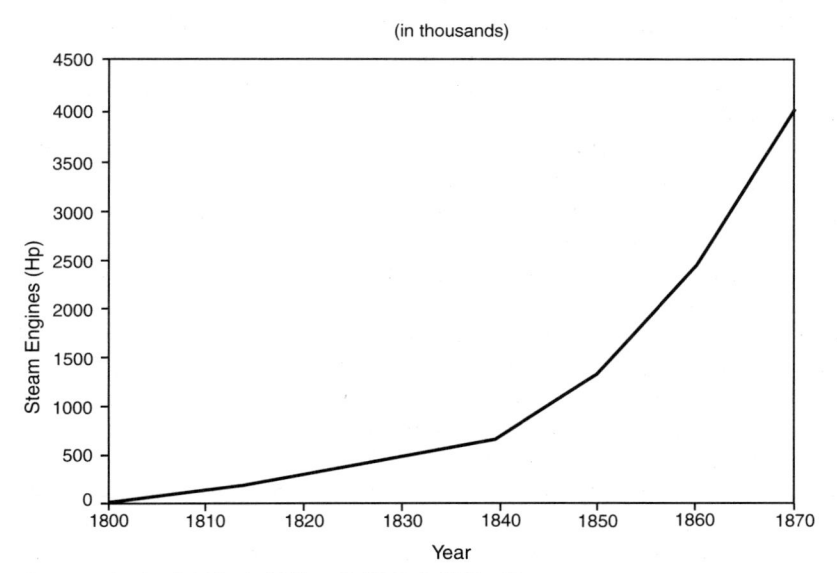

Source: based on data cited in Landes (1969), pp. 98, 104; Cipolla (1978), p. 57.

Figure 6.2 Steam engines (Hp) in the U.K., 1800–1870.

ton in the cylinder; the incoming steam created a vacuum and then air pressure pushed the piston downwards. The piston was connected to one end of a beam whose other end was connected to the rod of a water pump; this engine's main use was pumping water out of mines. Two technical features are important. First, the piston prevented cold water from coming into contact with the steam, so less energy was wasted. Second, as the piston's diameter increased, so the air pressure increased, which offered the potential of generating more horsepower with the same amount of steam.

James Watt's 1776 steam engine had a separate condenser for steam, which was a further improvement. Steam entered the space above the piston, drove it part of the way into the cylinder but was then cut off, leaving air pressure to do the rest. This meant that smaller amounts of steam produced more energy. Another significant improvement in efficiency resulted from Watt's collaboration with the engineering firm of John Wilkinson. Wilkinson made cannons for the army, and he used the same skills in steam engine production, which made possible an accurately bored cylinder to minimize the escape of steam from the gaps between the piston and the cylinder, resulting in a further improvement in energy efficiency.

Interestingly enough, older generations of steam engines coexisted with new ones, and all of them underwent improvement. For example, Von Tunzelman found that the diameter of cylinders in Newcomen engines increased throughout the eighteenth and well into the nineteenth century, with corresponding increases in horsepower generated[2] (cited in Stoneman 1983, p. 141).

The last stage in the development of steam engines in this period was the introduction of high pressure engines early in the nineteenth century. Richard Trevithick made some technical modifications that resulted in an engine with a smaller piston but which produced more horsepower. This version was lighter and cheaper, two features that were important to producing moveable engines later on. High pressure engines were further improved with the compound engine where steam passed to more than one cylinder, multiplying the energy output while economizing on fuel.

Technical considerations seem to be very influential in determining the rate of diffusion of steam engines. For most of the eighteenth century, they were adopted only in locations where there were no other sources of energy; that is, their fuel inefficiency implied that they were uncompetitive with other energy sources until after significant improvements first eliminated, then reversed the discrepancy.

A second important factor influencing diffusion patterns was *rela-*

Technological Diffusion Patterns

tive factor prices, which altered as a result of technical changes improving efficiency. For example, although Watt's separate condenser decreased fuel consumption fourfold (Mokyr 1990, p. 85; Landes 1969, p. 102), it was expensive to buy, which slowed its diffusion. Von Tunzelman compared the total costs of a (piston action) Newcomen engine and a Watt rotative engine before the 1790s, and found that the Watt engine was profitable only as long as the price of coal exceeded £1.7s. 10d per ton (cited in Stoneman 1983, p. 143). The threshhold price rose to £2.14s. per ton when the comparison was between the total cost of installing a Watt engine and an already-installed Newcomen engine. Similarly, although initially high pressure engines reduced coal consumption by threefold when compared to the Watt steam engine, Watt engines were gradually improved, and by 1845, the fuel efficiency advantage of high pressure engines was reduced to slightly less than twofold (Landes 1969, p. 103; Mokyr 1990, p. 90).

When it came to the diffusion of high pressure engines, however, technical considerations were critical in altering relative factor prices across sectors, depending on the use they were put to. For example, high pressure engines were successfully used to drain mines in Cornwall where they could be run at slow speeds to minimize fuel consumption, but they were less successful in textile manufacturing where high speeds were imperative. Hence by implication, von Tunzelman calculated that the diffusion of high pressure engines would only have been faster had the price of coal exceeded some threshold level (he used 12s. per ton) such that their fuel efficiency offset their high purchase price (cited in Stoneman 1983, pp. 143–44).

The influence of a third factor, *market structure,* is more difficult to assess, but seems relevant because of its influence on the ability to purchase new steam engines. For example, a Savery engine delivering 2–4 horsepower cost £150–£200 at the end of the eighteenth century, compared to a Watt rotative engine delivering 15–20 horsepower which cost between £600 and £1,000 (Landes 1969, p. 65).

Entrepreneurs in different industries showed varying levels of enthusiasm. Before 1800, four industries took the lead in using steam engines: mining (especially coal), canals, cotton textiles, and breweries. They were used for pumping water in the first two, and for turning shafts in the last two (Mathias 1969, p. 29). The iron industry is not on this list because it was only after 1780 that Cort's invention made use of the steam engine feasible.

After 1800, the iron, mining, railroad, and textile industries absorbed the largest number of steam engines. In textiles, cotton manufacturing took the lead, while wool followed after a significant time lag. Ninety percent of all cotton mills were steam-powered by 1850, and steampower dominated over waterpower by a ratio approaching 7:1 compared with a ratio of approximately 2:1 in the wool industry (Mitchell and Deane 1971, p. 198; Landes 1969, p. 104; Mathias 1969, p. 133).

Some correlation derived from empirical evidence and logical inference seem to imply that, given the increase in the purchase price of steam engines over time, only industries with relatively large economies of scale could justify the purchase of such expensive equipment. Both the cotton and iron industries bear this out.

The scale of operations in cotton manufacturing was small during the industry's "infant" stage in the eighteenth century. Most establishments were housed in subdivided old buildings or cottages, and fixed capital in the form of machinery was very low as a proportion of total assets. Even the first generation of spinning machines could be bought fairly easily. A forty-spindle jenny cost £6 in 1792, and a hand-loom cost between £7 and £10; the cost of a jenny was equivalent to the wages for two weeks of the forty women it replaced (Landes 1969, p. 65).

The ratio of fixed capital to total assets rarely exceeded 15 percent, and circulating capital, especially raw materials, accounted for most of the value of assets. Given the limited size and the nature of the capital structure of most firms, it is not surprising that it was not until 1785 that the first steam engine entered a cotton factory (Mathias 1969, p. 132).

The situation changed drastically in the 1790s when waterpower but more especially, steampower, was used in cotton mills, first in spinning, and later in weaving. Then both the average size of the firm and the proportion of fixed capital to total assets steadily increased. Arkwright's mill at Cranford, for example, employed 300 workers in the 1770s, but 727 forty years later. Jedediah Strutt spent about £15,000, two-thirds on fixed capital, to establish his mill at Belper in 1793. Fixed capital as a percentage of total assets is always relatively high when a factory is first founded, then it falls as output increases and more circulating capital is used. For example, the cotton mill of Old Knowe Cowpe & Co. started in 1786 with fixed capital accounting for 90 percent of its assets, a proportion that fell to 35 percent ten years later (Landes 1969, p. 75; Mathias 1969, p. 129).

The trend to increased scale was clearly irreversible; soon the largest spinning mills employed as many as 1,500 workers. "This signifies that technology had at once caused a revolution in the mode of production" (Mathias 1969, pp. 129–31), a revolution that was not about to stop. The next step came with the vertical integration of spinning and weaving that pushed the average size of the firm and its employment level to new heights. In Lancashire, for example, there were 1,500 cotton mills by the middle of the nineteenth century; about one-third were fully integrated, and on average, they employed 300 workers, 300 looms, and close to 20,000 spindles (Mathias 1969, pp. 265–66). It was only within this group of highly concentrated firms that the steam engine could be successfully utilized in large numbers, which helps explain why the cotton industry had a leading role in the diffusion of the steam engine during the first half of the nineteenth century.

There is a similar pattern of increasing concentration showing the interaction between technical change and industrial organization in the iron industry. Before Cort's inventions, the widespread use of charcoal limited the size of furnaces and thus restricted the typical output of a furnace to about 300 tons, which could be produced by ten men with a few dozen others employed to dig ore, and collect and transport charcoal. Entry costs were low; for example, the Walker brothers established an iron foundry in Sheffield for £10. But unlike textiles, there were also large establishments in the iron industry which early showed a tendency to increasing concentration. Darby's iron works at Coalbrookdale cost about £3,500 to establish; in 1759, the Carron works were begun with a capital value of £12,000, which increased to £130,000 just eleven years later. These are all examples of firms which pioneered in the use of coke (Mathias 1969, p. 125; Landes 1969, p. 12; Rosenberg 1982, p. 85).

These pioneering firms very early pushed the ratio of fixed to total assets to levels possibly approaching 50 percent, higher than in the cotton industry (Mathias 1969, p. 148). Entry costs rose, to approximately £50,000, as larger furnaces and their consequent economies of scale required larger plants. During the 1840s, it was not unusual to see employment levels of 1,000 men in iron plants; one of the largest employers, John Guest, employed 6,000 workers at Dowlais in Wales producing 20,000 tons of pig iron a year, with a capital that exceeded £1 million (Mathias 1969, pp. 269–70). The days of the small, independent forge were irreversibly over.

What is common to all these developments is that the increasing use of the steam engine was linked to the emergence of economies of scale in some key industries, and to a resulting tendency towards a more concentrated market structure. Given this, the spread of the steam engine also implied a built-in tendency to increasing innovation. That is, if fixed capital represented a relatively large proportion of total assets, then depreciation charges on that fixed capital would fall as a component of unit price the larger the output produced. This implied operating (increasingly large) plants close to their full capacity, but this cannot be done unless there is a market for selling that increased output. For an individual producer, the best way to sell an increased output is to grab market share at the expense of competitors by cutting prices below theirs; to do this profitably requires more investment in more efficient capital, hence the incentive to innovate.

During an inquiry of a Parliamentary Committee in 1833, a cotton spinner complained that "our profits are extremely low and I do not see any prospect that we have of improving it except by reducing the price still further and extending production" (cited in Mathias 1969, p. 141). It was entrepreneurs like this cotton spinner who were forced to adopt the steam engine (or other new technologies) during the nineteenth century by obeying the laws of capitalist competition. It is also no accident that joint-stock companies, which had advantages when it came to raising capital for new ventures, appeared and multiplied in precisely those sectors with high ratios of fixed capital. These sectors, iron manufacturing, railroads, and, to a lesser extent, cotton textiles, also took the lead in adopting the steam engine.

Two other factors played a role in the spread of steam engine technology. One was the *patent system*. At the beginning of the nineteenth century, when Watt's patents expired, prices fell dramatically, making his engines much more attractive, especially given their superior fuel efficiency. Also the existence of a *substitute technique*, waterpower, could limit the diffusion of steam power technology. Although waterpower was often inconvenient because of geographical or climatic factors, it was cheaper in terms of capital requirements, and water mills did undergo gradual improvements. In 1800, output generated by waterpower was four times larger than that generated by steam (Cameron 1985, p. 5). Only after various technical improvements and changes in market structure did the balance tilt in favor of steam.

HOW IMPORTANT WAS THE STEAM ENGINE?

Some scholars of the Industrial Revolution have questioned the importance given to the steam engine, using the concept of "social savings." This concept attempts to estimate the cost of additional inputs that would have been used if the second best alternative to any given innovation had been adopted instead; this extra cost is then expressed as a percentage of Gross National Product (GNP).

If, in 1800, waterpower had been used instead of the steam engines that were being used, Von Tunzelman estimated that Britain's GNP would have declined by a mere 0.2 percent (cited in Stoneman 1983, p. 233). Therefore, he concluded, the steam engine was not particularly important. But apart from the fact that very few steam engines were in use before 1800, this type of calculation underestimates the significance of technical innovation because some factors are not taken into account. Take the example of the cotton industry, which needed new sources of power for the three new spinning devices that had been introduced in the last quarter of the eighteenth century. Because existing steam engines were technically inefficient, cotton manufacturing located in areas with abundant water supplies, but these areas were not necessarily the most convenient in terms of market access or transportation.

But once these inefficiencies were ironed out, and steam power improved sufficiently to be used in cotton mills, location decisions became much more flexible. Although waterpower continued to be significant, the industry in fact became concentrated in Lancashire, around Manchester and Liverpool, which were more accessible locations. Transportation costs subsequently fell, and, in addition, some important externalities appeared. As urbanization increased, the pool of skilled workers grew larger, and some complementary specializations, such as bleaching and machine-making firms, also located in the area, developments which are unlikely to happen in remote villages.

None of these supplementary developments are taken into account in the social savings concept, which also ignores the fact that there would have been no railroads without the steam engine. Hawke estimated that if in 1865, there had been no railroads in Britain, GNP would have been lower by £28 million, or 4 percent (cited in Stoneman 1983, p. 232). Despite the fact that this is a significant amount because it was calculated as a marginal rate of growth (i.e., estimating what GNP would have been in 1865 compared to 1864), I believe this still underestimated the contribution of railroad transportation.

First, it was estimated by including freight transportation costs only, and it did not include the revenues generated from passenger traffic. The 400,000 passengers who used the Manchester and Liverpool line in 1830, its first year of operation, accounted for twice the revenues of transporting commodities, and this passenger/freight ratio remained the same until 1845. Half a million people traveled on the London and Birmingham line in 1839, when it first opened, a number that doubled six years later (Mathias 1969, p. 279); figures such as these are not inconsequential. Revenues from freight exceeded those from passengers only during the 1850s.

But more important, Hawke's estimates do not take into account the role of the railroads in widening the internal market by improving links between closely related industries, and between them and their customers. As Mathias noted:

> Steam power was the greatest of the industrial innovations developed in the course of the Industrial Revolution because it became the agent and instrument for applying basic innovations in so many industries and transport. By 1800 the continued momentum of advance in strategic industries like cotton spinning and iron was dependent on enlarging the uses of the steam engine, even though only a small proportion of productive effort in the economy then depended on the engine. Everyone knew that the greatest strides in technical progress lay in applying the steam engine and iron machinery to more and more processes in more and more industries. A contagion was in progress. (Mathias 1969, p. 134)

In other words, the steam engine became the central element of the "technological paradigm" that defined the Industrial Revolution. Its significance is evident by the fact that the speeding up of its diffusion path coincides chronologically with, and is probably the main cause of, the acceleration in the growth rates of national output that took place in the second quarter of the nineteenth century. It was at that time that the steam engine was technologically mature enough to be used in certain key industries, such as cotton and the railroads. This does not underestimate the importance of the technologies that appeared in the late eighteenth century, but these technologies needed more efficient steam engines to reach their full potential (and in turn may also have stimulated the maturing of the steam engine).

In summary, I have argued that looking at the adoption of certain key technologies helps understand the contribution made by different industrial sectors to the overall growth process. It may be that we may have to alter the "start" or the "maturing" of Britain's Industrial Revolution; what remains an important insight is that the beginning of truly modern industrialized economies occurred when these technologies acquired a critical mass in certain areas.

NOTES

1. Four terms are usually utilized in the conventional literature of technical change: (a) invention, the initial discovery or creation of something;

(b) innovation, the commercial application of an invention; (c) innovation improvements, which are technical improvements that transform and modify the characteristics of an invention; and (d) diffusion, which refers to the gradual adoption of a technique along temporal and sectoral lines.

2. For example, in 1712, a Newcomen engine used in Dudley had a 21 inch diameter cylinder producing an estimated 5 horsepower; by 1810, an improved Newcomen engine used in Whitehaven had an 82 inch diameter cylinder producing an estimated 100 horsepower.

ACKNOWLEDGMENT

The author gratefully acknowledges the editorial input of this volume's editors.

7
TRADITION AND MODERNIZATION: STATE, SOCIETY, AND THE DEVELOPMENT OF INDUSTRY IN EIGHTEENTH-CENTURY RUSSIA
Gennady Shkliarevsky

The eighteenth century was a period of dramatic changes in Russia. These changes, initiated by Peter the Great (Peter I, 1682–1725), involved wholesale borrowings of western institutions, technology, and even dress and manners. Yet the effects of this "westernization" were paradoxical. At the end of the century Russia was as different from the West as it had ever been, if not more so. While many Western countries were becoming more liberal and democratic, Russian autocratic rule remained essentially unchanged; indeed, with the ubiquitous police surveillance by the infamous Third Section of His Majesty's Personal Chancellery under Nicholas I (1825–1855), the Russian autocracy became even more oppressive. And while western countries were moving toward dismantling the system of indentured labor, serfdom persisted in Russia until the middle of the nineteenth century.

This chapter will focus on one aspect of the Russian modernization in the eighteenth century—the development of industry. Although the results of this industrial development, in terms of output growth, were quite impressive, they failed to generate an ongoing industrial expansion similar to the one experienced by western countries in the first half of the nineteenth century. Why this was the case, and what its implications were, is the subject of this chapter.

RUSSIA'S INDUSTRY IN THE EIGHTEENTH CENTURY

Traditionally, the emergence of Russian industry has been associated with the name of Peter the Great, although some "modern" industrial activity started as early as the sixteenth century. In the seventeenth century, iron and copper plants, some of them water-driven, operated in the regions north and northwest of Moscow. There was also a fair number of enterprises producing potash, weapons, gunpowder, leather goods, textiles (both linen and woolens), as well as salt works and liquor distilleries.[1] Some individuals—for example, the Stroganov family—were able to build vast commercial-industrial empires worth millions of rubles (Blackwell 1968, pp. 10–15). As one economic historian concluded: " . . . beginning with the seventeenth century, the economic and the social foundations upon which Russian industry of the eighteenth century rested become apparent" (Blanc 1974, p. 24). Although these early achievements were significant, they were overshadowed by the sheer extent of industrial activities and the growth of industrial output that occurred during and after Peter I's reign.

Peter I placed a high priority on the development of industry, which was part and parcel of his overall policy of modernizing the country. By promoting Russian industry, Peter I hoped to make the country economically self-sufficient and utilize its enormous resources. He believed that the success of his industrial endeavors would enhance Russia's prestige in Europe, since many countries would come to critically depend on Russian trade; but more important, he wanted to see his country rich and its population engaged in productive labor. In fact, many of his decrees related to industry made references to "the general good" and "the good of all the people" as justifications for the proposed changes.

Peter I aggressively pursued his goals. Following his first trip to Europe early in his reign, he imported Western technology, equipment, and specialists on a wide scale. He created government agencies for promoting industry, the most important of which were the Business College; the College of Manufactures; and the College of Mines (the latter two colleges functioned as one institution until 1722 due to lack of personnel). Peter the Great also issued numerous decrees designed to encourage nascent Russian industry, including "The Privileges of Colleges and Mines" (1719) and the "Regulations of the College of Manufactures" (1723). His government granted privileges and subsidies to domestic industrialists and merchants, and vigilantly protected them against foreign competition. In 1724, for example, the government introduced a protectionist tariff to benefit Russia's budding industry. It also used dumping (exporting abroad at prices below those prevailing in Russia) in order to increase Russia's share in international trade. One example of this occurred with iron which Russia sold on the European market for a price of 56 kopeck per pound, while on the domestic market the cost of iron was maintained at 66 kopeck per pound (ibid. p. 30–34).

Peter I's efforts produced impressive results. In addition to traditional industries such as the production of precious metals and copper, liquor distilleries, and salt works, the country's industrial sector included a vastly more expanded iron industry and such major new industries as woolens, armaments and gunpowder, and linen by the time of his death. According to one estimate, in 1725 (the year of Peter I's death) there were 226 large industrial enterprises in Russia of which only 21 dated back to the seventeeth century. A typical enterprise employed between 200–300 workers (Blackwell 1968, p. 17; see also Falkus 1972).

The metal industry was a real success of Peter I's industrial policies. During his reign, investments in the metal industry, both government and private, grew from 22,000 silver rubles in 1700 to 170,000 in 1725 (Kahan 1974, p. 63). These substantial investments produced impressive results. Russia was an importer of metal at the end of the seventeenth century, but became an exporter of iron by 1725, with England being its main trading partner. One of the giants of the metal industry was the Nevianskii plant—the largest enterprise in the industrial empire of the famous manufacturer Demidov—which had four furnaces and produced between 1,800 to 3,600 tons of iron a year (Blackwell 1968, p. 17).

Textile production was another major industry which developed dramatically under Peter I. As was the case with the iron industry, most enterprises in this industry were large and employed hundreds and sometimes even thousands of workers. For example, the linen enterprise producing sailcloth located in Moscow had 1,362 workers, the woolens factory of the merchants Schegolins in Moscow had 1,010 workers and 155 looms, and the Moscow linen enterprise of the Dutchman Jan Tamesz employed 600 workers and 336 looms (Daniel 1995, p. 6). A vivid indication of Peter I's success in developing Russian industrial production was the fact that by the time of his death Russian industry was able to supply a 220,000-strong army. Already in 1715, the army's artillery had approximately 1,300 domestically produced artillery pieces of various sizes. The yearly output of firearms exceeded

20,000 by 1720. Domestic textile enterprises produced the bulk of cloth for the Russian army and navy (Kahan 1985, p. 99; Kahan 1974, p. 63).

Several researchers have shown that in the years following Peter I's death, the evolution of the industrial sector continued unabated (Kahan 1974; Falkus 1972). For example, investment in the iron industry increased from 170,000 silver rubles in 1725 to 371,000 in 1735, and to 1,102,000 in 1745 (Kahan 1974, p. 63). By mid-century, the output of Russia's metal industry was higher than that of many major European countries. In 1740, Russia produced 31,975 metric tons of cast iron, which was more than the amount of metal produced by Britain (20,017 tons), France (25,979 tons), or Germany (17,691 tons) (Baykov 1974, p. 7). Russian metal production, which was only 59 percent of British output at the time of Peter I's death, exceeded British production by 50 percent in 1750 (Blanc 1974, p. 27). Approximately ten large linen factories opened during the decade after Peter I's death, in addition to the fifteen which were in operation in 1726. By 1760, there were forty-four large linen factories in Russia exporting 70 percent to 90 percent of their output abroad.[2] Some researchers have estimated that internal trade turnover at the time when internal custom tariffs were abolished in 1753–54 was 22 million rubles—an enormous sum for that period.

By the end of the eighteenth century, there were approximately 1,200 large industrial enterprises in Russia compared to 663 in 1767. The industrial labor force comprised nearly 200,000 workers. The Russian woolens industry—which was practically nonexistent prior to Peter I—had, according to one estimate, 152 enterprises. Most of them were medium and large size. For example, only two or three of the fifteen enterprises listed in the records had fewer than a hundred workers, while nine employed between one hundred and five hundred workers, and three had over a thousand.[3] The number of linen enterprises grew to an impressive 318 with a labor force of 29,303, compared with only ten at the time of Peter I's death in 1725. Russian exports more than tripled in value from 1762 to 1793. More than 45 percent of Russian exports in 1793 were in metals and textiles. The number of trade centers in Russia increased from 608 in the 1750s to 2,571 by the end of the 1790s (Pallot and Shaw 1990, pp. 196–97; Kahan 1985, p. 88).

EXPLANATION OF RUSSIA'S ECONOMIC BACKWARDNESS

Despite these impressive achievements, the development of Russian industry in the eighteenth century failed to ignite an industrial expansion similar to the expansion which occurred in many western countries during the first half of the nineteenth century. By the turn of the century, Russian industrial production began to fall behind that in western Europe and the gap continued to grow. Russia's defeat in the Crimean war (1853–1856) testified to its industrial and technological backwardness.

Many researchers have addressed this paradox, and have tried to explain what happened. Their explanations focus on a variety of factors ranging from the economic through the political to the mentality of the Russian people. Alexander Gerschenkron—a doyen among economic historians of Russia—considers that the country's initial economic backwardness by comparison with the western countries required a broad involvement of the government in industry. But this involvement, in turn, subsequently created obstacles to the emergence of a more market-oriented economy and more sustained industrial growth (Gerschenkron 1962; 1963; 1970). William L. Blackwell, who has studied the role of dissenters—Old Believers and Jews—in Russian economic development, views the repressive nature of the Russian state as being the main obstacle to the development of Russian industry which, he argues, was to a significant degree developed by the dissenters in response to persecution and restrictions imposed on them by the state (Blackwell 1982; 1968 pp. 19–23, 229–36).

In contrast to the above historians, Arcadius Kahan emphasized mentality, rather than economic or political factors. He saw the Russian economy in the eighteenth century as evolving essentially along the lines of a capitalist market economy—a view that has recently been cogently challenged (Daniel 1995). Kahan believed that the most important part of industrialization involved "sets of cultural phenomena that entail the creation of wants resulting from the acceptance of a new value system, the willingness to change traditional patterns of life, perseverance in the pursuit of particular goals, acceptance of new behavioral norms, the assumption of responsibilities and risks, and new types of decision making by a multitude of people" (Kahan 1989, p. 106). It was the slow evolution of this new mentality and values among Russian people that, Kahan suggested, presented a serious obstacle to the industrialization of Russia occurring earlier than it did.

The views of Soviet economic historians on this question were more uniform. Most of them saw Russia's economic backwardness in terms of class conflict. They argued that the interests of the landowners, who constituted the dominant ruling class in the Russian empire, demanded the preservation of serfdom and the feudal social order, and impeded the country's evolution toward industrial capitalism.[4] Only with the advent of *perestroika* in the 1980s did new interpretations appear in Soviet scholarship. Among recent post-*perestroika* contributions to this discussion, one should note the work by Evgenii Anisimov who emphasizes what he calls the Russian "police culture" as the main factor which hindered the country's development.[5]

The differences in these interpretations indicate the complexity of the problem. Although a short chapter cannot go into a detailed analysis of these various interpretations, one observation should be made: while these interpretations identify valid issues, they focus on individual aspects of the problem, rather than the problem as a whole. This chapter will provide an integrated analysis. It will examine the specific features of Russian industrial development distinguishing it from the development of industry in the western world, and then will relate these features to the more general cultural causes which produced them.

Government Intervention in Industry

Modernization in western Europe—of which industrialization was a part—evolved in the context of an emerging civil society. The rise of civil society was characterized by, among other things, the differentiation of the state from society, the separation of the public from the private sphere, and the recognition of the autonomy of the individual. The notion that individual members of society were endowed with natural and inalienable rights, and were free to pursue their own ends as long as they did not harm others was increasingly gaining acceptance in the West.

The two processes—the development of industry and the rise of civil society—in many ways complemented each other; they both contributed, for example, to the consolidation and institutionalization of private property which, in combination with free hired labor, became one of the cornerstones of west European capitalist economies. Indeed, the emergence of civil society and the development of capitalism were so important to each other that one may think about capitalism as an extension of the principles of civil society into the economic sphere, or conversely, of civil society as the transfer of capitalist principles onto the social and political plane.

Russia's eighteenth-century economy evolved in a very different context. One important difference which strikes a researcher is the degree to which the government was involved in the development of industry. Indeed, government involvement in industry was not uncommon in Europe, but still the involvement of the Russian government was unprecedented in its extent. In fact, in the eyes of the government there was no distinction between working in industry and serving the state. As Simone Blanc observed, the government viewed "work done in the 'factories,' by the owners as well as by the workmen . . . as being at the 'service of the state'" (Blanc 1974, p. 32).

The Russian state founded enterprises; granted monopolies and subsidies; provided access to labor and resources; determined the quality and quantity of output; granted exemptions from taxes, custom duties, and state obligations; and regulated and closely supervised the operation of enterprises including aspects which had little to do with production, such as the way workers spent their leisure time, their attendance at church services, and so forth (Kahan 1985, p. 3). It is also worth noting the arbitrary nature of this supervision. In exercising this supervision, the government and its agents showed little regard for law. In fact, it is difficult to apply the word "law" to the numerous decrees and regulations issued by the government; Russians themselves used the word *privilegii,* or "privileges," rather than "law." The institutional framework for directing industry was weak. The history of the Manufactures College is illustrative. Introduced in 1724 for the purpose of granting privileges and permits to set up enterprises, it was abolished in 1727, then reestablished that same year, merged with the Mining and Commerce Colleges in 1731, then separated again in 1741, and then, finally, put to rest in 1779 (Rieber 1982, p. 8). These constant changes disrupted the institution's work and rendered it ineffective.

In the absence of a strong institutional base, powerful satraps of the tsar exercised complete power, particularly in provincial areas where much industry was concentrated. V. N. Tatishchev, who was put in charge of the entire Urals region during the 1730s, enjoyed dictatorial powers. He had the right to assign peasants to enterprises, grant privileges, provide subsidies—and all at his whim. He openly took bribes and justified doing so by saying that he took them for the "righteous labors" (*za trudy pravednye*).

Lack of Property Rights

Government exercised total control over industry. The very concept of "private property" was alien to eighteenth-century Russians: neither Russian rulers nor the population made a clear distinction between private and state property. For example, enterprises which were originally founded by the state were often transferred to individuals, and then, later, confiscated by the state. Individuals who took over state enterprises were supposed to fulfill conditions imposed by the government. They were to supply the government with their products at cost and could, therefore, sell on the market only what was left after they fulfilled their government quotas. As a result, only a small fraction of their output was available for private consumption. For example, only two of the thirty woolens factories which operated in the 1760s produced cloth for the private market: one factory could use two looms for this purpose and another, three. In addition, the government usually specified the quantity and quality of the product. The producers frequently had to promise the government to make investments (often a specified amount) and expand production. Noncompliance with these conditions usually led to fines, confiscation, and even lashing, exile, or imprisonment (Pipes 1992, pp. 209–10).

The "privatization" of enterprises was not an entirely voluntary transaction. It was often implemented under duress and without the slightest regard for the wishes or interests of manufacturers. One author aptly describes Peter I's policy of enterprise transfers as "manufacturing manufacturers."[6] In 1711, for example, Peter I created the first Russian industrial company by forcing two merchants, Andrei Turka (Turchaninov) and Stepan Tsinbal'shchikov, to invest their money in it. The Shchegolin company was set up in a similar manner. When creating the Moscow Commercial Company, Peter I personally selected individuals from among the leading Russian merchants and sent soldiers to bring them to Moscow for "temporary exile." The state provided them with an interest-free loan on the condition that they should operate the enterprise properly. However, if they failed to do so, the government threatened to take over the company and punish the owners (Pipes 1992, pp. 209–10). A similar policy continued under Peter's successors.

Similarly, when owners set up enterprises with their own capital, the government showed no regard for their property rights. The case of the woolens mill founded by General Kormchin and Ivan Dubrovin with their own capital illustrates this point. Over a number of years Dubrovin, who managed the factory, failed to submit reports on the operation of the factory. In 1726, he told government officials, evidently under duress, that the factory had a sufficient amount of cloth to fulfill state orders. When he failed to deliver the required amount, the government dispatched a special commission which audited the factory and found no cloth available for delivery. In punishment for failing to fulfill state orders and providing false reports, Dubrovin's properties—not just the factory, but his other properties as well—were confiscated. Dubrovin himself was taken into custody and sent to St. Petersburg. In accordance with the decree issued on June 28, 1731, manufacturers who suspended the work at their enterprises or did not, in the opinion of the government, sufficiently expand their production could lose their status and property. Such was the case, for example, of Bogdan Myl'nitskii in 1740.

Not even noble landowners were exempt from government incursions on their property. Peter I's decree concerning the mining of iron ore stated that if a landowner failed to set up an enterprise to mine iron ore on his property, the government would force him to cede this privilege. Attempts to conceal information from the government about iron ore deposits incurred severe punishment, including death.

Petty Supervision

Peter I and his successors practiced a strict and often petty supervision over the operation of industrial enterprises. For example, according to the decree of 1731, managers of state or private iron plants could not utilize their resources as they saw fit; they were to use them "moderately and without excess." Government officials often prescribed what and how much enterprises should produce. In 1734, Tatishchev issued an order which, under the pain of death, forbade the metal plants located in the Urals to produce or sell abroad "guns, mortars, bombs, cannon balls, as well as other weapons, foils, spears, and other weapons" without his explicit permission. Even such wealthy industrialists as Akinfii Demidov were completely powerless before the government. In one instance, when government officials learned that a quarter of the furnaces at Demidov's plants were not operational due to a lack of funds, he was ordered to return immediately to the Urals (he was in Moscow at the time) and provide the capital required for operation.

In order to ensure government control, Tatishchev instituted the so-called *Schichtmeisters* (lit. supervisors) who exercised close supervision over the enterprises located in the Ural region. The *Schichtmeisters's* functions were to make sure that managers fulfilled a whole range of requirements. Not only did the latter have to produce and deliver goods of prescribed quality, expand production, submit timely reports, pay wages set by the government, and explore new deposits, they were also made responsible for building churches for their workers, establishing schools, setting up stores, making sure that the drinking establishments frequented by their workers stayed open only during specified hours, and that workers attended churches and went to confession regularly. Some of these gems of Tatishchev's bureaucratic "genius" were rejected by the Commercial College, but many were approved and put into practice.

Although the government officially enunciated policies designed to facilitate and simplify the procedure for opening new enterprises in several decrees issued in the course of the eighteenth century, in practice the granting of permissions was circumscribed by a number of conditions. The merchant Ivan Kuznetsov, for example, applied in 1739 for permission to open a small manufacturing shop in his own house and at his own expense. He had to promise that he would pay a duty of 50 rubles to the government over the next ten years, regardless of whether the enterprise was profitable or not. The government usually attached numerous conditions to subsidies and privileges granted to individual manufacturers. It prescribed how much of their own money they should invest, how they should run their enterprise, and often added on various petty regulations. Another example concerns the merchant Eremeev, who received permission from the government in 1736 to set up an enterprise. However, he had to promise to invest thirty thousand rubles of his own money into this enterprise. The decree of Peter I which lifted restrictions on mining gold, silver, and copper also stipulated that the producers should sell these metals exclusively to the government; needless to say, at prices set by the government.

Unfree Character of Russian Industrial Labor

Another important feature of Russian industrial development in the eighteenth century was that workers employed in industry were essentially unfree. By contrast industry in the West employed primarily labor that was free of feudal obligations. At the start of his industrial expansion policy, Peter forced convicts, vagabonds, prisoners of war, prostitutes, and soldiers' wives (who were placed in the same category as prostitutes) to work in Russian industrial enterprises under the threat of penal labor and even the pain of death. However, as industry expanded, other sources of labor had to be found.

Privately owned serfs then became a major source of industrial labor in Russia. Owners could force their serfs to work in industrial enterprises. In accordance with a decree of 1740, a landowner could make his serfs fulfill their servile obligations by working in a factory set up on his estate, if hired labor was unavailable or too expensive. As large segments of Russian industry came under noble control toward the end of the eighteenth century, noble landowners used serf labor extensively in their enterprises (Pipes 1992, p. 49). Under Peter I, merchants and other non-noble manufacturers were also granted the privilege, which was abolished later, of purchasing serfs for their factories (ibid., pp. 209–10).

In addition, in promoting industry, Peter I's government instituted the practice of assigning state peasants, who were legally freemen, to factories. They were called "assigned peasants," or *pripisnye* in Russian. The government through this mechanism could thus force entire villages into working for industry. Consequently, the status of the *pripisnye* was hardly different from that of the serfs. This treatment continued under later rulers. The Empress Anna issued a decree in 1736 which ruled that the "assigned peasants" and their families were to be permanently attached to factories; they could not leave one factory for another and were to be treated no differently than the serfs (Avrich 1977, p. 200). Finally, using the threat of penal labor, the government could force different categories of the population to work in factories; under Peter I, this could be done with former serfs who were freed by their owners or with individuals who owed taxes to the state.

Russian industry did also employ hired workers. They included free peasants, serfs who were allowed by their owners to work on a quitrent basis (lit. a payment made by serfs in lieu of required feudal services), and urban residents. Although the number of hired workers was lower than the number of indentured laborers, it was still significant. In some instances, as was the case in many industrial enterprises in the Urals in 1753, hired workers constituted as much as one-third of the total labor force.

The status of freemen was nearly identical to that of indentured laborers. In his study of the early period of Russian industrial development, William Blackwell observed that " . . . hired labor, which in some cases involved ten-year terms at negligible pay, was not always distinguishable from the various types of impressment that came to be used" (1968, p. 19). The government, which considered hired workers to be in the service of the state, set the example in treating hired workers as de facto unfree. It would transfer workers from one enterprise to another without any regard for their wishes or personal circumstances, often taking workers away from their families. In 1749, the government transferred seventy-two workers from the plant of a manufacturer named Tumenov, who poorly managed his enterprise, to the woolens plant of I. Gordenin. Needless to say, Tumenov received no compensation for his loss. In another instance, a certain General Irman requested in

1765 that a significant number of skilled workers be transferred from private plants to the Gornoblagodatskii and Kamenskii state plants. There are numerous other examples of similar treatment of workers by the state. In 1795, three hundred skilled workers were transferred from the Lipetskii to the Luganskii plant, one hundred were sent from the Aleksandrovskii plant to the Petrozavodskii plant, and in 1796, three hundred workers went from the Lipetskii plant to the Aleksandrovskii plant.

In view of the chronic shortages of labor and the paucity of legal constraints, manufacturers resorted to a variety of methods to keep hired workers in their enterprises against their will. Factory owners freequently confiscated their workers' internal passports. This prevented them from leaving the enterprise. In one documented instance, the well-known industrialist Nikita Demidov took away the passports of a group of carpenters who worked at his Siberian plant far away from their families.

Financial indebtedness was another method of preventing workers from leaving the enterprise. Since manufacturers usually provided workers and their families with housing, clothes, and food, the latter would often become indebted to their employers who would then demand that a worker should settle his account before leaving the plant. The case of Abyzov, an ethnic Tatar, is typical. Abyzov and his two children were sent to work at the plant which belonged to a certain Pokhodiashin to repay a debt of 96 rubles. Two years later, when Abyzov wanted to leave the plant, the management would not let him since according to their records, Abyzov now owed the plant 345 rubles. Abyzov ran away but was brought back in shackles and kept in chains for five days. The extensive use of such methods was a major factor in generating workers' discontent. When the rebels led by Emelian Pugachev during the famous uprising (1773–1775) in the reign of Catherine the Great captured the Zlatoustovskii plant, they destroyed 59,250 promissory notes recording workers' debts; 33,000 such notes were also destroyed at the Satkinskii plant.

Once a worker was deprived of his freedom, he was completely at the mercy of his employer. The latter could keep the worker's wages as low as he wished or could force him to relocate to another enterprise. The previously mentioned Nikita Demidov, for example, would routinely transfer workers against their will from his enterprises located in central parts of Russia to those located in the Urals and Siberia which experienced significant shortages of labor. For example, he forced a worker named Gavrilo Mishukov to move to the Kyshtym plant in 1758, and then, in 1763, to the gold mines in Ekaterinburg province. The position of apprentices, who constituted a significant part of the labor force in Russian industrial enterprises, was worse than that of hired workers. Their apprenticeship usually lasted twelve years, and their work conditions resembled those of serfs.

LACK OF CIVIL SOCIETY IN RUSSIA

The extent of government involvement in industry, the total lack of any institutional guarantees of private property or protection of the individual rights of both workers and manufacturers, and the extensive use of unfree labor, indicate that despite many similarities, Russia's industry evolved in a very different context than that of the western countries. In contrast to the West, where the development of industry was accompanied by the rise of civil society, the development of Russian industry took place in a cultural context which made little differentiation between state and society or between the public and private sphere, and which had no conception of individual rights, private property, or law (at least in the western sense). Thus, industrial development in the eighteenth century was not accompanied by those cultural changes which characterized the rise of civil society in western Europe. Despite numerous innovations introduced by Peter I and his successors, traditional culture successfully survived virtually intact.

It would be wrong to assume that the survival of traditional relations was due exclusively to the oppressive character of the Russian state. Nothing could be further from the truth. Indeed, there is much evidence to suggest that the attitudes which perpetuated these relations were shared by broad segments of the Russian population. In contrast to the West, for example, where the middle class sought to assert its interests vis à vis the rulers and feudal elites, the Russian middle class—the merchants and non-noble manufacturers—made no attempt to challenge the government and the established order. In his study of Russian merchants and entrepreneurs, Alfred Rieber explains this complaisance primarily by "the collective mentality and behavior of the merchants themselves," rather than just by the threat of reprisals (Rieber 1982, p. 8).

The writings of Ivan Pososhkov, a would-be manufacturer and an autodidact, are instructive. Pososhkov reflected the predominant attitudes of the middle class. His famous treatise *The Book on Poverty and Wealth,* for which Pososhkov suffered imprisonment, articulated very traditional views. He advocated a close unity between "the people"—merchants, artisans, manufacturers, and peasants—and the tsar, and the suppression of the nobility. He believed that the power of the tsar should be unlimited. The monarch, Pososhkov wrote, should be able to "order his people [to do] not only what serves the benefit of the homeland [*otechestvo*], but anything that he wishes, as long as this does not harm the people" (Platonov 1989, p. 26). In another passage, Pososhkov put it even more bluntly: " . . . the tsar is like God, he should do whatever he wants in his realm."[7]

Among the Russian lower and less educated classes—workers and peasants—belief in the paternalistic state was equally strong, if not stronger than among the middle class. This belief, for example, was one of the major inspirations behind the Pugachev rebellion (1773–75) during the reign of Catherine the Great. The image of the suffering, righteous, and redeeming tsar, which Pugachev assumed, appealed to the Russian lower classes, including workers, who joined his force in large numbers. In their petitions to Pugachev, workers in the industrial enterprises located in the Urals expressed their loyalty to the "righteous tsar" and asked for his intervention in redressing their grievances and punishing the nobility. They characteristically addressed him in a very traditional way as "our dear father" and "our red sun" and called themselves his "slaves."[8]

IMPACT OF TRADITIONAL RELATIONS ON ECONOMIC DEVELOPMENT

The survival of traditional relations between the state and society and the lack of differentiation between the private and the public sphere had profound effects on the economic development of the country. The rise of civil society in western countries led to the expansion of the sphere of autonomous action within which the individual could pursue his or her own goals. This expansion had beneficial effects on all aspects of western society, including economic development. Private initiative was a powerful force which propelled this development; its complex interplay with growing consumer demand in the context of the competitive market economy led to the unprecedented expansion of western economies and the increased prosperity of the population.

In the Russian case, the retrenchment of the traditional culture, which recognized the state as the sole legitimate agent of change, continued to restrict the sphere of autonomous action. As a result, private initiative and market demand played a limited role in the country's economic development. The needs of the state defined economic development. Once state priorities shifted away from industry, as was the case in the second half of the eighteenth century, there was little that could stimulate its development.

The survival of traditional attitudes also led to the wide use of indentured labor which greatly impeded the development of industry. Not only was this labor less productive than that of hired workers, but also its wide use discouraged technological progress. Few manufacturers in Russia were inclined to seek alternative ways of increasing productivity by making costly investments in new technologies. Instead, they tried to increase production by getting more workers and depriving them of their freedom.

Finally, the continued domination of traditional relations greatly weakened the urban middle class—merchants, artisans, manufacturers. Despite some patronage by the state during the reign of Peter the Great, the Russian merchant class failed to establish their position vis à vis the state and the nobility (Rieber 1982, p. xxii). In contrast to their Western counterparts who played an enormous role in the development of their economies, the Russian merchant class did not create effective organizations able to defend its interests. In view of the weakness of the urban middle class, it was the nobility that became the dominant force in the industrial sector toward the end of the eighteenth century. In the course of the several decades after the liberalization of industry and trade under Catherine II, the Russian nobility, which controlled much of the available land and had access to cheap serf labor, came to own all the distilleries, 64 percent of the mines, 78 percent of the woolen mills, 60 percent of the paper mills, 66 percent of the glass and crystal factories, and 80 percent of the enterprises producing potash (Pipes 1992, p. 212). In contrast to the West, eighteenth-century Russian industry became a rural rather than an urban phenomenon. The trading pattern was diametrically different from that in western Europe, with urban merchants selling agricultural products in the countryside and peasants taking their handicrafts to the city (Rieber 1982, p. 12). In western countries, modernization and the development of industry contributed to the growth of cities and of the urban population. The city became a fertile ground which nourished industrial growth. In Russia, by contrast, the urban population hardly grew in the course of the century and in 1800 constituted a meager 4 percent of the total population—an increase of merely one percent since 1724 (Falkus 1972, p. 28).*

---

*Editors' note: At the beginning of the eighteenth century, Russia was not the largest of the European powers. In 1725, its population was approximately 13 million, compared with 19 million in France and 7.5 million in Great Britain and Ireland (1700 figures). But its rate of population growth was much faster. In 1800, population figures for these three countries are, respectively, 36 million, 27 million, and 16 million; and in 1871, 87 million, 36 million, and 32 million.

CLASH OF MODERNIZATION AND TRADITION

As this chapter has demonstrated, Russia failed to capitalize on its successes in the development of industry because this development—a product of modernization—clashed with the Russian tradition which impeded its progress. Why did Russian tradition prove to be so durable? The answer probably lies in the very method by which Russia was modernized. In Russia, the state was viewed as the only legitimate agent of change. By modernizing the country from above, the state, ironically, reasserted this tradition. Thus, the way in which Russia was modernized helped to preserve the tradition.

This is not to say that modernization and borrowing from the West had no effect on Russia. They most certainly did. Despite modifications which these borrowings underwent when applied in Russia, they still preserved in embryonic form the dynamic elements of the culture which produced them. Indeed, the impact of these borrowings was ambivalent: not only did they strengthen and modernize the Russian tradition, thus contributing to its survival, they also generated trends which clashed powerfully with this tradition. The contradictory course of the Russian autocracy which tried to modernize the country and, at the same time, strengthen autocratic rule, could not but generate conflict which, one could argue, ultimately led to its demise.

NOTES

1. Much of the information and historical data used in this chapter comes from Russian-language sources. The interested student should consult the following (in alphabetical order); E. V. Anisimov *Vremia petrovskikh peremen* (Leningrad: Lenizdat, 1989); P. I. Liashchenko *Istoriia narodnogo khoziaistva SSSR,* 2 vols. (Moscow: Gospolitizdat, 1952); P.G. Liubomudrov *Ocherki po istorii promyshlennosti* (Moscow: Gospolitizdat, 1947); I. V. Maevskii and F. Ia. Polianskii, eds. *Voprosy istorii narodnogo khoziaistva SSSR* (Moscow: Izdatelstvo AN SSSR, 1957); E. V. Spiridonova *Ekonomicheskaia politika i ekonomicheskie vzgliady Petra* (Moscow: Gosizdat, 1952); and E. I. Zaozerskaia *U istokov krupnogo proizvodstva v russkoi promyshlennosti XVI–XVII vekov* (Moscow: Nauka, 1970).

2. See reference to Liubomudrov (pp. 76–77) in note 1; Arcadius Kahan provides a more generous estimate of 79 factories employing over thirteen thousand workers in 1763 in Kahan 1985, p. 88.

3. See Liubomudrov, pp. 52, 59. The largest factories were those belonging to the count Iusupov (1,386 workers), Osokin's factory (1,645), and the state factory near the town of Irkutsk in Siberia (1,933) (ibid.).

4. See, for example, Liashchenko 1952.

5. Anisimov 1989.

6. See the introduction by L. R. Lewitter to the eighteenth-century trea-

Tradition and Modernization in Russia 145

tise by a Russian autodidact, Ivan Pososhkov, *The Book of Poverty and Wealth* (Stanford: Stanford University Press, 1987), p. 114. Blackwell (1968, p. 17) also notes the forced character of such transfers.

7. D. N. Platonov, *Ivan Pososhkov* (Moscow: Ekonomika, 1989), p. 26, 31.

8. See Avrich (1972) and also Pokrovskii, et al., eds. *Pugachevshchina: Iz arkhiva Pugacheva (manifesty, ukasy, perepiska)*, vol. 1 (Moscow: Gosizdat, 1926). The petition of workers from the Votkinskii and Yugovskii plants provide good illustrations of this point (ibid. pp. 178–79, 200–201).

8
BEYOND THE "NATIONAL CONSENSUS": RECENT RESEARCH ON THE ORIGINS AND TRAJECTORY OF GERMANY'S INDUSTRIAL REVOLUTION

George S. Vascik

The literature on the economic history of Central Europe is terra incognita to many Anglo-American scholars and most of their students. It is a landscape with a few great peaks rising above a barren plain.[1] In his essay "The Paradigm of German Industrialization," W. R. Lee bemoans the fact that "this critical branch of historical research is still characterized by a certain backlog" (Lee 1991, p. 1). As a result, historians working on other facets of German history have worked with economy-based interpretative models that are outdated, superficial or inaccurate. Lee also shares Frank Tipton's conviction that "the study of German economic history has been distorted by a "national consensus," based upon the continuing subordination of economic history to political developments and the process of national unification" (Tipton 1974, pp. 195–6).[2]

There is no excuse for further ignorance, beyond the unwillingness of Anglo-American scholars to actually read German texts. In contemporary Germany, economic and business history are active fields of research, with strong institutional underpinnings. It is the goal of this chapter to provide English-speaking scholars and students with a review of the latest writing and research on industrialization in the area that became the German Empire. In doing so, it continues in a historiographic tradition, begun by Richard Tilly and continued by Karl Hardach, Frank Tipton and W. R. Lee, of periodically assessing the newest work in the field of German economic history.[3] It will begin by examining the notion of Germany's reputedly peculiar path to modernity, the *deutsche Sonderweg,* that has so informed Anglo-American scholarship since 1945. It will then examine important works by two scholars that summarize the status of the field in the German-language literature. After reviewing the English-language scholarship published in the years 1990–1995, it will conclude with an agenda for further research. I will argue that the German experience was one of evolution rather than revolution, that regional differences are important to understanding the course of the Industrial Revolution in Germany, and that politics—and political economy—must be reintroduced into our understanding of the process of German industrialization.

GERMANY'S "PECULIAR PATH?"

Since 1945, a majority of the English-language scholarship on the Industrial Revolution in Germany has taken place within the context of the *Sonderweg* debate. The phrase *das deutsche Sonderweg* refers to Germany's peculiar path to modernity, and is often used to explain Germany's aggressive, seemingly aberrant behavior in the first half of this century. *Sonderweg* theory has political, social and economic components. Politically, Germany was said to suffer from the failed revolution of 1848—the turning point where German history failed to turn. Lacking a successful bourgeois revolution, Germany remained under the rule of premodern élites, who used various techniques (namely revolution-from-above, nationalism and anti-Semitism) to hang onto power in a process that eventually led to National Socialism. Socially, Germany's politically neutered bourgeoisie chose to ape their superiors in a process Max Weber labeled the "feudalization" of the middle class.

Both notions of a political and social *Sonderweg* have come under sustained attack in the past generation, and it is a brave historian indeed who would embrace them in their pure form. The possibility of an economic *Sonderweg,* however, still has considerable explanatory power. This is especially true once one accepts that every nation experienced the Industrial Revolution in a different way—that the English road itself was "different" from other national experiences. As the chapters in this volume show, different countries and regions experienced the process of industrialization at different times, in different ways, and with varying intensities, none of which conformed to the English "norm."

The notion of a German economic *Sonderweg* is the intellectual legacy of two émigré scholars, Alexander Gerschenkron and Hans

Rosenburg. Gerschenkron's contribution came in his book *Bread and Democracy in Germany,* where he argues that large *Junker* landowners were responsible for many of the woes of twentieth-century Germany. That class of landowners, who existed primarily east of the Elbe River, provided most of the personnel who served in the higher ranks of the Prussian (and later German) government and military. According to Gerschenkron, the *Junkers* retarded the development of industrial capitalism in Germany. They fought the spread of parliamentarism before the First World War, and sought to undermine democracy during the Weimar Republic. Gerschenkron further argues that their beliefs informed much of National Socialist ideology. Until the *Junkers* were destroyed as a social and economic class, Gerschenkron argued, democracy in Germany would never rest on a sound foundation. In Gerschenkron's world, Germany's proper political and economic development was constrained by the persistence of pre-industrial elites. The model that he posited for German development fitted very well with a school of historiography (the social-critical movement) that became quite popular in the 1960s and 1970s.

Hans Rosenburg was the second person responsible for framing the *Sonderweg* debate. Rosenburg accepted much of Gerschenkron's economics and his sensitivity to the political determinants of economic development. He was particularly interested in the effect that the Great Depression of 1873–1896 had upon the political world of nineteenth-century Germany. For Rosenburg, the two pivotal events in Imperial history were the collapse of the *Gründerjahre* (1871 unification) boom in 1873, and the "Second Foundation" of the Empire in 1879. The economic collapse of 1873 was important because it came to signify, in the popular imagination, the limits of economic liberalism. The discrediting of economic liberalism served to discredit political liberalism, which, before the collapse was the most potent political force in Germany. The political/economic collapse of liberalism was ratified in 1879, when Imperial Chancellor Bismarck broke with his erstwhile liberal allies and embraced a governing coalition of Catholics and Conservatives, the so-called Second Foundation. In their eagerness to placate Bismarck, formerly liberal industrialists acceded to this new alliance—called the coalition of Iron and Rye—which was cemented by new tariffs protecting industry and agriculture.

ALTERNATIVE VIEWS

Although there are problems with the thesis advanced by Gerschenkron and Rosenburg, their work has been (and in my opinion, still is) highly stimulating. This work, and the *Sonderweg* theory that derived from it, has by and large carried the day in Anglo-American academe. Only in the last five or six years has the historiography begun to reveal the cracks in the *Sonderweg* edifice. German economic and business historians, moreover, never succumbed to social-critical orthodoxy. The preeminent German economic historian of the postwar generation, Knut Borchardt, very much cut his own path. Unfortunately, the bulk of Borchardt's work (save for several controversial pieces that attained a reputation as conservative apologetics) is not known in the English-speaking world. Borchardt, currently an emeritus professor at the Ludwig-Maximillians-Universität in Munich, has preferred the scholarly article rather than the monograph as a form of publication. Fortunately, his essay, "The Industrial Revolution in Germany, 1700–1914," in the Fontana economic history series, clearly lays out the Borchardtian synthesis (Borchardt 1991). While the Borchardtian synthesis falls short in numerous ways, these admitted shortcomings have provided the framework for the current generation of German research. As Rolf Dumke has written,

> By addressing central established issues of German economic development . . . and by asking intriguing new methodological and historical questions, Borchardt has in effect generated a set of research agendas that have been at the core of German economic history in recent decades. . . . However critical one might be of Borchardt's arguments, one thing is clear: they stand at the center of the debates in German economic history, provoking, challenging, and revising historical interpretations. (Dumke 1991, pp. 449, 457–8)

Hubert Kiesewetter has filled many of these gaps with his text *Industrielle Revolution in Deutschland, 1815–1914*.[4] Kiesewetter is one of the most articulate opponents of the "national consensus" in German economic history—the obsession of earlier German scholars with Hegelian notions of national unification and political periodization. For Kiesewetter, the key to German industrialization is to be found in the regional theory developed by Sydney Pollard.[5] His synthesis skillfully pulls together the vast number of regional studies that characterized German research in the 1980s. As a result, not unsurprisingly, Kiesewetter contends that it is impossible to speak of a national path to industrialization, but rather that different parts of Germany industrialized in different ways at different times.

REGIONAL DIFFERENCES

This position makes empirical sense. Clearly, Germany's regions developed different industrial characteristics at different paces. Silesia and Saxony already possessed highly developed manufacturing sectors before the French Revolution. The Rhineland and Westphalia developed into textile centers in the 1820s and 1830s. The Ruhr developed in the 1850s into a mining, iron and steel center. Berlin grew as a machine-building and railroad center from 1860 onward. The new chemical and electrical concerns that grew up after 1890 developed in yet other regions. Industrialization had not reached all areas within the Empire by 1890, and even after that date whole regions remained at a very low level of development.

Kiesewetter locates the cause for this differential development in the political sphere. As he states:

> The Industrial Revolution in Germany is deeply interwoven with the activities of the states.... Politics and economy are Siamese twins—the risk entailed in separating them is very high. This results less from the primacy of one over the other, than from their mutual interdependence throughout the process of industrialization. (Kiesewetter 1989, p. 19)

It is important to remember, he tells us, that prior to its dissolution in 1803, the Holy Roman Empire included over a thousand sovereign units. Under the peace settlement agreed to in Vienna in 1815, this number was reduced to thirty-nine—thirty-eight of which would later be absorbed into the German Empire in 1871. These units, through their individual political economic regimes, provided the framework for Germany's multitracked path. Moreover, by their constant competition with each other and with neighboring Great Powers, the German states, large and small, paid greater attention to economic development than might otherwise have been the case.

But how does one reduce to two dimensional linearity the constant, complex dialectic between economy and state in a competitive multistate system? Kiesewetter's solution is less than satisfactory. It leaves readers feeling that they are trying to shove too much into the regional comparative box without sufficient regard for the social preconditions and ramifications of industrialization.

This deficit is filled by another recent treatment of the process of industrialization by Richard Tilly, *Vom Zollverein zum Industriestaat* (1990). In many ways, this is a more satisfying treatment of this process, as Tilly casts his net more broadly than Kiesewetter does. Tilly's previous work concentrated on the banking industry and the process of industrialization in the Rhineland and northwest Germany. He is also a pioneer in the appreciation of regionalism's impact on the German experience. The result is Kiesewetter plus.

For Tilly, industrialization does not take place in a vacuum. The distinctive elements of the German path were the centrality of the state in the takeoff phase, the intensity of links between economic factors and political institutional ones, and the emergence of a vast pool of surplus labor.[6] Tilly's concentration on social factors distinguishes him from Borchardt and Kiesewetter. Although he begins his volume in 1834 with the founding of the German Customs Union (the *Zollverein*), Tilly believes that the 1840s were the critical decade of German industrialization. Tilly also puts the German phenomenon in international perspective, which is absolutely crucial if the German situation is to make broader historical sense.

Tilly's work has been criticized for being chronologically unclear and insufficiently conscious of the broader issues involved in the industrialization process.[7] This is an interesting critique, for while Tilly is distinctly concentrated in his approach, he is much more inclusive than most German historians, who tend to focus exclusively upon either the economic or the social aspects of industrialization. Tilly insists upon examining the social causes and effects of industrialization and places more emphasis on the importance of the *Zollverein* and the 1840s. Kiesewetter favors an earlier periodization and puts greater emphasis on the political constellations that shaped Germany's Industrial Revolution. Neither author's work is exclusive of the other; both can be referred to with equal assurance. Together, Tilly and Kiesewetter demonstrate how far German economic history has come in the last generation and how far it has yet to go.

RECENT SCHOLARSHIP

How does the recent English-language literature fit into this scholarship? Less well than one would hope. The work that was published between 1990 and 1995 in English is generally first rate—it displays meticulous use of the archival sources, theoretical sophistication, and proper direction. But there is simply not enough of it. Economic history is not particularly *au courant* in Anglo-American academe, which at the moment is much more taken with "culture," "the literary turn," and "historical memory." Moreover, the study of comparative economic history requires mastery of the local language and hours in the archives. As a result, a significant proportion of the English-language material has been produced by prominent German scholars like Rainer Fremdling, Carl-Ludwig Holtfrerich and Rolf Dumke.

A review of the major economic and historical journals indicates a bias towards the period after 1890, which Germans refer to as the period of high industrialization (*Hochindustrialisierung*). Two of every three English-language articles concentrate on the period after 1890. The imbalance in monographs is even more striking. At this level, three of four books on German economic history begin their analysis after 1890.[8] At the beginning of our time period, 1750 has so stubbornly become the year studies of the German Industrial Revolution commence that the period from the end of the Thirty Years War to the mid-eighteenth century is almost totally ignored.

Recent contributions to the field have been made in four broad areas: sectoral studies, political economy, studies in technology, and those using an international comparative perspective. While regional studies have been at the forefront of German work in the past decade, only one such work has appeared in English (Gunter Back's study of the Württemberg salt industry). Sectoral studies, which have also been an extremely productive area in the German scholarship, are likewise thinly represented in English. Wilfried Feldenkirchen, in his study of the role of banks in German industrialization, suggests that earlier characterizations of the dominant role of banks in German industrialization has been overstated. Rather than characterize the relationship between banks and industry as one in which industry remained heavily dependent upon banks for capital and direction, Feldenkirchen suggests that although the relationship between the two varied from sector to sector, in general terms their actual relationship was one of interdependence. The level of capital required within each industry, along with that industry's rate of growth, seem to have been the determining factors in structuring the relationship. In the heavy and electro-technical industries, for instance, Feldenkirchen finds that the banks' influence was greater, while the influence of banks in the engineering and chemical sectors was negligible (Feldenkirchen 1991).

As these two titles suggest by their singularity, what is desperately needed are English-language studies to supplement the large German literature focusing on regional and sectoral development.

POLITICAL ECONOMY STUDIES

Political economy and technology have fared better over the past decade. In "The Political Calculus of Capital: Banking and the Business Class in Prussia, 1848–1856," James Brophy investigates the relationship between capital and state. Specifically, he holds that "the emergence of commercial investment banks after the revolution of 1848 was an institutional breakthrough for modern capitalism and one of the central factors in the accelerated development of the Industrial Revolution in Germany between 1848 and 1871," arguing that these banks were the catalyst of Germany's economic "takeoff" (Brophy 1992, p. 149).

Brophy's work boldly takes on an extensive historiographic literature. His research debunks Karl Obermann's Marxist interpretation, which sees the growth of investment banks as part of a tacit alliance between the bourgeoisie and the Prussian state following the former's estrangement from the proletariat after 1848. He also takes to task Helmut Böhme, who sees in David Hansemann's abbreviated tenure as Prussian Minister of Finance and director of the Prussian state bank (1848–1851), an unwillingness on the part of both State and Capital to loose political and economic influence. Böhme, Brophy writes, conveys the mistaken impression that "leading businessmen uniformly sided with the Prussian state" (Brophy 1992, p. 151).

Rather than fixing on some chimeric "alliance," Brophy would have us recognize the emergence of the business class as an additional force in Prussian politics after 1848. To illustrate this contention, he explores the controversy surrounding the royal decree of 12 July 1856 to ban *commandité* banks. His conclusion: Prussian businessmen were "[C]onsistent neither as unfailing parliamentarians nor as obedient subjects of the crown" but were nonetheless resolutely unwavering in pursuing bourgeois social and economic goals" (Brophy 1992, p. 152). In Brophy's model, the ambivalent position of Prussian bankers toward the State was part of a strategy of successful negotiation.

In an analysis of tariffs and market structures contributed to Lee's volume on German industrialization, Rolf Dumke rehabilitates the fiscal interpretation of the foundation of the German Customs Union (*Zollverein*), positing that historians' criticism of that model results from a misunderstanding of economists' methodology (Dumke 1991, p. 98). According to Dumke, the most important factor behind the creation of the *Zollverein* was the otherwise unattainable revenue gain that resulted from a more optimal size of customs administration. The financial difficulties experienced by the German states in the *Vormärz* (the period between 1815 and the revolutions of 1848), linked as they were to political instability and the pressure for constitutional reform leading to more representative forms of government, led these states to seek "new and politically neutral" forms of revenue. Thus, "the peculiar political constellation and the unusual geography of the German states" not only generated pressures for more revenue, but also suggested the Customs Union as one solution.

TECHNOLOGY STUDIES

Two students of technology have also published important works in the 1990s. Rainer Fremdling has contributed two articles to the literature. For the Lee volume, he analyzed the effects of foreign competition on the development of German industry in the early stages of industrialization. Fremdling concludes that "new fuel technology spread continuously and gradually, with new and old techniques being interwoven in numerous combinations" (Fremdling 1991, p. 55). Moreover, Fremdling's analysis of the data suggests that foreign trade boosted rather than hindered the modernization of the German iron industry. The *Zollverein,* in turn, facilitated a process of import substitution, which enabled the German iron industry to learn from and eventually outcompete its British counterpart.

The most ambitious contribution, not only in the history of technology but in the entire question of German industrialization, is by Eric Dorn Brose, *The Politics of Technological Change in Prussia* (1993). Brose demonstrates that a straight and determined path of state-driven industrialization in Prussia is more historical imagination than empirical reality. Rather than offer the reader a chronological narrative of Prussian industrialization in the *Vormärz,* Brose offers a thematic assessment of the culture of technological change. After surveying the historiography of modernization theory and Prussian industrialization, the author offers six self-contained sketches of the interests shaping Prussian modernization. What arises from this assessment is the understanding that there was a diversity of interests regarding industrialization within the Prussian government, and that one direction was never preordained.

In the government's Business Department, for example, the liberal Christian Beuth pursued an aesthetic industrialization. Forsaking the British model, which had produced "chamber pot" industrial cities, Beuth envisioned a harmonious marriage between city and countryside. Industry was to proceed in the two spheres simultaneously, under the tutelage of an elitist, technocratic bureaucracy, within a free-market environment.

In contrast to the Business Department, a protectionist attitude pervaded the Mining Corps. The Corps was influenced by the perspective of the noble mining interest concentrated in the province of Silesia. These mine-owning nobles were keen to protect their local political and economic hegemony and their position within the Prussian state. They feared that free-market industrialization would lead to the disruption of their paternalistic world.

The military constituted yet another realm of decision making and interest advocacy. Army bureaucrats vacillated between antipathy to and interest in industrialization. They recognized the military utility of industry and railroads, but were loathe to adjust to the social consequences of industrialization upon strategy and tactics. King Friedrich Wilhelm, as supreme warlord and head of state, presided uncertainly and uneasily over the contested, broken terrain created by his bureaucrats.

Given the dissonance within the Prussian government, it is not surprising that industrialization proceeded unevenly and produced an unexpected result. Brose argues that early success in achieving a laissez-faire economy was quickly eclipsed by an economic reaction that accompanied the political reaction contained in the Carlsbad Decrees (1819). Nonetheless, anti-modernist interests did not triumph in Prussia. The military, which initially balked at the prospect of industrialization (and indeed limited railroad development), in time became a leading proponent of railroad growth and government intervention in industrial development.

Brose concludes his analysis with a bold assertion: much as the bureaucratic advocates of modernization favored a state presence in the industrialization process, which would channel its negative impacts into acceptable forms, the impetus for economic development lay beyond the government's domain. Brose argues that Prussia ultimately industrialized, not along the lines laid out by bureaucrats, but rather in response to the consumption demands of its prosperous agrarian sector. The result was an urban, nonaesthetic industrial model that all the competing elements within the bureaucracy had tried to avoid.

COMPARATIVE STUDIES

Two comparative studies complete our list of English-language works on the German industrial revolution. Hubert Kiesewetter, in "Competition for Wealth and Power," (1991) explores the economic rivalry between Germany and Britain. Kiesewetter insists that the competition between Britain and Germany started much earlier than has been previously assumed, tracing it back to 1815. The belated foundation of the German Empire in 1871 caused many observers to overlook the fact that many German states had already undertaken vigorous policies, of which the German Customs Union was but one example, that successfully promoted economic growth. Britain's industrial revolution, though envied, "could not be and was not imitated by Germany" (Kiesewetter 1991, p. 298). By the time that German industrial dynamism came to be most threateningly felt in Britain, British industrialists were already locked into their own peculiar production structure. Germany was not bothered by aging industrial plants and outmoded thinking. Lacking the foreign political obligations that entangled the British, the German government could more easily support industrial development. The result of this struggle for wealth and power was that the German government became convinced that if economic competition led to war with Britain, German economic superiority would carry the day.

The second comparative article is "Tired Pioneers and Dynamic Newcomers? A Comparative Essay on English and German Entrepreneurial History, 1870–1914," by H. Berghoff and R. Möller (1994). This piece examines an old chestnut—the notion that British entrepreneurship, as the result of British cultural and educational inertia, had waned by 1870 and was supplanted by a more dynamic brand of technically educated, state-supported capitalism practiced in Germany. Berghoff and Möller compare British and German entrepreneurs in four categories: recruitment patterns, education, social identities and involvement in public life. The authors focus their analysis on six cities (Birmingham, Bristol, Manchester, Bremen, Dortmund and Frankfurt), and use the biographies of 1,328 British and 1,324 German entrepreneurs in business between 1870 and 1914.

The authors found that in both England and Germany most entrepreneurs were already middle-class businessmen before they started their own firms. Few began life in the working class or the nobility. In the sample that the authors have collected, few entrepreneurs became members of the nobility as the result of their careers. Not a single businessman from Dortmund was ennobled; those from Frankfurt who did achieve noble status gave up their active business careers. Few of the British entrepreneurs in the authors' database became noble, but those who did generally continued their business careers. Berghoff and Möller generalize from this data that Germans generally felt that it was necessary to give up their careers before ennoblement, but other studies, particularly Werner Mosse's study of nineteenth-century Jewish businessmen, indicates that this was not the norm.[9] Perhaps, even at 1,324 souls, Berghoff and Möller's database is too small and at only three cities too restricted.

The authors found it very difficult to compare the education of the two different groups of businessmen because of the differences in their national educational systems. It is clear, however, that although few had a university level education, most had a classical rather than a scientific, "practical" education. Of the two groups, the Germans were more likely to have a business-related degree. The greatest difference between the two groups was in real world experience: 72 percent of the German entrepreneurs had lived outside their home country for several months, while only 22 percent of their British counterparts had a similar experience.

The clearest differentiation uncovered by Berghoff and Möller's study came in the public sphere. English businessmen were more generous donors to causes outside their profession, while the Germans were more generous to their workers. Both nationalities were equally active in local government and school politics and administration. On the national political level, English businessmen were more active in seeking parliamentary seats than their German counterparts, although the limited geographic scope of this study allows no meaningful comparison.

FUTURE RESEARCH

Where can American scholars make their greatest contribution in the next decade? The three great practitioners of social/economic historical analysis, Charles, Louise and Richard Tilly, have an answer. In an article published in the *Journal of European Economic History* in 1991, they argue that "we must [strike] that great misnomer, the Industrial Revolution, from our conceptual vocabulary" (Tilly 1991, p. 660). They argue that the Industrial Revolution was not a compact, sudden upswing in the economy and more specifically did not necessarily occur in the factory. Although the phrase still sounds too precious, they suggest that the whole concept of the Industrial Revolution should be replaced by that of an Industrial Evolution.

Moreover, they argue that the current understanding of "economic and social history as base and superstructure, cause and effect," needs revision. The Tillys' solution is "to de-economize economic history and re-economize social history"; in other words, to open up economic history to include an analysis of "rights, power, coercion, state action, and related 'institutional' factors." At the same time, social history must be opened up to "new treatments of the interdependence among different forms of production both material, biological and social" (Tilly 1991, p. 647). The Tillys would direct this new social and economic history into seven interrelated fields of inquiry: gender inequality, mobility of labor and capital, institutional change, state formation, economic growth, economic structure, and international variation. A cynic might note that save for the first item, these topics have been on the professional agenda for some time. More important, no doubt, is the trio's call for a reintegration of the social sciences. In no place is this reintegration more needed than in the study of economic history, where economists and historians have found it increasingly difficult to talk with one another. Although I would be loathe to argue with the Tillys, one question does remain: how should their directives be applied in the German context? First of all, we should start off with the realization that some important areas of study are simply off the map. Dense social history, important as it is to understanding the causes and effects of industrialization, is impossible for American graduate students and probably for most of their mentors—it takes too long and costs too much. Tightly defined studies of specific regions and sectors of the economy, on the other hand, can produce useful results in an acceptable time frame, while still contributing to the advancement of our common knowledge. Studies of individual industries, the local branch of an industry, or individual businessmen are eminently doable and would contribute to the English-language discourse. The role of religious and ethnic minorities in German industrialization is a still underdeveloped area of research. In the past ten years there has been a growing literature on the role of Jews in the German economy, but none of this work has concentrated on the role Jewish entrepreneurs played in Germany's industrial revolution. The descendants of the French Huguenots, who played an equal if not more important role in the process of industrialization, have yet to find their proper place in the literature. Americans scholars could also make their mark through the device of international comparative history.

Lastly, it is essential that we rethink the whole chronology of German industrialization. Even the most expansive studies only begin in 1750. Why? Was there nothing important that came before? If one is to begin one's analysis before 1815, why not pick a truly significant date and begin in 1648? Choosing a chronological framework for the study of German industrialization ultimately means that we have to deal with politics and political economy. If we are not to fall into the trap of the "national consensus," that means that we must look beyond Prussia and deal with the other states in particularist Germany.

NOTES

1. One example of such a peak is Gerald Feldman's magisterial study of German hyperinflation, *The Great Disorder: Politics, Economics and Society in the German Inflation, 1914–1924* (Oxford: Oxford University Press, 1993),

which was reviewed and placed into perspective by Charles Kindelberger, *Journal of Economic Literature,* vol. 32, 1994, pp. 1216–25.

2. Tipton's monograph *The Regional Development of the German Economy* (Middletown, CT: Wesleyan University Press, 1978), has been largely instrumental in turning this situation around.

3. Richard Tilly "*Soll und Haben:* Recent German Economic History and the Problem of Economic Development," *Journal of Economic History,* vol. 29, 1969, pp. 298–319, and Karl Hardach "Some Remarks on German Economic Historiography and its Understanding of the Industrial Revolution in Germany," *Journal of European Economic History,* vol. 1, 1972, pp. 37–99.

4. Readers seeking an English review of Kiesewetter's work should see the review by Ilaria Zilli in *Journal of European Economic History,* vol. 23, 1994, pp. 419–21.

5. See Sydney Pollard *Region und Industrialisierung. Studien zur Rolle der Region in der Wirtschaft der letzen zwei Jahrhunderte* (Göttingen, 1980), and Richard Tilly and Rainer Fremdling *Industrialisierung und Raum. Studien zur regionalen Differenzierung im Deutschland des 19. Jahrhundert* (Stuttgart, 1979).

6. See the review by Constanza D'Elia in *Journal of Economic History,* vol. 19, 1990, pp. 709–12.

7. See the review by Joerg Voegele in *Business History Review,* vol. 64, 1990, pp. 804–15.

8. This conclusion was reached after surveying the following journals: *American Historical Review, Business History Review, Central European History, Economic History Review, Essays in Business and Economic History, Explorations in Economic History, German Studies Review, German Yearbook of Business History, History of Political Economy, Journal of Economic History, Journal of Economic Literature, Journal of European Economic History, Journal of Modern History, Historical Abstracts.*

9. Werner Mosse, *Jews in the German Economy,* Oxford: Oxford University Press, 1989.

Part III
Consequences

INTRODUCTION

The theme of the chapters in this section concerns the lasting impact of the Industrial Revolution, especially on the living standards of ordinary people, and also on whether it can be duplicated. Industrialization expanded the output of manufactured goods and also stimulated change in agricultural practices, raising output levels there too. This effectively removed the Malthusian constraint that had previously prevented significant long-term population growth. However, this gives rise to several questions. Did living standards rise because of the increase in output? Or was population growth greater than the increase in output? Or were there other developments occurring which affected how people lived and what they thought?

The issue of the impact on living standards is taken up by Casey Harison, who compares some of the available evidence from Britain and France. He shows that this evidence can be interpreted either in support of the position that living standards declined, or that they rose. (The key to the paradox lies in what exactly is being measured, and the time frame of the measurement.) James Briscoe analyzes competing philosophic interpretations of industrialization as it occurred in France. There was a great deal of skepticism in France about the benefits of industrialization, and partly in response, several official studies were made to determine exactly what the living conditions of the poor were like; examples from these are included.

Finally, and providing a bridge to present day efforts at initial industrialization, Christine Rider looks at the role of technological change in the industrialization process. Although new technology involves labor saving mechanization, in the nineteenth century and in her specific example of Japan, market expansion enabled an overall expansion of production, effectively preventing long-term unemployment. However, given the globalization of markets today and the trend to economies of scale in increasing production facilities, newly industrializing countries may not be able to offset unemployment caused by mechanization, which has severe implications for their standard of living.

9
THE STANDARD OF LIVING OF ENGLISH AND FRENCH WORKERS, 1750–1850
Casey Harison

"Standard of living" describes the relative well being of individuals and is often used as a general measure of the economic progress of a society. It is a familiar idea today, yet both the concept and even the very possibility of a substantial improvement in living standards are, historically, relatively recent developments. As the economic historian Joel Mokyr has written:

> We are, after all, living in an exception . . . (since) only in the last two centuries has Western society succeeded in raising the standard of living of the bulk of the population beyond the minimum of subsistence. (Mokyr 1990, p. 302)

The idea emerged after the middle of the eighteenth century, when the optimistic view of human nature implied in the Enlightenment and the productive potential of industrialization made a general improvement in the quality of life seem attainable. Since the late eighteenth century, citizens typically have expected that one function of governments and of economic systems such as capitalism or socialism is to map out a route for the improvement of living standards. The concept has also been an excellent tool for scholars to use to measure the costs and rewards of industrialization. One "lesson" of the history of industrialization is that it requires time for industry to improve a society's living standards. Bridging the gap between the promises of the eighteenth century and the conditions of life of industrial workers was at the core of what Europeans in the first half of the nineteenth century called the "social question." Answering this "question" meant, among other things, raising the standard of living.

This chapter surveys and compares the standard of living in

England and France during the first century of industrialization (roughly 1750–1850). These two countries offer excellent examples to consider, because there is a great deal of information on each for measuring the standard of living, and because by the start of the nineteenth century both nations had political and economic systems in which the promise of an improvement in the standard of living was implicit. Particularly in the case of England, there has been a lively "debate" among scholars about whether the emergence of industry was characterized by a rise or a decline in living standards. One aim of this chapter is to survey the literature on that debate; another is to gain some perspective on the issue by comparing the English experience with France, England's continental neighbor, whose path to industrialization differed in important ways from the so-called "English model." Signs of improvement or decline during industrialization have been especially apparent in the living standards of the working class, whose wages and health conditions provide a focus for this chapter.

DEBATE ON THE STANDARD OF LIVING

Popular histories of nineteenth-century England have often begun with the premise that industry brought significant material improvements to the lives of the workers who labored in her factories. One author states unequivocally that "It was the mark of this country's industrial success that through industrialization (England's) vastly increased population attained a higher standard of living than ever before" (McGrandle 1973, p. 75). Yet more than a century earlier, at a time when English industries led the world in production, the very opposite assessment had been offered by Friedrich Engels in *The Condition of the Working Class in England* (1844), a work that Karl Marx may have used in formulating his "General Law of Capitalist Accumulation," and in the construction of one of the most influential critiques of the living standards of the industrial proletariat.[1] Clearly, the relationship between industrialization and standard of living is one that has inspired quite different assessments.

The modern scholarly debate on the standard of living began with the publication of papers by Eric J. Hobsbawm in 1957 and R. Max Hartwell in 1961. Hobsbawm offered the *pessimistic* point of view that the growth of industry in England was marked by declining living standards. Hartwell countered with the *optimistic* argument that the conditions of English workers under industrialization improved, particularly after 1815. These two perspectives have since come to represent the classic counterpoints on the question. For Hobsbawm and Hartwell, a consideration of living standards was important because it went to the heart of two issues regarding modern change: first, whether the material benefits and productivity of industrialization have outweighed the costs (including urban overcrowding, pollution, and the exploitation of persons and resources); and second, whether changes in the standard of living are best understood in the *short term* or the *long term*. Since they staked out these positions more than a generation ago, other scholars have carried on the debate by searching for evidence that will identify changes in the living conditions of the working class. Depending on the measures selected or the way one looks at or manipulates these measures, a variety of interpretations about the standard of living are possible. Over the last two decades, the debate on England's standard of living for the years 1750–1850 has been notable for the sophistication of the methodologies devised and for the rigor with which they have been employed.

France's standard of living (*le tariff de la vie humaine* or *le niveau de vie*, using French terminology) in this period has not inspired the kind of polemic it did in England. This difference may be due to the fact that while France's economic development paralleled England's in important ways, it differed in other, equally significant, ways. For many years, France was thought of by economic historians as an "also ran" (Clough 1939) or as the "ugly duckling" of the Industrial Revolution (Heywood 1992, p. 10); a society that "took stagnation for granted" and that, according to the provocative language of one scholar, had developed " . . . within her body psychological and institutional antibodies to the virus of modernization" (Landes 1969, pp. 236, 528, 530). Over the last twenty years, however, scholars such as Patrick O'Brien and Caglar Keyder have offered a *revisionist* interpretation of the so-called French "lag" (*décollage*). The revisionists have argued that France followed a "different path" to industrial modernity than England that was not necessarily less productive and was perhaps more "humane" than England's, and, in any event, was more suited to her history and culture (O'Brien and Keyder 1978). For the revisionist school of interpretation, the "English model" is unpersuasive and the *retard française* (French lateness) a false problem (Asselain 1984, p. 217). However, the interpretation struggle continues: a recent "econometric" history of France (Lévy-Leboyer and Bourguignon 1990) reasserts the older interpretation that economic change in France happened slowly, while Francois Crouzet's *Britain Ascendant* attempts to reconcile the traditional with the revisionist view (Crouzet 1985).

The different paths to industrialization taken by England and France are partly reflected in the way that the two societies have perceived, accepted, rejected, or accommodated to economic change, but also in the ways that the improvement of the standard of living has been thought about. Historically, there has perhaps been a stronger inclination in France than in England to be skeptical about the rewards of industry. Accordingly, a debate or discussion over the standard of living has not presented itself so forcefully there.

MEASURING THE STANDARD OF LIVING

The difficulty of assessing past living standards may be judged by quoting one author who, after devoting an entire book to the topic, concluded that "'Standards of living,' either today or in the past, cannot be measured exactly" (Dyer 1989, p. 274). This kind of skepticism about arriving at the "truth" about the standard of living is common. Two problems in particular have plagued the endeavor: finding evidence, and the subjective nature of judgments about living standards.

Over the last fifty years or so, researchers have struggled to find the best measures for the standard of living. While this chapter focuses on statistical analyses of data, not all of the historical evidence on the standard of living relies so heavily on quantitative assessment. Much descriptive evidence also exists, to be found in memoirs, contemporary fiction, and in the surveys of public health experts [and see the following chapter]. As demonstrated below, the statistics for this period provide mixed appraisals of the standard of living, especially if looked at over the long run. Yet the descriptive evidence for the First Industrial Revolution seems to point overwhelmingly to the presence of urban poverty and to a quality of life for the working class that appeared to be worsening. Thus, while the *long-term* trends for the standard of living show improvement, two running themes found in the *short-term* descriptive literature of the period are working class misery, and the perception of imminent social rebellion brought on by lowered living standards.

One difficulty in measuring the standard of living is finding information which covers a period long enough to permit useful temporal comparisons. Fortunately, a good deal of statistical information of this sort is available for both England and France. But still, because the standard of living is defined partly by the expectations of societies in particular times and places, there are different opinions about the validity or the meaning of these measurements. Thus, for example, a high standard of living in the United States in 1997 is different from a high standard of living in, say, Bolivia in 1997, or in France in 1800. The most useful measurements of living standards are those that have some consistency over time and can be used to make comparisons—namely those that demonstrate either an ability to acquire more (e.g., higher wages), or those that show clear results (e.g., lower infant mortality).

Wages and Measurement Problems

Wages are perhaps the most widely employed and the most useful measure of the standard of living. They are important because, historically, industrialization has been accompanied by the spread of wage labor, and because an improvement or decline in wages relative to movements in prices obviously has a direct impact on the quality of life. *Real wages* represent actual purchasing power; the higher the real wage of a worker, presumably the higher is the standard of living.

Although tracking real wages seems like a common sense way to measure the standard of living, it is nonetheless an approach that should inspire caution. Typically, the wages that have been measured in the past are those earned by adult males; looking only at these, it is easy to argue that the standard of living of both English and French workers improved during the first century of industrialization. However, this narrow view has serious drawbacks, since it does not describe how wages earned by adult males met the needs of entire families. The wages of women and children, both of whom constituted significant parts of the working population during this period, have rarely been taken into account (Horrell and Humphries 1992, pp. 849–80). Also, the measurement of wages over the long run does a poor job of accounting for short-term costs. That is, the question that looms over the issue is whether a rise in the standard of living in the long run can be considered an improvement if it comes at the cost of a decline and more misery in the short run. In the debate over real wages, some scholars argue that months and years reveal more about the standard of living of wage earners than do half centuries or longer periods. For the long term, all of us can afford to be optimistic about the standard of living, although it is the short term that counts socially and politically. There are also times when wages are more helpful in informing us about consumer habits, diet, investment strategies, and labor activity than about real income (Scholliers 1989, pp. 4, 10).

Other problems that need to be accounted for when using wages as a benchmark for the standard of living include the seasonal or cyclical rhythm of many types of work; the impact of war and military recruitment (the period under consideration coincided in England and France with the Seven Years War of 1756–63, and the Revolutionary and Napoleonic Wars of 1792–1815); recurrent economic downturns; population growth; and the degree to which the daily wage formed just one part of a worker's remuneration (Schwarz 1985, pp. 31–33).

WORKERS' WAGES AS A MEASURE OF THE STANDARD OF LIVING

But allowing for these difficulties and employing them carefully, wages can serve as a qualified measure for the standard of living. Several authors have produced valuable studies of the standard of living based on an estimate of wages. L. D. Schwarz showed that wages in London in the first half of the nineteenth century can be assessed with some accuracy, at least for adult males (ibid., p. 25). Basing his calculations on data from the building trades, Schwarz wrote that real wages declined after 1750, increased after 1815 when the price of bread fell, but did not attain the level of the 1740s until a century later (ibid., pp. 25,31).

Schwarz's argument is the latest addition to what might be called a "debate-within-a-debate" on whether the real wages of English workers, and thus their standard of living, rose or fell during the first century of industrialization. The position of Peter Lindert and Jeffrey Williamson is that real wages rose in the period 1820–1850 (Lindert 1983, pp. 131–55; Williamson 1985). The counterargument is offered by Crafts and Harley, who hold that improvement in real wages, as well as the rate of growth in English industry, has been overestimated (Crafts 1985; Crafts and Harley 1992, pp. 705–30). The Crafts-Harley *revisionist* interpretation also argues that the idea of an "English model" of industrialization should be reconsidered (Crafts 1985, p. 2). The revisionists have not gone so far as to say that England did not contribute in truly important ways to industrialization, or that the nation was not a great economic power in the nineteenth century; indeed, Crafts wrote that the early *pessimistic* analysis of the standard of living has been overstated. Instead, the revisionists have proposed a nuanced view of industrialization that is less England-centered. Schwarz put the revisionist viewpoint this way: "What is at issue is the conceptual framework within which the question of living standards is set. It is misleading to see developments in England as necessarily different from developments in continental Europe" (Schwarz 1985, p. 35). Schwarz himself places emphasis on similarities between London and other European cities, noting that London was not an exceptional manufacturing center, and was more comparable to continental cities like Paris, Berlin, and Leipzig than to English industrial towns like Manchester and Halifax (Schwarz 1992). The revisionist position on real wages and the standard of living is that they generally declined during the period of initial industrialization before 1830.

There has been less research on the history of wages in France than in England. For France, the consensus has been that wages did not keep up with grain prices in the half century before the Revolution of 1789 (Schwarz 1985, p. 30). Grain prices are a crucial measure of the standard of living for this period, since bread was a staple of the European diet. This decline in real wages contributed to the start of the Revolution, but because it coincided with the early rise of industry in France, it may also be seen as a reflection of the relationship between industrialization and the standard of living. Wages did climb, slowly, in France until about 1825, but then fell through the 1850s, and only regained the levels of the 1820s in the 1870s (O'Brien and Keyder 1978, p. 70). Throughout the period in question (1750–1850), national wage rates in France lagged behind those in England. As the *revisionist* authors O'Brien and Keyder note, however, a national wage comparison is deceptive since it "still provide(s) an unrepresentative indicator of relative levels of welfare for the majority of British and French families, because the share of the population who depended on wages for their livelihood varied significantly between the two societies" (ibid.). Revisionist historians comparing the levels of French and English production assert that long-standing assumptions about the sluggishness of the French economy in an "Age of Industry" supposedly dominated by England are incorrect. Though the French economy has long fared poorly in comparison with that of England, a recent study of Paris and London in the mid-nineteenth century found that 15 percent more Parisians than Londoners were occupied in manufacturing, and that by several measures, Paris was more productive than London at a time when England was reckoned to be the world's great economic engine (Ratcliffe 1994, pp. 263–328). Clearly, the difficulties of comparing the different styles and levels of English and French production require that our perceptions about the standard of living in these two societies be nuanced.

More research is required on the history of real wages before a definitive comparison between England and France may be made. For now, it may be said that during the first century of industrialization, with exceptions during some years, there was little or no improvement in real wages. Because income growth was irregular, unemployment and underemployment were perennial problems. This situation was accompanied in both countries by the widespread impression of a lowering of the quality of life.

HEALTH OF THE WORKING CLASS

Wages are an important gauge of the standard of living, but there are other useful measures which offer historical insights into the issue. One such measure is the health of the population. There is much descriptive evidence that the health of the urban working class in England and France during this period was not good, and in many specific cases, deplorable. We can still read lurid accounts of slums and paupers during the era of early industrialization in the novels of Charles Dickens or Emile Zola. Public health experts such as William Farr in England and Louis-René Villermé in France were very concerned about the impact of industry on working populations, finding abominable living conditions and low life expectancies in the slums of London and Paris to support their apprehensions. Contemporary writers and investigators such as Farr and Villermé almost uniformly attributed the unwholesome conditions they found to industrialization (Coleman 1982).

As with wages, however, finding evidence upon which to base conclusions about the health of working class populations is a complicated task. One way to assess the health of societies during this period is to review the epidemic diseases new to Europe in the first half of the nineteenth century, for these were diseases which seemed to find a home in densely populated and dirty industrial cities. Among them were typhus, cholera, and tuberculosis, all serious health problems through much of the century. The epidemic that most concerned contemporaries was the cholera epidemic of 1830–33, which affected tens of thousands of persons across Europe. Because the working class suffered the highest rates of infection and mortality in London and Paris, some observers linked the disease to poor living conditions exacerbated by industrialization. The response over the next decades in both cities were efforts at what would today be called "urban renewal," an important purpose of which was to alleviate the conditions believed to breed disease and to improve the living conditions of working class neighborhoods. In the case of London, Schwarz writes that the only "really great improvement" in working class life during the first century of industrialization was the decline in the death rate from 40–50 per 1,000 persons in 1750 to 23 per 1,000 in 1841 (Schwarz 1992, pp. 236–7).

Innovative use of source materials has characterized research on health during the period of early industrialization. One author, for instance, used parish birth registers from England's industrial north to assess infant mortality, discovering (in contrast to Schwarz's assessments of London) a rising rate of mortality that shows that living conditions did not improve substantially through the mid-nineteenth century (Huck 1993, pp. 528–50). Another way to "measure" health is to examine the height of individuals, using as data the rolls of military recruits, criminals, and other groups whose physical dimensions are recorded institutionally. It is known that stature is affected by diet, so judging the health of a population through this kind of *anthropometric* history is possible. Such studies have generally found a decline in height, implying a fall in living standards during the First Industrial Revolution. Examining the height of poor boys and soldiers in England, groups which were most likely to come from predominantly working class populations, John Komlos concluded that "there is hardly a sign of a nutritional upswing . . . at any time during the eighteenth century, and after a weak and temporary improvement (after 1815), the decline in stature persisted well into the nineteenth century" (Komlos 1993, p. 128). A similar study based on the height of male and female criminals born in Britain between 1812 and 1857 showed a definite decline in average height during rapid industrialization, with the most noticeable downturn occurring in the 1840s, "suggest(ing) that there was a major deterioration in environmental, nutritional or employment conditions for British workers in this period that is not reflected in real wage data" (Johnson and Nicholas 1995, pp. 470–81). A recent work on the "biological standard of living" of a later period (1850–1930) looked at weight at birth, and demonstrated (unsurprisingly) that working class women living in poor areas, doing difficult work and without access to good health care produced smaller, less healthy babies (Ward 1993, pp. 5, 115, 121, 139).

Some anthropometric studies have also been done for France. Data on French military recruits in the first half of the century showed individuals whose physical stature was "stunted" (Komlos 1994, pp. 493–508). Even the middle and upper class students of the École Polytechnique (a prestigious French engineering school) suffered a decline in stature in the first half of the century—suggesting that declining living standards may have had an impact that went beyond the working class. In the second half of the nineteenth century, health conditions improved in France as they also did in England. Data on military recruits from Paris suggests that better food and hygiene under the Second Empire (1852–1870) produced healthier populations during the Third Republic (1870–1940), so that by 1900 in Paris, "Laborers... were probably stronger, freer from chronic disabilities, and better able to resist disease than their ancestors" (Berlanstein 1984, p. 53).

The anthropometric studies are innovative and provide a useful profile of working class populations. However, as with studies of wages, they must be used with care when considering large historical developments such as industrialization. In the cases given above, one interpretation maintains that the decline in stature was not the result of industrialization, but was rather a reflection of a natural demographic or "Malthusian" crisis that, in fact, industry was eventually able to "solve" through improvements in food production, preservation, and distribution (Komlos 1993). In England, while "The decline in the biological well being of the population ... supports those who point to widespread poverty in the early stages of the industrial revolution ...," the evidence also "... points to the demographic explosion and not to the industrial revolution itself as the original cause of the adverse developments" (ibid, p. 142). The "stunted" heights of military recruits in France may be interpreted as the product of "habits" promoting low living standards which persisted even when food with a higher calorie content became available, the rigidities of these consumption habits, and the importance of food in budgets "limit(ing) the increase in demand in France for many goods and retard(ing) the progress of industry" (Lévy-Leboyer and Bourguignon 1990, p. 30). Thus for the years 1852–1862, the percentage of the average French family budget spent on bread and meat hardly changed (declining from 67 percent to 63 percent for bread, and rising from 11 percent to 14 percent for meat), even when incomes were rising and a greater variety of foodstuffs were available. In the second half of the nineteenth century in both England and France, diets and calorie consumption improved, with predictably positive results for the health of workers.

CONCLUSION

During the years 1750–1850, contemporary assessments of the effects of industrialization and its impact on the standard of living were generally negative. One can easily find sources ranging from contemporary novels to the reports of public health inspectors describing the unhealthy conditions their authors believed resulted from industry. Contemporary observers were also certain that these social and economic conditions engendered moral decay and political unrest.

The historical assessment of this period, based largely on statistical analysis, has been more mixed, varying over the last four decades between the pessimistic and optimistic views laid out by Hobsbawm and Hartwell. The divergence of scholarly opinion over the question of the standard of living is greater for the "First Industrial Revolution" than it is for the "Second Industrial Revolution." Commenting on the lack of agreement about the earlier period, Schwarz argues that it may be because the relationship between industrialization and the standard of living has been overstated. "While the 'industrial revolution' can hardly be ignored, the question of its direct (and even indirect) impact on living standards in London—and perhaps on much of the rest of England—requires both caution and scepticism" (Schwarz 1985, p. 36). Other authors note that gains in the standard of living in one location have been paid for by losses elsewhere, an argument that supports the pessimist case that "the gains of the winners . . . were largely, though perhaps not entirely, offset by the setbacks suffered by the losers" (Mokyr and O'Grada 1988, pp. 210–31). Revisionist historians like Crafts and Harley ask whether we can affirm the seeming "historical discontinuity" of this period, and whether it is still convincing to argue that England's industrial experience of 1750–1850 is the best model with which to view other national experiences (Crafts and Harley 1992). Over the last two decades, the revisionists have undermined many of the early optimistic views while challenging the premise of an "English model." Others, relying especially upon anthropometric analyses, question whether the decline in living standards in this era can be attributed to industrialization.

For both England and France over the long term (roughly 1750 to 1950), there was improvement in the standard of living. Gains in purchasing power and in health were experienced by workers after 1850. Still, the optimistic view must be qualified by considerations of regional variation in quality of life; the fact that, because workers were tied to the wage system, recessions and depressions had a more drastic impact on their standard of living than on that of the upper classes; and that even after 1850, a great gulf remained between the living standards of lower and upper classes. The long term improvements in living standards are important and should be recognized, but they should not mask the fact that the costs of economic change were borne disproportionately by the working class. Even an optimist such as Williamson wrote that "British capitalism did breed inequality . . . (which) seems to have been a product of the forces associated with the Industrial Revolution" (Williamson 1985, p. 200). There were improvements in working class life in cities such as London, but in fact much of the daily life of urban workers did not get better with industry. In some ways, as Schwarz noted, the quality of life in the early period of industrialization declined from earlier times (Schwarz 1992, p. 235). And for women and children, about whose condition we do not know nearly as much as we should, the insecurities of life probably remained greater than for men.

The differences in the standard of living of English and French workers during the years between 1750 and 1850 reflect the different paces at which the two nations industrialized. Clearly, economic change affected both nations in crucial ways. However, the rapidity and breadth of the rise of industry in England as compared with France, where the process took longer, meant that the intensity of distress and social inequality may have been greater in England. In comparing the advance of industry and its impact on the standard of living, we may also want to include considerations of the role of culture. One recent economic survey of industrialization in France argued that the nation "managed to avoid the scale of distress" of English workers because of the ". . . underlying shrewdness and economic rationality of the French population" (Heywood 1992, p. 71).

To conclude, at present there is an impasse in the debate on the standard of living, as neither the pessimistic nor the optimistic camps have clearly proven their case (Komlos 1993, p. 116). It may be that in the future a consensus will take shape about industrialization and its impact on living standards; for now, much effort remains focused on determining the best measurements to use. The measurement of real wages was recently criticized as not being sensitive enough to the issues of locale, gender, and age. It is to be expected that as the debate on living standards continues, scholars will further test measures reflecting the economic fluctuations such as recessions and depressions that had an immediate impact on working class lives, consider more closely the standard of living of women and children, and look more toward the use of biological indicators of well being such as height and calorie consumption.

A belief that improvement in the standard of living is possible through economic expansion and technological ingenuity—crucial aspects of the industrialization process—characterized the eighteenth, nineteenth, and twentieth centuries. That belief has been borne out for some nations in the long term, though with the growing understanding that of necessity the short-term costs must be accounted for. Today, there is a realization that industrialization, or to use the contemporary synonyms, "growth" and "development," is not infinite and unlimited, and that the costs of improved living standards—including pollution, the exploitation of resources, and the exacerbation of divisions between rich and poor nations—are part of the equation of industrialization.

NOTES

1. Cited in Jeffrey Williamson (1985), p. 1–2.

10
THE DEBATE ON THE CONDITION OF THE WORKING CLASS IN FRANCE CIRCA 1840: A STUDY IN IDEOLOGY

James B. Briscoe

It is no longer easy to say what the term "industrial revolution" denotes. Whether intended as a concise description of the sustained process of economic development or as a brief for a causal explanation of the acceleration of growth in the eighteenth century, it is now likely to bring more controversy than clarity into any account in which it appears. Perhaps concepts, like tools, wear down after hard use, and this has happened to the "Industrial Revolution." But industrial or not, revolutionary or not, the economic, social, and demographic changes that occurred in more or less distinct regions of Western Europe and Britain between the mid-eighteenth and mid-nineteenth centuries seem to belong to a connected historical process and to require a connected explanation. The changes seemed then to do so, and the years between 1830 and 1850 were filled with investigations, analyses and prolonged controversy over the transformations that one contemporary writer at least did not hesitate to describe as *"une révolution industrielle"* (Buret v. II 1979, p. 45).

This chapter gives an account of how this controversy arose in France. It is concerned with France rather than Great Britain because, while the process of industrialization may (or may not) have occurred more rapidly in the latter country, it was in France that public debate was, if anything, more intense and more prolonged. The main reason for this, of course, was that in the immediate past France had experienced social and political transformations in the form of revolution rather than evolution. The foundations of society—political, social, economic, and cultural—seemed less solidly grounded there, and change—from whatever direction—seemed more threatening. And it may have been so.

Our concern is with contemporary perceptions of the impact of industrialization and especially with the formation of ideologies that sought explicitly to shape and define those perceptions. Ideology here is conceived as a relationship between a body of discourse and a given social context. That is, ideological discourse aims to change social realities through the act of interpreting or re-presenting them. An ideology consists of both "empirical and normative statements about the world as it is and as it ought to be" (Hartley 1983, pp. 14 ff); its orientation is practical; it has, or intends to have, a strong link with behavior; it "impels to collective action." The debates concerning the impact of industrialization, it will be argued, were, in this sense, essentially ideological in nature. The writers whose works are considered here intended not just to describe the social changes wrought by industrialization, but equally or principally to affect them. Their works were informed by interests, prejudices, programs and what would today (unhappily) be called "agendas." At the center of these controversies and the starting point for our consideration of their ideological implications is the complex and closely articulated body of doctrines, values, and programs that came, in the nineteenth century, to be known as liberalism.

LIBERALISM

Liberalism arose in the seventeenth and eighteenth centuries primarily as an attempt to justify the existence of a sphere of individual autonomy in the face of the growing authority of the absolutist state, the associated demands of a monolithic established church, and the barriers imposed by a social order still dominated by conceptions of hierarchy, privilege and the corporative organization of economic life (Laski 1962). In the first instance, liberal writers based their claims, openly or implicitly, on the then-radical conception that the happiness—and the material well being—of individuals was in its own right, without reference to any higher or transcendent source, an autonomous value and a valid end, even the chief end, to the furtherance of which society and the state should be directed. In the natural law tradition, which was one of the progenitors of liberal doctrines, individuals were considered proprietors of their own selves: this entailed, among other claims, the right to free, uncoerced religious and intellectual development; hence demands for religious liberties and for freedom of expression and of the press. It led also to the claim that valid political obligation must be voluntarily assumed, and loyalty to authority freely given, not compelled. And, central to the purposes of this chapter, it led to the claim that individuals should be free to exploit their own powers—notably their own labor—in furtherance of their individual interests, to achieve their own needs and wants, and to increase their own happiness. As they owned their own labor, they had, it followed, a proprietory claim to the products which it created. Property, it was also claimed, secured individual autonomy by promoting self-sufficiency. It was a condition of freedom and consequently only property owners could be free.

Paralleling these arguments based on inherent rights and ends was an instrumentalist argument which later became the utilitarian position. Individuals, pursuing their own interests and goals, would, on this view, also maximize the sum of social well-being and progress. And, more radically, it was claimed that the social interest was nothing more than the sum of individual interests. Government and monopoly corporations, as it appeared from empirical observation and a priori reason, were not well suited to the task of giving intelligent direction to social or especially economic activity, whereas individuals, thanks to the concordance of their interests and initiatives through the divine order of providence, the providential order of nature or the simple mechanics of untrammeled markets, were.

At first liberalism presented chiefly negative and corrosive analyses. Its criticisms fell upon the range of institutions and practices particularly identified with the French state under Louis XIV and with what in due course would be styled the "old regime." But liberal writers also projected alternative political, social and economic forms, positive conceptions of an imagined society that acquired more concrete substance in the eighteenth century, first in England and Holland, then, from the 1760s on and especially following the Revolution of 1789, in France. By 1815, the end of the revolutionary era and the beginning of the Bourbon restoration, France had substantially remade itself in accordance with liberal ideas, though contemporary writers like Benjamin Constant and Charles Dunoyer considered that too much of the old regime still remained. During the next fifteen years, the ideological conflict between liberal and conservative conceptions of society ("liberal" and "conservative" taken in the nineteenth-century context, which differs significantly from the present, as will be seen) raged anew. With the Revolution of 1830 which expelled the last Bourbon king and installed the "bourgeois monarchy" of Louis Philippe (of Orleans), the ascendancy of liberal doctrines and of liberal practices and policies seemed assured. But it was precisely at this conjuncture that liberal conceptions of society received their most sustained and, it may appear, their most damaging criticisms. The issue at the center of the new controversy was the impact of industrialization upon society and particularly upon those most directly involved in industrial activities, the men and women who were often, though controversially, described as "the working class" (a term first used, in the singular, in 1794). These debates marked the opening of the now superannuated controversy between "optimists" and "pessimists" (over the impact of industrialization on workers' "standards of living" in particular), the issues then were broader than disputes over real per capita income or weekly meat consumption. They went to the heart of the liberal conception of society and its defense of industrialization as a manifestation of individual initiative and social progress. To put the issue briefly and baldly, the writers whom we shall characterize as critics of the liberal view—some were conservative or traditionalist, others are best described by the new term socialist—argued that industrialization brought the impoverishment and moral dissolution of the working classes; that these problems were essentially social, not individual in nature; and that their causes were rooted in the doctrines and practices of laissez faire capitalism and liberal individualism. Liberal defenders, in contrast, maintained that the alleged evils of industrialization were fictitious or exaggerated; that its benefits, even to the working classes, far outweighed its costs; and that, in all events, if some workers were suffering, the fault lay in their own failings—above all moral failings—which neither government nor society could ameliorate; or even if they could, should not attempt to alleviate since it was contrary both to justice and to the ethic of individual responsibility to relieve individuals of the consequences of their actions.

THE ISSUE OF POVERTY

Changes in vocabulary and in forms of discourse are sensitive indicators of shifting terms of argument. The phrase that in the 1830s and 1840s seemed to epitomize the condition of the working classes, to concentrate associations and images, was *la misère*—"poverty" in the most literal meaning but connoting a broader nexus of economic, social, and cultural phenomena. To Victor Hugo, it was "a nameless thing" on which he wrote, over a period of nearly twenty years, a very great and a very long novel (Chevalier 1973). Eugène Buret, whose views will be considered below, defined the concept more concisely;

"*La misère*," he said, was "pauvreté moralement sentie" ("poverty morally felt"). It was "the impoverishment, the suffering, and the humiliation that results from forced privations alongside the legitimate expectation of well-being . . . A man belongs to *la misère* when he is no longer able alone to bear his poverty and that of his family" (Buret 1979, p. 112–13).

Poverty, certainly, had long existed in France—nothing in contemporary society could compare with the terrible famines that had ravaged the countryside in previous centuries; but, concentrated in industrial cities and districts, modern poverty seemed more menacing. "The signs that presage a social revolution are everywhere evident," wrote the former prefect of the Departement du Nord, the vicomte Villeneuve-Bargemont (in a 1834 work entitled significantly "Economie politique chrétienne"): "Europe seems to be struck with terror and vertigo—*la misère des classes ouvrières* has become the great question of the present epoch." What was most disturbing to this writer and to many others was that poverty no longer seemed natural or inevitable; it now appeared to be one of the main products of industrial development—its "fatal complement," Buret believed. Or, as another titled critic, the baron Bigot de Morogues, wrote in 1832, "nowhere is there more poverty than where there is immense wealth." This "*paupérisme éffrayant*," he claimed, was the direct result of the development of *la grande industrie manufacturière* (Bigot Morogues 1832). The growing impoverishment of workers—so at least critics believed—challenged the comfortable association of industrial development with social progress. It is unlikely that poverty or even the culture of poverty that Hugo called *la misère* was more widespread in France in the nineteenth century than earlier. What did change were perceptions of the direction of its historical development. For the revolutionaries of 1793, *mendicité* was the "leprosy of monarchies"; under the republic it would be found only in history books. And in 1827, in an influential work, Charles Dupin still associated poverty with the infertile and underdeveloped regions of the country. But by 1834 Villeneuve-Bargemont would define *paupérisme* as "the general, permanent, and progressive distress of the working population." What was being questioned, then, was not just poverty, but the complex of social and economic relations that appeared to create and reproduce it alongside and, critics claimed, as a consequence of, industrial growth and the prosperity it created for a fortunate few. The belief that *la misère* had become the normal and perhaps irreversible condition of industrial workers led some writers to doubt the viability of a society in which prosperity and misery exist in such proximity.

THE MEANING OF INDUSTRIALISM

The term "industrialism" itself seemed novel enough in 1839 to require clarification. Reporting to the *Société industrielle de Mulhouse* on the results of an essay competition on the subject "industrialism in its relation to society, from a moral point of view", an aptly named Dr. Weber offered this definition: "we may understand by 'industrialism'—if this term is adopted into the French language—the more and more pronounced tendency in civilized countries toward that vast production that converts cities and entire districts into immense workshops" (Villermé 1989, p. 543). What appeared most remarkable about the process of industrialization was the industrial city itself, that is, the concentration and increasing scale of production in a particular region. Steam engines, power-driven machinery, and factories—though instrumental in fostering concentration—appeared to be subsidiary phenomena; and in the 1830s much production continued in workshops or adjacent rural districts (handloom weaving especially). It was the industrial city "in its ensemble" that the social investigator Louis Villermé called *la fabrique* (Villermé p. 83). In consequence, for Buret and Villermé, as for many other contemporary writers, working and living conditions in these cities were two aspects of the same problem. Certainly, for vivid description and stark contrasts, no subject offered more scope than the squalor and misery that middle-class observers recorded with almost anthropological interest. Nothing better illustrates the chasm that was opening between the classes in France than the belief that conditions in working class districts of industrial cities had in effect created a different civilization, or rather the absence of a civilization.

> There, if you dare to enter you will see with every step men and women branded with vice and *la misère,* half-naked children who rot in filth and suffocate in hovels without light and without air. There, on the doorstep of civilization, you will encounter thousands of men and women who, through degradation (*à force d'abrutissement*), have fallen back into *la vie sauvage.* (Buret, 1979, p. 67–68)

Or, from an 1832 report by the Sanitary Commission of the Department du Nord:

> It is impossible to imagine the appearance of these habitations of the poor if one has not visited them . . . grinding poverty—intolerable, murderous . . . dark cellars, infected air, walls covered with a thousand forms of filth . . . [for beds] dirty, greasy boards . . . covered with damp and putrescent

straw ... furniture encrusted with grime ... windows always closed ... everywhere piles of garbage, ash, remains of vegetables collected in the streets ... the air, hardly breathable, has a dull, nauseating, slightly acrid smell—the smell of filth, the smell of garbage, the smell of humans. (Villermé 1989, p. 136)

These were, of course, descriptions of the poorest of the poor. Villermé, who three years later visited the same street in Lille, found the above portrait "by no means exaggerated," but added that only a few blocks away other workers lived in relative comfort. What seemed most damning about the condition of the working class was not that they lived always and everywhere in misery, but rather that they could never escape from the threat of falling at any time into indigence and the state that Buret called *"denûment,"* stripped of all security and means of support.

A New Term: Proletarian

Another term that came into general usage in the 1830s in France and that focused perceptions of the condition of the industrial working class, was "proletarian" (*les prolétaires*—the collective *prolétariat* first appeared in 1832). In the previous century, the term had denoted somewhat generally the urban, indigent poor with clear and often explicit reference to classical Rome. But around 1830 it took on a more precise and critical sense: *"les prolétaires"* tended specifically to refer to industrial wage-workers whose impoverishment and lack of independence and security arose as a direct consequence of the system of productive relations. In 1827 the economist Simonde de Sismondi denounced the "new world where *la misère publique* never ceases to grow along with material wealth, and where the class that produces everything comes closer each day to being reduced to having nothing.

We are ... in an entirely new social condition ... We are tending to separate completely all forms of property from all forms of labor, to destroy all relationships between workers (*journaliers*) and masters, to remove the former from any association with the profits of the latter ... The new social order brings into conflict all those who possess and all those who work. (Sismondi 1827, p. 358, pp. 438–39)

In 1837 he added, "the fundamental change that has come about in modern society ... is the introduction of *le prolétaire* ... One could even say that modern society depends for its existence upon *les prolétaires.*"

The socialist Saint-Simonian movement was most responsible in the early 1830s for popularizing the term "proletarian" in France. It introduced as well a new meaning of the term "exploitation"; previously used in the sense of the exploitation of land or capital, it was employed in Saint-Simonian discourse to describe the exploitation of labor ("the exploitation of man by man" was their phrase) that created the conditions of proletarianization—deskilling, reduction to the status of dependent wage-workers, and separation from ownership or control of the instruments of production. The new connotations of "proletarian" are exactly conveyed in the following passage from an 1832 article by the Saint-Simonian Jean Reynaud:

> I call *prolétaire* those men who produce all the wealth of the nation, who possess only the daily salary of their labor, and whose work depends upon causes over which they have no control; who retain each day from the fruits of their efforts only a small portion incessantly reduced by competition; whose future rests on the fleeting hope of the uncertain and unregulated movement of industry, and who can foresee no aid in their old age except a place in the poorhouse or an early death. (Reynaud, 1832, pp. 12–20)

All critics of industrialism deprecated the growing separation of classes—one might say the emergence of a class society; it is no accident that the singular form "the working class" ("*la classe ouvrière*") tended in the nineteenth century to supersede older plural terms. In place of the (perhaps idealized) traditional social structure in which gradations of wealth and property were supposed to form hierarchical, "organic" relations between orders, masters working alongside journeymen and apprentices, paupers receiving charity from the more fortunate, industrial society seemed to create an unbridgeable divide between workers and owners and to close off any possibility of social ascent. In contrast to liberal claims that through hard work, savings, and "prudence" (especially in the matter of family limitation), anyone could rise to the highest ranks of wealth and honor, socialist and conservative critics alike asserted that poverty and "proletarianization" had become the permanent and inescapable condition of industrial workers. Even Villermé, who was by no means unsympathetic to the values and institutions of his society, noted with dismay that the growing scale of industrial enterprises and the capital required to purchase machines engendered the concentration of wealth in the hands of a small number of "*hauts barons manufacturiers*" (great industrial barons), who confronted "a multitude of proletarians" (Villermé 1989, p. 534).

Working Class Impoverishment

The impoverishment of the working class, many critics claimed, was a necessary consequence of the system of competition, which they denounced as "anarchy" and a "war of all against all." Competition occurred on two levels: first between enterprises, which forced manufacturers constantly to find ways to reduce costs of production, labor costs in particular. And second between workers themselves as they competed for scarce positions. The fact that there seemed always to be a surplus of "hands"—labor shortages were rarely observed or considered—meant that workers had to take what wages were offered and that these steadily declined towards some minimum subsistence level, though that too appeared subject to downward adjustment. The need to reduce wage costs led to the introduction of labor-saving machines, which created further imbalances between labor supply and demand and induced further reductions in the competitive wage rate. The plight of handloom weavers, which Villermé described in vivid detail, offered the best example of this process. International rivalry intensified the conflict, particularly since French industry had to compete against more highly mechanized British factories, and, French critics charged, against the more proletarianized British labor force.

But it was the cycle of industrial crises—trade depressions, which struck French industry at regular intervals—that appeared to be the most pernicious and destructive consequence of industrial development. In cities in which a large part of the population depended directly or indirectly upon a single industry—cotton, wool, or silk, coal or iron—a precipitous drop in demand and production created unemployment and, in consequence, *la misère,* on a massive scale. All observers agreed upon the disastrous effects these crises had on working families, whose savings, if any, were quickly exhausted, plunging them into a state of poverty, misery and *"denûment,"* which public and private efforts were completely inadequate to relieve. Many writers, both conservative and socialist, followed Sismondi in attributing trade depressions to overproduction and recurring market gluts. This underconsumptionist theory of economic crises—as Keynes noted, a staple element in the "Victorian underworld" of nineteenth century economic heresies—held that in an industrializing, competitive economy there was a constant tendency toward insufficient aggregate demand, since, as workers' salaries fell toward subsistence levels, they were unable to take up the increasing output of manufactured goods. Profits, which in consequence gathered a larger proportion of income, accrued to a diminishing number of owners, who had limited needs and little taste for cheap factory goods. Outlets for all these products could only be found overseas, but market expansion led to heightened competition on an international scale and encouraged greater mechanization, which increased output but reduced both the number of workers and their wages, further increasing capital's share of income and exacerbating the shortfall in effective demand. The result, it was claimed, was a recurring cycle of overproduction and depression that became more severe with each iteration.

DEFENSE OF SOCIETY

Liberal writers, of course, rejected these criticisms of the competitive system. J-B. Say, the most widely read and influential economist in France in the early nineteenth century, dismissed the possibility of general market gluts and argued that aggregate supply and demand must always be equal—the doctrine still known as Say's Law (and still a matter for controversy). In any event, the dominant opinion in the July Monarchy, among legislators and industrialists at least, opposed interference in the operation of competitive markets. "Nothing could be more dangerous," Say wrote, "than those views that lead to the regulation of the use of property." (J-B. Say "Revue Encyclopedique," tome 23, pp. 18–31) And in 1827 the prominent liberal publicist Charles Dunoyer denounced critics of the competitive system who "attack society in its most active principle of existence, in its most efficacious means of development." (Dunoyer, Esquisse des doctrines auxquelles on a donne le nom d'industrialisme, "Revue Encyclopedique," tome 33, pp. 368–94) What he described as the "violent division of society between entrepreneurs and workers" arose from differences in activity, capacity and conduct; if superior application did not bring superior rewards, the motor of self-interest would splutter to a halt destroying "all principles of activity, honesty and virtue." As for the poor, he wrote, they must learn to depend upon their own forces and not be allowed "to speculate on public charity. . . . All must be certain that they will be subject to the penalties of their indolence or their lack of foresight." The view that poverty was an individual rather than a social problem was widely held in 1840. Responding to an inquiry into the causes of poverty, the Conseil général of La Drôme wrote that "pauperism comes naturally from the lack of order and economy, from the habit of cabarets and gambling, from sickness and serious accidents, as well as the voluntary or involuntary lack of work." And the Conseil of l'Aisne gave as the chief causes, "lack of foresight, ignorance, and immorality among the inferior classes." (Tudesq 1967, II, p. 566 ff).

Strikes and demonstrations by workers protesting wage cuts or demanding regulation of working conditions regularly met with official disapproval and, on occasion, with repression. When, shortly after the July Revolution, several thousand metal workers demonstrated in Paris for a reduction in the working day from twelve to eleven hours, the prefect of police posted a proclamation warning that fixing of salaries or hours of labor was "contrary to the laws that consecrate the principle of freedom of industry," and added for good measure that it was also proscribed by article 415 of the penal code (which forbade workers to "form coalitions to hinder or suspend work in a workshop . . . or to increase the rate of wages"). The most violent manifestations of working class unrest came in the silk-producing city of Lyon where, in November 1831 and again in April 1834, workers seized control of many districts and raised banners proclaiming as their objective "to live by work or die fighting." The first uprising was settled by negotiation, but the second brought military intervention and bombardment of the city. Although these disturbances were widely attributed to the activities of "agitators" (Saint-Simonians and republicans in particular), and a parliamentary commission reported in 1832 that "the true and indeed only permanent obligation of the government is to procure for industry the liberty and the security that make unnecessary, if not dangerous, all other public interference," (Georges Bourgin "La crise ouvrière dans la seconde-moitie de 1830," *Revue historique* 198, Oct–Dec. 1947, p. 204) the Lyon insurrections were instrumental in creating the impression of an impending social crisis. In 1835, following the second upheaval, the prestigious Academy of Moral and Political Sciences received 4000 francs from the Minister of the Interior to carry out an inquiry in order "to determine, as exactly as possible, the physical and moral condition of the working classes." The Academy entrusted the principal task of investigation to Dr. Louis-René Villermé.

INVESTIGATION OF CONDITIONS

Villermé was an inspired choice for the task. By profession a medical doctor, he had already gained a reputation as one of the most eminent investigators of conditions of public health and welfare in France. He had published detailed studies of prison conditions and delivered numerous communications to the Academy and other learned societies on such issues as comparative mortality rates and the physical stature of workers. He represented a type of individual at once common and exceptional in the nineteenth century, a "generous spirit" of independent means who devoted his life to philanthropic works. In 1835 and 1836 Villermé traveled to the major textile producing areas of France in order to carry out a scientific, empirical investigation into all aspects of working class existence. On these visits, he wrote, he not only observed workers in factories and workshops, he went into their homes, shared their meals, and followed them, not without some distate and difficulty, into taverns and grog shops. "I was the confidant of their joys and their complaints," he wrote, "the witness of their vices and their virtues" (Villermé 1989, p. 82; henceforth cited as V). In 1839 he presented his report to the Academy and at the beginning of 1840 there appeared his two volume *Tableau de l'état physique et moral des ouvriers employés dans les manufactures de coton, de laine et de soie* (Portrait of the physical and moral condition of workers employed in the cotton, wool, and silk industries), the most famous of the investigations into the condition of the working class in nineteenth-century France.

It is impossible in a brief chapter to do justice to the richness and variety of Villermé's observations. The work was filled with vivid descriptions of living and working conditions in more than a dozen cities; it included numerous tables detailing workers' salaries and expenditures by year, by trade or profession, by age, sex, region, and industry with estimates of the cost of living and family budgets, calculations of birth rates (carefully distinguishing between legitimate and illegitimate births) and death rates. Villermé reported scrupulously on the conditions he observed and did not hesitate to denounce or condemn practices and behavior, both on the part of workers and of owners, but fundamentally he accepted the existing structure and organization of industry; he did not, and did not wish to, challenge the foundations of the society of which he was an eminent member. As Francis Démier wrote, Villermé's goal was to establish precise and limited reforms designed to restore both the economic and the moral equilibrium that he believed to be endangered by the rapid growth of industrial capitalism.

Poverty and misery he certainly found, especially among workers in the cotton industry in Lille and the Upper Rhine. There, he saw "frightful poverty, profound degradation, vices . . . how many of them are bady housed, badly clothed, badly fed, pale, thin, worn down . . ." he wrote. In Thun and Mulhouse these unfortunate workers were referred to by "the expressive and strange epithet of 'White Negroes' "

(V, p. 358). But such conditions occurred mostly among workers employed in factories producing the plainest and coarsest cloth; in printed cotton mills and in wool and silk districts, laborers were better off, though he was revolted by the smell and unsanitary work involved in preparing raw silk (V, p. 303 and 495). While noting that workers in large spinning mills suffered from the heat, humidity and cotton dust, and often contracted lung inflammations and a "terrible phtisie," he also calculated that these factories afforded many more cubic meters of air space per laborer that the cramped rooms in which weavers worked (V, p. 485 and 501).

After comparing workers' budgets and expenses, he concluded cautiously that in most industries, in normal times (he meant, of course, in periods of prosperity), salaries were sufficient to support a working family adequately, though hardly in comfort, provided—and this was a large qualification—that at least two or three members had regular work and were not disabled by sickness or injury. To cite one example from dozens, he calculated that in Lille, a family of four, if husband, wife, and one child each worked 300 days, could earn 915 francs in a year; food and housing on a modest scale would cost 798 francs (738 francs on food alone!), leaving 117 francs for all other needs, such as clothing and medicine, etc.—not enough, he judged, to allow a margin for savings, misfortune or imprudent expenses (V, pp. 146–7). Incomes varied, of course, according to profession, level of skill, and demand; they depended as well upon age and sex. Villermé noted that an unmarried man between the ages of twenty and forty, steadily employed, could live easily from his salary and realize some savings, while a single woman, earning roughly half a man's wage, would live in poverty. If they married, their combined salaries, even for poorly paid workers, would support, "with prudence and no vices," two infants. But, he added, "supposing a third child, unemployment, sickness, lack of economy, habits or even a single instance of intemperance, this family would find itself in the greatest need, in terrible poverty." In any case, the margin between sufficiency and want was narrow. A rise of 10 centimes in the price of bread would significantly affect the family's condition. After the age of forty, salaries declined and the likelihood of bad health increased; without savings there would be no security in old age. Moreover, these calculations assumed regular employment. But Villermé noted with dismay that commercial crises, "of which the more or less regular occurrence is a condition of industry," exposed the majority of workers to the greatest poverty (*une grande misère*); "lacking work, they lack everything" (V, p. 538). Even those who succeeded in finding work in hard times were often employed only three or four days a week for six or eight hours instead of the usual thirteen. Under those circumstances, wages dropped below a level that would enable a worker to support himself and his family. "If industry, organized as we see it now, is one of the most admirable phenomena of our society," Villermé concluded, "when there is a crisis, it is one of the most terrible: multitudes of workers fall into extreme distress (*une horrible détresse*) which strikes principally at the weakest, those who earn the smallest salaries" (V, p. 539).

It was not, however, the material condition of workers that Villermé found most disturbing. Despite the poverty and squalor in which many families lived, most workers, he insisted, were at present better housed and fed than they had been twenty or thirty years before—far better than in the previous century—and the cost of necessities such as bread and clothing was lower (V, p. 237, p. 367). For Villermé the most insidious aspect of industrial civilization was rather its corrosive effect upon the morals of the lower classes. Indeed, questions of the physical condition of the working classes were inseparable, as the title of his work indicates, from concerns about their moral condition. And this was depicted in the darkest hues: drunkeness, prostitution, violence, illegitimacy, cohabitation, sexual immorality of all sorts— but especially drunkeness. Repeatedly Villermé deplored the intemperance of workers. Drink—he actually wrote this—"is the curse of the working classes" (or almost: "*l'ivrognerie . . . c'est le plus grand fléau des classes laborieuses*"). The subject, indeed, led him to this intemperate outburst: "At first they [workers, mostly men] drink spirits without pleasure . . . to keep up with the others; but soon indifference gives way to enjoyment [*une sensation agréable*] and then to an irresistible desire and a constantly growing passion . . . from this point, drunkeness destroys savings, the proper upbringing of children, the happiness of the family . . . it turns the inebriate into an idler, a gambler, a brawler, a troublemaker . . . it degrades him, besots him, ruins his health, shortens his life, destroys his morals, scandalizes society and leads to crime" (V, p. 389).

Villermé was shocked by the coarseness of workers' language, particularly in workshops and taverns where the sexes intermingled and children were often present. In the department of the Upper Rhine, he noted, the morals of workers in textile factories "pass for the most dissolute" in the region; the principal cause of this corruption, he believed, was "the reunion of both sexes in the same workshop, especially during the night" (V, p. 103). Nothing was more common in these factories than to hear words and conversations "injurious to decency [*qui blessant la pudeur*]." And actions followed words: illegitimacy rates in the region had risen steadily over the past fifteen years. Elsewhere in the district, in the printed cotton factories of Dornach, he observed many girls and women "among whom the cut of their clothing, the coquettry of their behavior, and the expressions on their faces, betrayed morals which were hardly chaste" (V, p. 104). And in Lille, visiting the cellars inhabited by the poorest of the poor, he figuratively averted his eyes but recorded this lurid scene:

> I saw lying together [in the same bed] individuals of both sexes and very different ages, most without chemises and repulsively filthy. Father, mother, the elderly, children, and adults, pressed and packed together. I will stop here . . . the reader must complete the picture for himself; but I warn him, if he is equal to the task his imagination must not falter when confronted by the revolting mysteries that take place in these impure beds amid the darkness and the drunkenness. (V, p. 134)

Despite these expressions of scandalized prudery, Villermé's objective was not to deplore or condemn the behavior of factory workers or that of the lower classes in general. He intended to produce a clinical diagnosis, not a moralizing tract. The central question, he wrote, was to determine whether the development of modern industry was responsible for creating "the present state [in which] workers in factories lack sobriety, prudence, foresight, good morals and are often impoverished by their own actions." The answer he gave was not calculated to reassure the Academy:

> The evil is not new, but it is greater than ever; it results principally from the habitual assembly of workers in large workshops, which are like *serails* where workers of both sexes and all ages intermingle; and from their stay in cities, especially large cities, where numerous factories create agglomerations of population. It comes also from free competition, that cause of the growth and prodigious expansion of industry, but also of the frequent overproduction of manufactured goods, of bulging warehouses and the collapse of the value of inventories, of the ruin of numerous factory owners, and of the many crises and many oscillations in the rate of salaries that are so injurious to workers. (V, p. 561)

It goes to the heart of the "unhappy consciousness" of Villermé that, having presented the problems of industrialization so starkly, he was unwilling to propose, or perhaps he was unable to envision, means to effect reforms adequate to resolve them. He dismissed, after almost perfunctory attention, contemporary efforts to ameliorate the poverty of workers; public and charitable institutions, mutual aid societies, savings banks, and vocational schooling, though they might assist those suffering from temporary misfortune, were powerless to combat moral degradation. In Villermé's eyes, the industrial city and its corrupting environment had become an all-dominating evil. He advanced a not especially convincing proposal to decentralize industry by relocating factories to the countryside. Since, he noted, mechanized factories tended to employ mostly women and children, in a rural environment men might again "turn their vigorous arms" to agriculture with the happy result that industrial crises would no longer expose entire families to destitution (V, p. 539). In the end, however, mindful of his audience and the milieu in which he lived, Villermé concluded with an appeal to the good will of the "heads of industry," in their own interests, as well as in the interests of society, to concern themselves with the moral improvement of their workers, so that "in place of the complete abandon in which the majority [of owners] leave their workers [and] in place of the exclusive thought of exploiting their condition, there might arise a more generous and more humane aim, a patronage that would be as profitable to them [the owners] as their egoism" (V, p. 573).

There was one practical reform for which Villermé fought passionately and, in the end successfully—legislation to limit the working hours of children. Radical critics, to say nothing of many workers, had for decades demanded public regulation of the length of the working day. Extensions of work, often with no increase, or even reduction in the daily wage, were a frequent cause of strikes and labor disturbances in the nineteenth century. But among middle class legislators, at least, there was implacable hostility to interference in the "freedom of contract" between masters and workers. However, the case for safeguarding minors against abuse and exploitation in the work place was stronger; they had not entered into a free contract, and society had a clear and overriding interest in protecting the next generation. Villermé portrayed the condition of these most defenseless workers in the harshest light. It was usual, he wrote, for children as young as six years of age to be employed in spinning mills for thirteen hours a day or more. Since they were awakened before dawn to reach the factories by the beginning of work, "they must remain on their feet for sixteen or seventeen hours each day and for at least thirteen hours in a fixed place [tending the spinning machines] . . . this is not labor, not a job, it is torture; and it is inflicted upon infants from six to eight years old" (V, p. 415).

Even if they wished to, Villermé added, individual manufacturers could do nothing to shorten the hours because children's parents, who depended on their earnings, would send them to other factories where they could receive a full day's wage. To protect these children, even against their parents, was, he wrote, "a necesary, indispensable law of humanity" (V, p. 423). In this crusade, he prevailed, and in 1841, due in part to Villermé's report and repeated appeals, the French legislature passed, not without heated debate, a law to limit work to eight hours a day for children aged eight to twelve yeatrs and to twelve hours for those between twelve and sixteen with further restrictions on night work. But, since penalties for exceeding these limits were set at a nominal twelve francs per violation (up to a maximum of 200 francs), and no inspectors authorized, the measure, like similar legislation in Great Britain, remained largely ineffectual.

CRITICISM OF ANTIPOVERTY REMEDIES

Eugene Buret's study of the *Poverty of the Working Classes in England and France* appeared a few months after Villermé's *Tableau;* it too had been written in response to an initiative by the Academy of Moral and Political Sciences, which in 1838 and again in 1839 offered a prize of 5000 francs for the best work examining "the nature of poverty, its causes, and the forms in which it appears in various countries." Since the Academy specifically requested investigations into "the most useful applications of the principle of voluntary or private association to relieve poverty," it is somewhat puzzling that Buret's work should have been awarded the prize; his critical intentions were evident from the subtitle of the book, "On the nature of poverty . . . and on the inadequacy of the remedies that have been proposed for it . . . " In contrast to Villermé's careful balancing of the benefits and costs of industrialization, Buret did not hesitate to challenge the existing economic system directly. He certainly did not lack ambition; the work, which ran to two volumes totaling almost a thousand pages, was intended, he said, to form part of a larger study with the imposing title of "The Poverty of Nations." The "phenomenon of poverty," he wrote, deserved the attention of economists just as much as the science of wealth; in particular, it was necessary to determine whether poverty "develops under the influence of the same causes; whether it is the counterweight and inevitable compensation for wealth" (Buret 1979, v.1, p. 13, henceforth cited as B).

The image Buret repeatedly employed to depict the present economic system was that of conflict, indeed of war, for *"la misère* is a matter of life or death for societies" (B II, p. 318. He wrote of "the brutal violence of the industrial war," of *"la guerre perpetuel"* created by the system of competition and *"la guerre intestine du capital et du travail"* ("the intestine war of capital and labor") which was the "dominant fact" of the existing economic order [*"l'économie sociale actuelle"*]; and finally of those "industrial armies which have paid with their weariness, one could say with their blood, for the admirable conquests [of industry] . . . No defeated army ever presented a more lamentable spectacle than this triumphant industrial army" (B I, pp. 23, 26, 66–67; II, p. 337).

In modern societies, he wrote, there had arisen a basic contradiction between the "economic regime" that governed industry and the "moral principles upon which our civilization rests" (B I, p. 53). Just when men had become free politically, they were "enslaved" by an economic system that resembled, in many respects, the feudalism that the French revolution had overturned. Were not, he asked, those "great mercantile individuals whom one calls capitalists" successors to the noble landowners of feudal times, and were not *"les proletaires"* the modern equivalent of serfs? (B I, p. 59; II, p. 69). That this new concentration of wealth did not result from legal privilege but rather from "a fact" made it all the more menacing "because [today] it is the fact that creates the law" (B I, p. 59). Throughout the book, Buret constructed an extraordinary indictment of the automonous and "fatal" operation of the modern economy that produced its effects independent of the will of individuals. Reading many passages, it is necessary to recall that they were written when Marx was still pondering the mysteries of Hegelian philosophy at the University of Berlin. What "condemns without redemption" the present economic order, Buret wrote, is "that it cannot be other than what it is" (B II, p. 200). Owners were not to blame for the insufficiency of salaries or the excessive length of the working day because these matters were determined by competitive market forces. As for the immorality and vice of the lower classes, they too, Buret insisted, were trapped in a "fatal circle:" material poverty led to moral poverty and vice versa; "the two evils are mutually entangled . . . In a word, *la misère* comes not from the actions of men, but from the power of things [*la puissance de choses*] . . . capital is a *power* that commands labor" (B I, p. 82; II, p. 204). The most dangerous "economic fact" [*le fait économique le plus funeste*] was the "absolute separation" of labor and capital that created a "perpetual conflict" between owners and workers (B II, pp. 136, 337). He asserted as a general proposition, "confirmed by all evidence," that "the physical and moral condition of workers is in exact proportion to the position they occupy vis à vis the instruments of [labor]".

The argument proceeded along lines reviewed earlier. Industrialization, by increasing the scale of production and the capital required to compete successfully, excluded workers from ownership or control of the "instruments of production"; mechanization encouraged replacement of skilled labor by women and children; competition engendered a downward spiral of wages and created "manifest hostility" between owners and workers; the growing size of productive units increased the "chasm" between capital and labor as more and more workers found themselves reduced to the status of "proletarians," dependent upon their daily wages for survival; overproduction together with the concentration of wealth and workers' lack of purchasing power led to recurring industrial crises that destroyed security and savings and brought impoverishment and degradation. (It was strange, Buret noted, to give the name of "crises" to those "periodic phenomena" which had become "the normal state of . . . industry" (B I, p. 186). In summary:

> The dominant fact of the present social economy . . . that which determines all the others . . . is the more and more absolute separation that exists between the two elements of production—capital and labor . . . It is here, in the constitution or rather the lack of a constitution of the public economy [sic], that the fundamental cause of the poverty and degradation of the working classes is to be found. (B II, p. 337)

After these fulminations, Buret's proposals for subduing the demons of industrial capitalism appear rather tame, though also, it may be said, rather modern—anticipating the reforms of the twentieth century. He proposed, of course, legislation to regulate working hours and wages. Like Villermé, he envisioned relocating factories to the countryside—no one, it seemed, had a favorable opinion of industrial cities. In order to associate workers with ownership of enterprises, he suggested investing workers' savings in industrial property—an early version of pension plan capitalism. However, he did not favor nationalization or public ownership of industry since "there are no citizens except on the condition of a direct participation in property." To reduce concentration of wealth, he recommended inheritance taxes on the order of 20 to 25 percent (at the time inheritance taxes were less than 5 percent and often below 1 percent) and an income tax "proportional to real wealth." To overcome the political separation of classes and to provide workers with legislative representation (in France during the

July Monarchy only substantial property owners had the right to vote), he proposed creating a "Chamber of Labor" in which owners and workers would sit side by side. And to oversee the "public economy" he envisioned a "Grand Council of Industry" which would regulate production and maintain a stable balance between output and consumption. Most important of all, to free the nation from *la misère*—the permanent possibility of poverty and destitution—he considered it essential to guarantee each citizen "steady and assured employment."

LIBERAL RESPONSE TO CRITICISM

The most extreme, though also characteristic liberal response to these criticisms came from Charles Dunoyer. To turn from Buret's astringent criticisms of competition and industrial capitalism to Dunoyer's truculent and uncompromising defense of the same institutions is to pass from one universe of discourse to another. All the social and economic evils in Buret's account are positive virtues for Dunoyer. "Freedom of labor [*la liberté de travail*], competition, machines . . . the accumulation of capital, far from being the causes of poverty, are the most powerful instruments of prosperity" (Dunoyer 1842, p. 20, henceforth cited as D). To place Dunoyer's account alongside Buret's is like bringing together ideological matter and antimatter that annihiliate each other when they come into contact. It was not surprising that Dunoyer responded so violently to criticism of the system of "free competition;" for thirty years he had been one of the most vigorous champions of liberal individualism and laissez faire economics. In numerous articles, lectures and books, he repeated his conviction that freedom arose only from individual initiative and competition, not from the actions of governments or society. After 1830, he viewed with mounting indignation the succession of attacks upon "the most just liberty in the world" ["*une liberté bien naturelle légitime . . . la liberté la plus juste du monde*"], that is, the system of free competition among individuals (D, p. 14), until in 1842, dismayed that the latest criticisms (the books of Villermé and Buret) had come, not from "eccentric socialists" but from respectable writers whose works appeared under the sponsorship of the prestigious Academy, he dispatched to the leading economic journal a review article entitled "On the objections that have been raised in recent times against the regime of competition". To summarize its arguments, Dunoyer first denied categorically that poverty had increased in modern times, What was "openly manifest" was rather the "progress of material well being" among all classes,. Even the least fortunate members of society participated in the benefits of civilization:

Condition of the Working Class in France 199

They enjoy [at present] more liberty and security . . . they can more easily find work, they walk on streets that are cleaner, more spacious and better lit. They work in cleaner workshops at less dangerous work. They profit equally with the rich from the amelioration of all the objects of public and common usage. (D, p. 11)

It was also untrue that the poor had become more numerous. Looking at land tax rolls, Dunoyer calculated that at least 24 million of the 34 million inhabitants of France owned some form of property (there were six million tax payers and he assumed an average family of four persons); furthermore, business tax licenses had risen from 887,000 in 1817 to 1.4 million in 1840, indicating that nearly six million persons were associated with the ownership of businesses, which left at most four million out of the 34 million inhabitants of the country in the doubtful category of "proletarians" (D, p. 7).

Second, he asserted that it was more than a falsehood, that it was a calumny to maintain that the middle classes had achieved their position in society as a result of privilege, and that they formed, in consequence, a new aristocracy. On the contrary, he claimed, they had risen to prosperity and respectability through a "glorious progress of democracy . . . by hard work, by saving, by a vigilant and hereditary morality from generation to generation" (D, p. 13).

Third, what of Buret's proposals for "associating labor with the fruits of capital"? They violated, Dunoyer insisted, that "fundamental law of humanity and of society" which made the condition of each individual "the direct result of his conduct, in direct proportion to the activity, intelligence, morality and persistence of his efforts" (D, p. 34). Workers could justly demand from the wealth created by industry only the portion due to their own contribution, that is, to their labor. And that, Dunoyer wrote (long before Fisher and the rise of theories of marginal value product) "is exactly represented, when nothing hinders the liberty of the transaction, by their salary" (D, pp. 29–30).

Finally, attempts to regulate labor markets and to remove them from the pressures of competition, would, he claimed, only exacerbate the crises which critics of the industrial system denounced so fiercely. Those writers in fact caused great injury to workers by encouraging them to imagine that there could be any remedy for crises except to prepare themselves during periods of prosperity "by a little foresight [*un peu de prevoyance*], moderation and savings" for inevitable downturns. If instead workers disregarded "the clearest warnings," spent all their earnings, and "multiplied with a bestial fecundity," the suffering they endured should be regarded as the consequence of their "passions and stupidity [*sotisse*]." The real evil in modern society, Dunoyer added, warming to the subject, was the workers' "immoderate expectations":

> The principal cause of poverty in these times—which is above all a moral poverty [*une misère morale*]—[is] the immoderation of desires and the little care that the inferior ranks take . . . to proportion their needs to their resources. (D, p. 37)

It was not the case, however, that Dunoyer regarded poverty as an unmitigated evil. "Even with the best possible social organization, poverty, like inequality, is to a certain degree inevitable . . . it is an element of social progress . . . inseparable from civilization."

> It is necessary that there should be in society those infernal regions into which families that conduct themselves badly are in danger of falling . . . Poverty is this redoubtable abyss [*ce redoutable enfer*], placed before fools, dissipates, debauchers, and all sorts of vice-ridden individuals, to warn them, if that is possible; to receive and punish them if it is not . . . [*La misère*] offers a salutary spectacle to the saner portion of the least fortunate classes . . . it exhorts them to the difficult virtues they must master in order to improve their condition; [it] renders possible and even easy patience, moderation, courage, economy, and that last restraint, the most necessary of all, that they must observe to limit their fecundity. (D, p. 43).

If poverty and sickness should lead to the reduction of an "overabundant population," Dunoyer concluded, that result might be considered "almost as a necessary evil [*presque comme d'un mal devenu nécessaire*]."

SIGNIFICANCE AND IMPACT

The term "ideology" is often employed in a pejorative and dismissive sense. To label a work as "ideological" is to bracket consideration of its arguments and turn attention towards the motives or politics of its author. In contrast to social science, ideology is regarded as "distorted," "warped," or "contaminated" by virulent partisanship, anxiety, fear or by sheer wickedness. Above all it is claimed, ideology is false. As a leading American sociologist wrote, "the problem of ideology arises where there is a discrepancy between what is believed and what can be [established as] scientifically correct." The question of what can be (or could be or has been) established as scientifically correct concerning the condition of the working classes in France in the nineteenth century is one which may be left for another occasion; it is irrelevant to understanding the significance and impact of the writings of Villermé, Buret and Dunoyer. Their ideological character does not arise from their correspondence or lack of correspondence to some objectively determined social reality, but from their rhetorical and discursive strategies and from the techniques by which they implicate and reorient concepts, words, and patterns of discourse in new semantic fields of meaning and intention. As the anthropologist Clifford Geertz wrote, "the function of ideology is to make an autonomous politics possible by providing the authoritiative concepts that render it meaningful . . . [it] names the structure of situations in such a way that the attitude contained toward them is one of commitment" (Geertz 1973, pp. 218, 230–31). The historical significance of the debate over the condition of the working classes, as it developed in France during the formative decades of the 1830s and 1840s, does not lie in the fact that these works present competing descriptions of social realities, but in their competing attempts to define the meaning of those realities—in the creation of ideologically charged conceptual fields that shaped perceptions and actions in the nineteenth century and that have continued to a significant degree to do so up to the present time.

11
TECHNOLOGICAL CHANGE, UNEMPLOYMENT, AND THE LATE INDUSTRIALIZING COUNTRIES: THE EXAMPLE OF JAPAN

Christine Rider

INTRODUCTION

The technological changes associated with the Industrial Revolution increased society's ability to produce things by making human beings more productive at work. Today's workers, using inanimate energy sources like steam power or electricity, can produce quantities of output far beyond the wildest dreams of our great-great-grandparents. The past two hundred years or so have also seen structural changes accompany these technological changes. Probably the change that has affected most people is the shift in occupational status from artisan or independent peasant farmer to wage earner; most people today are employees, not independent producers.

This chapter looks at the connection between productivity-enhancing technological change, the shift to wage earner status, and unemployment, in all aspects of the process of industrialization. Rising productivity may make some workers redundant; employee status is not permanently guaranteed over the worker's lifetime; hence income insecurity may increase over time. I will try to assess the policy implications of these changes, to see if there are differences between those countries which industrialized in the nineteenth century and those trying to industrialize today. I will also look at Japan, one of the first late-industrializers (so-called because it started the industrialization process in the late nineteenth century, a hundred years or so after the first industrializer, Great Britain). Japan is an interesting example because it adapted the then-new labor-saving technology, but avoided its unemployment-creating effects. However, this type of adaptation becomes harder for twentieth-century late developers, for reasons that are associated both with the nature of technological change itself and with the reality of international competition. The goal is to apply some of the lessons of modern history to modern economic problems.

Why Is This a Concern?

In today's market economies, a money income is needed to buy the things one needs. If most people are wage earners, they are concerned, first, that they will continue to have a job, and second, that the income they earn will be sufficient to meet their needs. No income source is permanently guaranteed in any type of economic system. In preindustrial agricultural economies, people were at the mercy of recurrent harvest failures, plagues, internal unrest, wars, and so on. Some of these have, to a certain extent, been controlled, but unemployment and underemployment have become new worries in industrialized market economies. If alternative nonmarket sources of income are not available, or if there is no socially provided "safety net" such as social security, periods of unemployment can have devastating economic and noneconomic effects on the jobless and their families.

Although unemployment has several causes, I will focus only on what economists call technological unemployment, which occurs when a change in technology requires fewer workers than previously. Developing countries shifting from a predominantly peasant agricultural economy to a more diversified, commercially oriented one, are particularly affected when adopting modern industrial technology because the shift to higher productivity activities by definition requires a smaller labor input for every unit of output. If their population is also increasing rapidly, it is easy to see that the problem of finding meaningful, productive employment for a growing labor force will be more difficult.

THE INDUSTRIALIZATION PROCESS

When people are economically active, they produce the things needed to support life—food, clothing, shelter, entertainment, health care and so on. This production requires what economists call economic resources: the natural resources (plants, mineral ores, for example) that people turn into usable things with the help of tools, machines, and equipment (the economists' "capital"). "Technology" simply refers to the combinations, or recipes, in which these resources are used.

In the last two hundred years, technological change has typically involved the development of increasingly sophisticated machines which use fewer natural resources and less labor, and which have made workers more productive, able to produce more output than before. Whether this increase in output translates into a rising standard of living depends on the distribution of income (a partly political question not covered here) and the rate of population growth. If output increase is matched or exceeded by population increase, then output per head does not rise, and neither do living standards. Some economists call this extensive growth, and distinguish it from intensive growth, which occurs when the capacity to produce increases faster than population.[1]

Historically, many societies have experienced extensive growth; fewer have experienced intensive growth, and these typically only in the period since the Industrial Revolution. In fact, the point at which extensive growth turns into intensive growth—a process which can take a considerable period of time—is commonly referred to as an industrial revolution, but the turning point is not automatic.

Economic historians have shown that many preindustrial economies were very innovative in responding to various stimuli, such as population pressure or the demands of military leaders, but these alone were not enough to shift the economy to a higher growth path. This required not only innovations in production techniques, but other changes as well. The economies that successfully passed through a turning point period also experienced political change, such as the development of the nation-state, and have imposed internal order. Other economic changes, such as improvements in infrastructure and transportation which reduce transportation costs, increases in food output, and the stimulation of market-oriented manufacturing, then became easier. It is important that once an economy shifts to a higher growth path, barriers that could prevent continuing economic progress are removed, which requires competent government action. In general, it seems that creating a favorable environment for innovative economic activity is a more important requirement for economic development than anything else.

Characteristics of a Modern Industrial Economy

Historians are divided over whether the turning point, the economy's shift to a higher productivity, higher growth path, was revolutionary (a relatively abrupt discontinuity in economic progress) or evolutionary (showing innovative behavior over long period of time). But they disagree less over the characteristics distinguishing modern industrial economies from preindustrial ones. First, their output includes a larger proportion of manufactured goods and what might be called business services (banking and insurance services, for example, as distinguished from personal services, like household servants). Second, this characteristic is paralleled by a shift of the labor force out of agriculture and into nonagricultural occupations in industry, transportation and construction. Third is a characteristic already noted, the prevalence of high productivity activities, where the increase in productivity is made possible by the adoption of new technologies, such as the use of inanimate power sources like steam or electricity. Industry is significantly affected by this increase in productivity, and in general, both the capital-output and the capital-labor ratios rise.[2]

Fourth, more capital equipment is used, and installing new equipment is how the new technologies, which make the increase in productivity possible, are introduced. Fifth, there is an increased role for trade. A few very large countries, such as the United States, can rely on internal market growth; most others experience an export-led shift to intensive growth, because access to expanding export markets is necessary to justify the investment in a larger production capacity. Finally, urbanization often increases. Modern factory industry tends to locate in a limited number of areas where there are good transportation linkages, access to commercial or financial expertise and where other external economies[3] make certain locations more attractive than others.

An Economic Growth Model

Economists usually assume that the industrialization process does not involve persistent, long-term unemployment, although temporary labor market dislocation is likely, especially in the early stages of the shift out of agriculture into industry. If new skills are fairly easily learned or if skills acquired in one type of work can be fairly easily transferred to another, the process of reallocating labor can be accomplished relatively easily.

In a market economy, how do economic agents know what to do, and therefore how many resources will be allocated to each activity? In the idealized world of standard neoclassical economic theory, where factors can be substituted for each other and where there is a huge menu of technological choices, the answer depends on price signals. Relative factor prices influence the choice of technology. Typically, a country beginning to industrialize will be short of (expensive) capital but have a lot of (cheap) labor, which theoretically can be shifted out of agriculture without agricultural output falling. This is because if too many people work in farming, each has only low productivity; shift some out, and the remainder can work more efficiently so output per capita rises; if done correctly, there need be no loss of output. The relative prices reflecting this initial scarce capital/ample labor situation, according to this simple model, will be high interest rates and low wages, hence the appropriate technology for new industry should be a labor intensive one, using a lot of the resource the economy is relatively well endowed with.

The model then goes on to hypothesize that this use of labor intensive technology will absorb the (low-cost) labor no longer employed in agriculture, and permit the export of labor intensive products in which the economy has a comparative advantage. Over time, as the development effort succeeds, surplus labor disappears and capital accumulates. Relative prices change to reflect this new situation so that wages rise and interest rates fall, and tend to converge to resemble those in already-developed countries. The implication of this (oversimplified) growth theory is that all countries can develop; any differences between them are the result of different patterns of preferences. (Differences are also due to market imperfections or biased policy choices if pure market signals are not permitted to control the development process.)

The Underdevelopment Paradox

A quick survey of recent development efforts today fails to show either completely successful development efforts or convergence (see Boxes 1 and 2). Instead, underdevelopment persists, and the income gap between developed and developing countries seems to widen (see Box 3). Some economies are also characterized by economic dualism, where two independent sectors coexist, each featuring a different level of productivity. The most common example is the coexistence of a small, modernized, high productivity industrial sector, surrounded by (and with few linkages to) a large, technologically stagnant, low-productivity agricultural sector. The so-called traditional sector— agriculture and small scale-and artisan production of traditional consumption items— remains large partly because its employment levels remain high, while under-employment, a situation where

Box 1
Have Developing Countries Developed?
I Income Growth

Income or output (Gross Domestic Product, or GDP) per capita is a commonly used measure of economic well-being because, in a money using, market economy, it is an indication of each person's statistical share of output produced. So if this figure grows over time, it can be assumed that output has also grown, and, if people have a larger share of a larger output, then their living standards have gone up.

Surveying United Nations' statistics indicates that, yes, most countries have had a positive rate of economic growth in GDP per capita, but often at a painfully slow pace. Taking the ten very poorest countries and comparing their progress over the nine years 1983 to 1991 shows that their average income per capita (expressed in US$, adjusted for purchasing power parity) rose from $320 to $398, an annual average growth rate of 2.7 percent. (Eight countries were still on this list at the end of the period, and were joined by two countries which had a negative growth over the period.) Going to the other extreme, the ten highest income countries showed an average growth rate of 6 percent over the same period.

Admittedly, these are the two extremes; many countries between these two extremes demonstrated remarkably fast rates of growth. And a note of caution: making international comparisons is limited by a lack of accurate, comparable statistics (especially for lower income countries), and is complicated by different data collection systems. The income figures in these boxes are presented purely for illustrative purposes; a more thorough analysis is needed to reach scientifically verifiable conclusions. (Computed from Table 24, United Nations *Statistical Yearbook,* 1993.) See Box 2.

> **Box 2**
> **Have Developing Countries Developed?**
> **II Food Grain Consumption**
>
> Monetary measures are notoriously unreliable for low income, developing countries because a large part of economic activity does not take place for a market; therefore no monetary measures are available to value it. To deal with this problem, economists have developed other measures to estimate economic well-being. One important alternative is food grain consumption; the implication here is that even in a nonmarket economy where independent producers grow their own food, a rise in food grain consumption represents an improvement in living standards. Unfortunately, the evidence seems to indicate that low income developing countries are losing this battle, while middle income and high income countries are gaining.
>
> | | Kilograms per capita | | |
> | --- | --- | --- | --- |
> | | 1961–64 | 1970–73 | 1976–79 |
> | World total | 312.1 | 342.8 | 362.1 |
> | Developing countries | 223.0 | 229.7 | 239.9 |
> | —Low income | 207.1 | 202.7 | 202.4 |
> | —Middle income | 238.1 | 255.6 | 275.7 |
>
> Source: FAO, from Table 7.2, p. 102, World Bank *World Development Report 1981*.

workers really do not have enough to do, also helps account for the low productivity levels (see Box 4).

What accounts for dualism? There are several explanations. One is continuing high rates of population growth. A second is the use of modern technology which has been designed to fit the resource endowment of the high wage, developed countries—ample capital, scarce labor—but which is less appropriate to the developing countries. That is, the latest technology, which tends to be capital intensive and labor saving and appropriate to the resource endowment of the high wage countries, is transferred. There need not be mass technological unemployment (or its corollary, underemployment in the traditional sector) if production expands faster than labor is being released, so that it is easy to re-absorb displaced labor. But this depends on the extent of

> **Box 3**
> **Have Developing Countries Developed?**
> **III Income Gap**
>
> If the Gerschenkron thesis (that there are catch-up advantages for an initially backward economy) is correct, we would expect that more rapid growth by developing countries as they borrow technology narrows the income gap between rich and poor nations. But at least for those at the very top and at the very bottom of the world income scale, this is not true: the gap has widened in the most recent period of history.
>
> In 1983, ten high income industrialized countries (absolute level of GDP per capita, expressed in US$, ranged from $10,246 to $14,492) had an average GDP per capita of $11,633. This was thirty-six times larger than the average GDP per capita of $320 of the ten countries at the bottom of the income distribution. (The range was from $96 in Cambodia to $495 in Myanmar.) By 1991, the average high income country GDP per capita was $18,371, forty-six times the average low income of $398. (But note the caution at the end of Box 1. Statistical information derived from Table 24, United Nations *Statistical Yearbook* 1993. See also "Globalization and Economic Convergence," especially Table 29, "Position of Countries in World Income Distribution, 1965 and 1990," in *UNCTAD Trade and Development Report, 1997*, pp. 69–101.)

market expansion which an individual small country has little control over. So while it appears to make sense to import the latest technology, the result can be extensive unemployment or underemployment and persisting dualism, as the new technology pushes surplus labor into the traditional sector. Furthermore, because there is consequently little opportunity for wage increases, domestic market expansion for the output of the modern sector remains limited.

Even when these economies' industrial sectors grow at historically high rates, the labor-saving bias of imported technology implies that growing unemployment is very likely. This situation is compounded by another trend—the tendency for new technologies to generate economies of scale, which means that larger plants produce absolutely larger levels of output at much lower per-unit costs than smaller plants (hence reemphasizing the need for market expansion).

Box 4
Have Developing Countries Developed?
IV Unemployment Levels

Does development increase output, economic activity, and generate meaningful employment? An accurate estimate of employment and unemployment is the hardest of all the measures considered here, because of widely different country measures. National definitions of employment and unemployment differ from recommended international standard definitions, according to the United Nations (*Statistical Yearbook* 1993, p. 317), which makes intercountry comparisons very difficult. The measurement of underemployment is also difficult: if a person has a job or is self-employed, how can one determine that they do not have much to do? So these figures may perhaps be only indicative of a problem that needs more investigation; they are offered to give an idea of the diversity of experience (or statistical collection methods) of some high income and low income countries, for three years.

Unemployment Rate, %

	1983	1991	1995		1983	1991	1995
High Income				**Low Income**			
Australia	10.0	9.6	8.5	Algeria	—	21.0	23.8***
Belgium	11.9	7.0	9.3	Angola	19.0*	—	—
Canada	11.8	11.3	9.5	Jamaica	26.0	15.7**	15.9***
Japan	2.6	2.1	3.2	Pakistan	3.9	6.3	4.8****
Luxembourg	1.6	1.4	2.7****	Philippines	4.9	9.0	8.4
United States	9.5	6.6	5.6	Puerto Rico	23.4	16.6**	13.7
				Sri Lanka	—	18.5	12.5

*1986 **1990 ***1992 ****1994

Source: Table 31, UN *Statistical Yearbook* 1993; Table 32, UN *Statistical Yearbook* 1995.

As one development economist first noted in the early nineteen seventies, "the elasticity of industrial employment with respect to output has not only been low but apparently falling over time" (Ranis 1973, p. 387). The outcome? either increasing unemployment or pressure on the agricultural and services sector, and both will increase if technological improvements in agriculture and service industries also have a labor-saving, capital-using bias. These are quite likely: modern farming techniques are much more mechanized and use inputs, like fertilizers, from capital-intensive industries such as the chemical industry. In services, computer technology has transformed information-providing and paper-handling activities, while food preparation techniques in fast food restaurants permit more customers to be served by fewer people.[4]

Again, if total economic activity and output grow fast enough to absorb all the newly available supplies of labor, any unemployment is likely to be only temporary. But if this does not happen, the problem also becomes a sociopolitical as well as an economic one: the potential for instability increases as larger numbers of people have little real productive activity, and instead have too much idle time to reflect on their disadvantages.

POTENTIAL SOLUTIONS

Some remedies have been suggested, but are unlikely to solve the problem. Faster economic growth is not an answer, as it is too expensive and capital intensive, and anyway exacerbates the unemployment problem if demand is not growing fast enough. Although possible, a government-run program of public works to hire the unemployed is unlikely. Development economist Gustav Ranis thinks that the main problem is that available technological choices are limited, not unlimited, as the simplified theory described above implies, and therefore decision makers probably cannot find a technological mix that is complementary to the actual resource endowment. If the latest technology from the advanced countries is the only one that is relevant—because of the need to be competitive in the international marketplace—then only its factor proportions matter, but they are unlikely to be the most "suitable" for the developing country (Ranis 1973).

Some people believe that even advanced technologies can be adapted to suit a particular country's needs better. Unfortunately, the borrowing country may not be able to adapt: the ability to adapt and innovate depends on the skills and managerial and entrepreneurial ability available. Almost by definition, these skills are in short supply at the beginning of a development effort. And the need to adapt gets more difficult as the technology gap widens and the newest technologies become more sophisticated.

Intensive growth, which characterizes industrialization, involves capital deepening, a much more complicated process than simply providing units of homogenous labor with more units of homogenous capital. Ranis described it as follows: "As capital per head increases [capital deepening], this means that the typical worker has learned to cooperate with more units of capital of increasing technical complexity" (1973, p. 393). Adaptation is not simply a minor adjustment in one particular process. It is easy, but wrong, to think of production as a one-stage process in which raw materials go in at one end, and finished goods come out at the other. Reality is more complex. Production of most things involves many stages, surrounded by secondary and complementary processes dealing with related production, materials handling, goods distribution, warehousing, marketing, financing and so on, and how much labor these activities use should also be taken into account. There are two more complications: how innovative trends influence technological development; and the reality of competition in the international environment. David Felix (1974, 1977) has described the issues as follows. Technological innovation reflects past experience in the developed countries. Typically, capital accumulation occurs at a faster rate than labor force growth, so wages tend to rise, encouraging the mechanization of the production process. At the same time, the size of plant needed for efficient operation at lowest cost has grown. So historically, there has been the simultaneous development of economies of scale, a rising capital-labor ratio and lower unit labor and unit capital costs. Today firms often search for new technologies that will generate dynamic scale economies which need less labor and which will lower costs, because lower costs can be passed on in the form of lower prices as part of a strategy to increase (global) market share. If successful, large firms headquartered in the advanced countries continue to be dominant in the international economy. Their strategy also helps explain the widening income gap between countries and the difficulties facing industrializing countries today.

These countries face a dilemma. If the economic world is like the one described by traditional growth models, then they could develop by adopting labor-intensive technologies. But in the real modern world, where they must compete in an open international economy, such a strategy puts them at a disadvantage because older technologies are often less efficient (i.e., use more resources) than modern large-scale technologies, and therefore are less competitive.

Even lower wage rates will not help if productivity per worker is less with the older technologies. They could try other options such as encouraging activities using artisan techniques or industries with low capital-labor ratios, but there are increasingly fewer of these, and competitiveness is still a problem. Also it is unclear whether the market for the output of "traditional" goods made by these industries is growing: it has been eroded by the rapid spread of consumption patterns based on high-income, developed country habits.

Some politicians favor using protectionist and import substitution policies to protect domestic industry in the industrialization effort, but they are not a long-term solution. The rules of modern international trade discourage the use of tariffs and quotas to protect domestic companies, and import substitution policies can reinforce dualism. Hence given all these problems and unsatisfactory "solutions," it is easy to understand the appeal of adopting the latest technology: at least it seems to promise international competitiveness.

But here too there are difficulties. Scale-intensive plants can be operated efficiently only if producing a large output, which forces the company into the export market to make up for the small domestic market. However, the marketing expertise necessary to make such large scale export sales is probably not available domestically, forcing recourse to the services of foreign companies which have it; the potential cost is loss of control by domestic companies. A second difficulty is the high start-up costs large plants impose. A third difficulty arises with their large demands for supplementary activities, such as business and handling services, education and training, communications, and transportation, for example. These are all less likely to be well developed at the beginning of an industrialization effort, problems that become more difficult to solve the wider the technology gap.

FIRST GENERATION LATE INDUSTRIALIZERS

The first country to achieve industrialized status was Great Britain, which started the process of modern industrialization in the eighteenth century. If industrial status is achieved when the share of industry in output exceeds that of agriculture, and when there is a larger proportion of the labor force employed in industrial than in agricultural activities, then this status was achieved later by France, Germany, the United States and Japan.

Was it easier for countries in the nineteenth century to industrialize? Evidence seems to indicate that it was, mainly because the technological gap was smaller, modern factory technology was largely based on artisan techniques, and protectionism was used to protect domestic industry from international competition. As development economist David Felix remarked, protectionism worked then because it was "suited for building a skill and entrepreneurial base for private technological creativity when the base is still heavily artisanal, when the pace of the international demonstration effect is moderate, and the international product differentiation game non-existent" (1974, p. 232). That is, it worked in the conditions of the 1880s, which were very different from those of the 1980s.

Nineteenth century development was not problem free, of course. Countries did develop dual economic structures, but dualism tended to be moderate and self-liquidating, unlike twentieth-century dualism. In the twentieth century, the tendency of technological innovation to generate increasing returns makes dualism more persistent while at the same time, eliminating the potential for an innovative artisan or traditional sector. International competition squeezes out the traditional sector long before the modern factory sector can grow sufficiently to provide employment opportunities for displaced workers. In the nineteenth century, the industrial share of both employment and output grew together, mainly because traditional small enterprise was often dynamic enough to absorb labor released from agriculture, so although it eventually shrank, by that time the modern sector had expanded sufficiently to provide employment. In contrast, in the twentieth century, the share of employment lags behind the growth of output (Felix 1977, p. 199). Also traditional consumption patterns favoring output from the artisan sector persisted, providing an early example of product differentiation.

But in the twentieth century, demand for "traditional" goods has shrunk, for several reasons. The quality of factory-made products has improved, especially at the top end of the market, while economies of scale made them increasingly competitive in price. Western consumption patterns have spread rapidly throughout the world, no doubt helped by improvements in communications, the spread of western movies and television programs, and the efforts of sophisticated western mass marketing techniques. The result has been an accelerated shrinkage of demand for the output of traditional industries which became less important as a source of demand for labor.

To summarize the argument so far, a modern industrialization effort is more difficult to accomplish in the twentieth century. The technological gap between advanced and developing economies is wider, and introducing modern industry requires a higher level of supportive entrepreneurial, managerial and technical skills, plus associated complementary industries and infrastructure, to be competitive in a global economy. Consumption patterns in developing countries are more likely to resemble those in high-income countries, reducing the market for the output of indigenous traditional industries in favor of mass produced goods. The growth of a modern factory sector has involved the adoption of technologies that increase economies of scale and reduce labor needs per unit of output; expanding meaningful employment opportunities consequently becomes harder. But protecting domestic industry with tariffs or adopting other protectionist policies is either ruled out by international trade conventions or can provide only a short term solution. In addition, the so-called solutions may put pressure on financing requirements and on the balance of payments (issues which are important but which will not be discussed here).

LABOR-USING INDUSTRIALIZATION

During the first few decades of their initial industrialization, the first generation of late industrializers managed to avoid persistent unemployment and underemployment. I will now present the example of Japan to see if there are any easily identifiable factors that contributed to a successful industrialization effort. It is likely that successful growth needs the presence of both positive forces encouraging change and the absence of negative factors blocking growth. In other words, the removal of barriers to change is necessary, but must be done without in turn creating new rigidities to continuing development.

PREINDUSTRIAL JAPAN

Japan is a particularly good example to use as it was the first Asian country to industrialize—and it industrialized relatively rapidly—and until recently, it had a smaller unemployment problem than most western industrialized economies. Before 1868, Japan was a low-income, predominantly agricultural, closed economy, although much more urbanized compared with similar preindustrial economies. Since 1868, Japan rapidly transformed itself into a high income, high exporting industrial economy.

Preindustrial Japan had much in common with most western European feudal economies, with one major exception: Japan was isolated from the outside world from the middle of the seventeenth to the middle of the nineteenth centuries. Earlier, Japan fell within China's sphere of influence, but was one of the few Asian countries to successfully resist the Mongol invasions of the thirteenth century.

Some limited trading links were subsequently made by Portuguese, Spanish, Dutch and English traders, but these were broken for fear of European aggression and fear that Christianity would undermine traditional Japanese values. So in the seventeenth century, Japan effectively closed itself from the outside world. No ships capable of long voyages were built; no Japanese were permitted to travel abroad; and only very limited trade, mainly with China, was permitted through Dutch traders.

Civil unrest punctuated the early phase of the period of isolation, but peace was restored once the Tokugawa *shoguns* overcame resistance from the other feudal lords (*daimyo*). They imposed centralized control over Japan, established a period of peace for the next two centuries and gave their name to an era. Although there was an emperor, he remained a ceremonial, powerless figurehead at Kyoto; real power was concentrated in the hands of the *shoguns* who ruled from Edo (modern Tokyo). The *shoguns* got rid of potential opposition to their rule by requiring the *daimyo* (who numbered about 200) to spend alternate years at court in Edo; otherwise they lived in castle towns in their own regions. Because of the extended peace, neither the lords nor their warrior retainers (*samurai*) had any military functions to perform. The *daimyo* were responsible for local government, and provided a market for luxury goods made by urban artisans, but the *samurai* were essentially parasitic.

Population growth was modest throughout the Tokugawa period; 21 million were counted in 1721 and approximately 35 million in the 1860s. About 80 percent of the population were feudal peasants who, like their European counterparts, were tied to the land. They too were subject to various feudal restrictions and requirements—such as the type of crop that could be planted. The lord was entitled to at least 30 percent of their rice harvest, and dues to the samurai were also paid in rice. Taxes of this sort averaged about 50 percent of output, but could be higher.

Although some agricultural innovations were made during the Tokugawa era, such as improved irrigation techniques and greater use of fertilizer, agricultural productivity remained low and farms small. Probably more important as an example of change was the growth in independent commercial activities, often combined with farming, towards the end of the period. Examples include silk reeling and weaving; production of cotton fabrics, paper, mats, umbrellas and lacquerware. Other examples, which were more often located in towns, included brewing, whale processing and production of earthenware (Miyamoto et al. 1965, p. 545). The town merchants (*chonin*) were often involved in trading these items or arranging for their production in a manner similar to the European "putting out" system, by providing raw materials to workers who then worked on them at home. However, their main functions were to handle sales of the lords' rice and provide them with credit. Merchants often became rich, but never rose in social status.

MEIJI RESTORATION

The Japanese economic and social system was already beginning to disintegrate in the last half of the Tokugawa period. Commander Perry's gunboat diplomacy is usually credited with forcing open the Japanese economy in 1853, but even without it, some sort of change was likely, as strains on the social structure had intensified.

Previous population growth ended, partly as a result of several natural disasters—a plague in 1773, and famines in 1783–87 and 1832–36. The *Shogun* came under financial strain: tax revenues were lower as a result of the natural disasters, and because dishonest officials embezzled funds. The *daimyo* fell into debt to city merchants, who were also feeling pressure, a result both of increased taxes levied on them and of *daimyo* refusing to pay back loans. Poor harvests reduced the *samurais*' stipends, which were paid in rice. Many *samurai* could no longer maintain their previous lifestyles, so they simply abandoned their feudal loyalties, and either took jobs in cities or became bandits. There were some peasant revolts in protest against deteriorating conditions, and some of the most distant *daimyos* became more actively involved in resisting the *Shogun's* authority.

So perhaps it was no surprise that the intrusion of foreigners in Commander Perry's "black ships" helped push the system towards collapse, a breakdown reinforced by the imposition of unequal treaties on Japan in 1858 and 1866. These treaties gave extraterritorial, legal and trading rights to Americans (and later on to Europeans) and imposed restrictions on Japan's freedom of action in commerce and taxation. Japan was not permitted to impose any duties higher than 20 percent on imports, meaning that newly established Japanese companies could not be protected from competition from well-established foreign companies. The effect forced Japan out of isolation and into the status of a vulnerable economy open to the outside world.

Internal reaction to this humiliation helped stimulate what Reynolds (1993) would call a "significant political event," and which he thinks is vital for the transition from extensive to intensive growth. The *Shogun* had agreed to the treaties, but the Emperor refused to ratify them; he was supported by those *daimyo* who were already opposed to the *Shogun's* authority. A civil war broke out which ended in 1868 with the removal of the Tokugawa *Shogun* from power and the accession of the Emperor Meiji to the throne. Thus drastic internal changes in constitution and government paralleled the economic changes forced on Japan from outside.

Preparing for Industrialization

A period of significant institutional reform followed the Meiji Restoration, paving the way for later industrialization. Similar in intent to European mercantilist policies, these reforms both removed barriers to growth and helped establish a favorable environment for modern industrial activity. The most important ones involved building a modern infrastructure of railroads, postal and telegraph services, improving education, reforming the monetary system, and establishing a banking system. Because Japan had been isolated for so long, and because economic activity had been tightly controlled, the government had to take a dynamic role in forcing economic change. By the 1880s, government spending accounted for 40 percent of total capital formation, although many of the early government-established "modern factories" and productive facilities were later sold off.

These early years were difficult ones. Peasants suffered most from the reforms, particularly because the burden of new money taxes fell on them. Many sold their land and became tenant farmers—the proportion of farm land held by tenants rose to 46 percent by 1913—but most farms remained extremely small. Japan's handicraft industries of paper, sugar and cotton were devastated by import competition, and early enthusiasm for westernization flooded the country with western products. Japan's major exports of raw silk and tea did not earn enough to offset these imports, so the balance of payments was usually in deficit between 1868 and 1914. However, foreign trade also produced benefits. Imports of foreign technology and capital goods helped build up domestic manufacturing ability. Soon exports of finished textiles became more important than exports of primary products, and because so few people in Japan could afford to buy imported goods, the balance of payments problem eased.

There were significant changes before 1905. The share of agriculture in the labor force fell to two-thirds, while the share of manufacturing and construction rose to nearly one-fifth, and commerce and transportation, employment categories that typically grow as the economy becomes more industrialized and diversified, also expanded. Between 1868 and 1905, real national income doubled while population increased by only 25 percent.

Industrial Adaptation

Japan industrialized in order to counter the perceived threat of western domination, and because, unlike Europe, it had little experience with preindustrial development, it borrowed already-existing industrial technology. However, as familiarity with modern industrial technology grew, an extensive process to modify and adapt it to suit Japanese conditions, especially the availability of ample supplies of cheap labor, took place.

This is most obvious with the cotton textile industry, which became Japan's single most important manufactured export by 1913. The industry began its modern development in the 1880s. All the new mills established at this time were exact copies of Lancashire mills, with machinery imported from a single supplier. Almost all the capacity in the cotton textile industry was controlled by the industry cartel, which operated a market sharing scheme with its members. Although cartelization is considered to be a restrictive practice under Anglo-American law, its effect in Japan was to minimize information and start-up costs, and to keep all member firms on the best practice frontier. The cartel kept up to date with foreign practices and encouraged cooperation on technical questions; the result was that all firms knew about the most efficient practices. Domestic industry could not be protected by import barriers (a major provision of the unequal treaties), giving an incentive to adapt the most advanced technology available to Japanese conditions in order to meet global competition head on. Some people thought that using older, more labor intensive techniques was more appropriate for a labor surplus, capital short economy, but the requirements of international competitiveness indicated otherwise.

Although imported textile technology at that time was more capital intensive than indigenous Japanese textile technology, it actually utilized more labor than in English mills. For example, capital stretching in Japan meant operating a three-shift system, so that more labor worked with the same capital equipment. In spinning, each operative minded fewer spindles than in England, again increasing labor requirements for each unit of capital. Also, cheaper Indian cotton was used which broke more often than higher-grade cotton, so more labor was needed to join the broken threads.

Labor-using Processes

Similar modifications were apparent in other areas. For example, people rather than mechanized belts were used to move materials and goods. In railroads, nineteen Japanese workers were employed per mile of track compared with only seven in the United States. The continuing use of older technologies, especially in cottage industry or small scale production for sale undertaken within the household and often combined with farming, saved capital. The construction of factory buildings and other industrial plants typically accounts for at least half of the total investment in fixed capital; because cottage industry used household labor, there was no need to construct new industrial buildings, which released resources for other purposes. Small-scale activity was important for the production of many traditional Japanese items, such as mats, umbrellas and traditional clothing, as well as the early stages of the silk industry (raising silk worms, silk reeling).

In 1878, cottage industry accounted for two-thirds of industrial output, but the proportion fell as development continued. However, it was important for two reasons. It absorbed labor that would otherwise be unemployed if factory industry was the sole source of industrial employment. It also helped develop a skill base on which to build future industrial expansion:

> By scattering familiar but improving machinery over large numbers of scattered miniplants, large amounts of unskilled labor could be deployed in both direct production and in satisfying the resulting increased demand for transportation and handling activities. In this fashion, Japanese entrepreneurs were able to, first, incorporate pure labor services and, later, domestic ingenuity and skills into the industrial production process, largely for export. (Ranis 1973, p. 402)

Labor absorption in this early phase of Japanese development was also helped by the persistence of traditional patterns of consumption, a sharp contrast to the rapid adoption of western consumption patterns noted in many low-income developing countries today. Early in the industrialization process, the government tried to limit imports of western consumer goods, which, combined with the persistence of the traditional small family farm, helped maintain traditional lifestyles. Even as late as 1955, approximately one-half of consumer expenditures in Japan were for indigenous commodities, produced by traditional, usually small scale, industries (Rosovsky and Ohkawa 1961, pp. 488–89). Also Japanese housing is modest, permitting greater construction industry efforts in industrial and commercial building.

JAPAN'S ECONOMY

By 1914, the first stage of industrialization was complete. The share of manufacturing in national output had risen from about one-fifth in the 1880s to about one third. The reserve army of labor had been absorbed, but industrialization had taken place without a western style agricultural revolution. Although agriculture accounted for a smaller share in total output and employment, this was due more to a shift to higher productivity occupations: the absolute level of farm output did not decline. The average farm size was small and there was little evidence of a consolidation of scattered farms or of a mass exodus of newly landless peasants.

It seems rather that the continuing importance of the rural sector provided for incremental increases in the industrial labor force and in traditional goods for domestic consumption. This is indicated in the economic statistics. The primary sector accounted for 64 percent of national income and for 76 percent of the labor force in 1878–82, and for 36 percent and 59 percent respectively in 1913–17 (Ohkawa and Rosovsky 1960, p. 63). This labor force proportion of 59 percent seems high, but it should be remembered that farm work was often combined with traditional industry. A better distinction would be between agriculture combined with handicrafts and small scale traditional production on the one hand, and modern factory production on the other (Taeuber 1960, p. 17).

Although this section has covered only the initial phases of Japan's industrialization, it illustrates a development pattern that is modern but still distinctively Japanese. It shows that an industrialization effort can adapt modern industrial technology to take advantage of the initial resource endowment of capital scarcity and ample labor, while the continued strength of the agricultural sector and traditional industries contributed to the persistence of traditional consumption patterns. This combination helped modify the adverse social impact associated with much of European industrialization: landless Japanese farmers did not emigrate or provide a large mass of unemployed workers. Once modern factory industry was well established, even though new technologies were capital using and labor saving, the continued growth and dynamism of the economy continued to provide sufficient employment opportunities until relatively recently.

CAN LATE DEVELOPERS REPEAT JAPAN'S EXPERIENCE?

On paper, it seems that a newly industrializing country should find it easy to catch up to the already-industrialized ones. Arithmetically, all it needs is a faster rate of growth, which is easier to achieve when the industrial base is small, and easier in industry than in agriculture. In a nutshell, this is the Gerschenkron Thesis, which holds that there are advantages in starting late: mistakes can be avoided by using existing technological knowledge, and it is less costly to borrow knowledge than to discover it.

Unfortunately, this argument has two flaws. First, it overemphasizes the arithmetic at the expense of the cultural and structural changes that are also necessary for a successful development effort. Second, it ignores the reality that technological innovations have tended to increase the potential for economies of scale. In an international economy, the choice of technology is not in fact very large. If the latest, most sophisticated technology dramatically lowers per unit costs, international competitiveness dictates the adoption of the latest, best practice technology. But trying to adapt these technologies, as Japan did at an equivalent stage of its industrialization, gets harder the more sophisticated they are.

In the nineteenth century, technological advances were rooted in and often generated from the artisan experience, and the borrowing country's ability to adapt them to local conditions was within reach of local artisans' experience. In Japan, moreover, the government played a strategic, and encouraging, role in this process. The state helped "overcome the initial obstacles to industrialization . . . by providing external economies, breaking bottlenecks, and solving the problem of 'lumpiness' or the need for investment in unprecedentedly large lumps . . . " (Miyamoto et al. 1965, p. 567). What was also important was that local skills were involved in the industrialization process from the start. This contrasts with, for example, Latin America or imperial Russia or many developing countries today, where foreign entrepreneurs were relied on to get the development process going, making it more difficult to achieve a truly internally self-generated development effort. In Japan, on the other hand, once some of the initial hurdles had been overcome, the government withdrew from direct involvement and found other ways to encourage the industrialization effort, leaving local entrepreneurs to continue.

A successful, adaptive industrialization strategy is much more difficult now. On the production side, the emergence of and need to exploit dynamic scale economies has removed the opportunities for adaptation by local artisans, and have also increased the financial requirements and managerial skills necessary to administer large scale operations. On the consumption side, the continuing globalization of consumer markets has two effects. One is the international demonstration effect, the copying of high income country habits, often in response to the internationalization of culture. If this effect is strong, then the traditional sector in the developing country will shrink much faster because consumer preferences shift toward the output of modern factory industry. As noted above, this process was much slower in Japan. Traditional consumer preferences were retained and the traditional sector continued to produce, providing a continuing, although eventually declining, demand for labor, while also encouraging innovative activity.

The second effect emerges because the domestic market is small. If the country hopes to industrialize using modern technology, local markets are too small to justify large-scale, cost-efficient production, implying a move into export markets to provide the necessary demand that will. But a country at the beginning of a development drive does not have either the production or the marketing expertise to sell effectively in international markets. An effective marketing effort requires using foreign companies' expertise, an option that does little to help the domestic development effort and which is likely to increase the tendency towards dualism. What has often happened is that a foreign company is attracted to the low wage country by the promise of tax breaks, free trade zones and the like. It establishes a low cost production enclave as a base for exporting to overseas markets. Foreign multinationals make only limited adjustments to local conditions and needs. They tend to transfer a (capital intensive) technology intact to the enclave, but retain the growth-enhancing design and creative functions for the home country (Felix 1977, p. 86). So although it appears as if the developing country has modern industry, there are few contacts between it and the rest of the economy; fewer opportunities, therefore, for knowledge to be disseminated and adapted.

Special Factors

Interestingly enough, although many developing countries today seem anxious to attract foreign direct investment, Japan was not, and took advantage of a loophole in the unequal treaties. Although they opened Japan to the international marketplace, they did not protect foreign rights to direct investment in Japan by companies wishing to establish production facilities. Consequently non-Japanese companies were kept out, and the Japanese retained control over production. The role that multinationals typically play now in developing economies by taking on risks and in meeting large finance capital needs was done by the *zaibatsu,* integrated commercial and financial groups that came to dominate the Japanese economy after the First World War.

Some other special factors which do not exist in the twentieth century also worked in Japan's favor. When Japan began to industrialize, international trade was expanding, which made it easier to initiate an export-led industrialization strategy. But isolationism dominated the interwar period, and although trade expanded again after 1945 amid greater consciousness of the need to retain an open trading environment, it has not been as encouraging for developing countries. One reason is that the greatest expansion of trade has been in industrial goods and between industrialized countries, which reinforces all the problems an inexperienced, new industrializer has to face in order to compete.

If the late developer attempts to earn foreign exchange by exporting primary products, it faces competition from synthetic substitutes, produced by the already-industrialized. In any event, demand increases only slowly for such products. Technological innovations have reduced wastage of raw materials used in industrial processes, and in general, the income elasticity of demand for primary products is lower than for manufactured goods, meaning that their sales do not increase as fast as incomes increase.

Japan was also lucky here. Its major foreign exchange earner in the late nineteenth and early twentieth centuries was silk (first raw silk, then an increasing amount of processed silk). Japanese exports expanded because European silk producers were devastated in the 1860s and 1870s when a disease killed off silkworms. Such occasional events do not happen often. If they do, it is important to use the gains to diversify the economy, as Japan did, so that the gains can become long-term ones. A recent experience where this did not happen concerns the rapid run-up of the revenues of the oil exporting countries in the 1970s. Few of them, whether in the Middle East, West Africa or Latin America, used this windfall to develop a diversified economy.

A final special factor concerns population growth; living standards can only rise if output increases at a faster rate than population. Population growth in Japan was modest as compared with rates in developing countries today. This means that the pressure for extremely rapid economic growth sufficient to raise living standards is intensified.

SUMMARY

In conclusion, economic development that raises living standards is much harder today for newly industrializing economies. A variety of factors—the development of dynamic economies of scale in production technologies, the internationalization of consumer markets and the adoption of western consumer preferences, and more rapid population growth—make it difficult to avoid technological dualism and mass unemployment or underemployment. In the nineteenth century, when these pressures were either less or absent entirely, a flourishing traditional, small-scale or artisan sector provided both employment and a source of indigenous skills and innovators. But now, such sectors shrink rapidly or stagnate in the face of modern competitive pressures.

The solution does not lie in protectionism, to insulate domestic producers from the outside world because it rarely encourages innovative behavior. It is impossible to duplicate past successes, because the environment today is so different. But lessons can be learned from experience. For example, it has been suggested that the success of the Asian Tigers (Taiwan, South Korea, Singapore especially) owes much to government intervention to direct research efforts, control trade and hold down domestic consumption, in ways similar to Japanese efforts at a similar stage of development. Perhaps the most relevant insight is that policies encouraging development are outward-looking ones which also encourage local technological creativity and adaptability in the production process. The focus should be shifted away from trying to attract foreign capital and technology, whatever the cost, because the cost in terms of dependency and dualism is probably too high. Instead, they should consider the importance of building up human capital through education, better nutrition and health care; support local design capability and technical expertise to encourage the adaptation of modern technology; control the impact of the international demonstration effect; and, in general, aim to promote a sense of pride in local production and achievements.

NOTES

1. See Reynolds (1993) for a discussion of this.
2. The capital-output ratio measures the amount of "capital" needed to

Technological Change: The Example of Japan 227

produce one unit of output; it typically rises during industrialization as production becomes more mechanized. The capital-labor ratio measures the relative proportions of equipment and people; it too rises as machinery is substituted for labor, and as workers have more and better equipment to work with.

3. An external economy exists when an improvement in one industry results in falling costs for another. For example, if a company providing transportation services replaces (slower) sailing ships with, for example, (faster) steampowered ships, then all companies using these shipping services will find their costs of transportation falling as less time is taken moving goods.

4. For the mathematically inclined, the argument can be expressed in simple mathematics. Let Y = output, L = labor, and t = time. Then Y/L = productivity (output per capita) = y, $\Delta y/\Delta t$ = rate of productivity growth; $\Delta Y/\Delta t = (\Delta y/\Delta t) + (\Delta L/\Delta t)$; i.e., output growth must keep pace with both productivity improvements and labor force growth. Demand must also be considered because output has to be sold. If demand for output does not increase as fast as productivity, it is easy to see that this will have a depressing impact on the demand for labor.

Part IV
Conclusion

INTRODUCTION

As John Komlos points out in the concluding chapter of this collection, the Industrial Revolution continues to be one of the most intriguing topics for historians. It is a watershed in human existence for many reasons. Probably its most significant aspect is the complex of developments making up the Industrial Revolution that permitted human societies to break through the Malthusian ceiling, which had previously checked the growth of human population. That is, although we can identify previous periods of growth in both population and in economic activity, they always came to an end. Only since the Industrial Revolution has expansion seemingly become the characteristic of modern societies.

What is important to remember, Komlos tells us, is that the Industrial Revolution is more than just a technological shift; many other social, economic, and institutional aspects were also undergoing improvement. These improvements were also experienced in many different areas of Europe, not just Britain. Hence Komlos provides a valuable contribution to the "reconceptualization" of the Industrial Revolution, which gives a much more nuanced view of the processes of change. Especially useful will be the discussion of the antecedents of eighteenth-century growth; the roots of the Industrial Revolution are to be found in the accomplishments of prior centuries.

12
THE INDUSTRIAL REVOLUTION IN COMPARATIVE PERSPECTIVE
John Komlos

It gives me considerable pleasure to contribute to this anthology written by participants in the summer seminar for college teachers that I organized in 1995 on the "Industrial Revolution in Comparative Perspective," sponsored by the National Endowment for the Humanities (NEH). I think it is appropriate that Krieger Publishing decided to undertake this publication not only because of the scholarship it represents, but also because it is symbolic of the value of the summer program and its contribution to American higher education. In a sense, this book can surely be interpreted as a return on taxpayers' investment. Yet, society's gain is much greater than that. From my European perspective, the small private liberal arts colleges and satellite state university campuses, which provided the home bases of most of the contributors, are part of the strength of the American educational system.

Everyone is all well aware of the importance of education in the modern world. As the globe shrinks, its importance will surely increase, not only in the realm of technology, but also in the sense that it fosters the ability of different cultures to coexist and communicate with one another peacefully. However, we need to appreciate not only the famous research institutes, not only the universities whose faculty receive Nobel prizes, but also the thousands of less well-known colleges and universities with dedicated faculties striving conscientiously to provide a solid educational experience for their students. Their faculties are doing the footwork that provides the very backbone of our democratic society. In addition to providing opportunities for personal advancement for which America is still known, the education at these institutions enables the average citizen to put the greater issues of life in a larger historical and philosophical context.

They provide vision to the local élites that run America in the counties and municipalities. These are the people who interpret the laws and regulations. These future citizens are given a moral and intellectual foundation upon which to draw when faced with the difficult problems that confront all of us sooner or later. Those small decisions are actually the ones which define the sensibility of a society. They provide political order and stability; deliver justice; define the context of change; and generate the atmosphere which makes America a welcoming place. Without these academic institutions America would be a less humane, less democratic and less just place to live. I find that the European societies are worse off for not having similar nurturing institutions. Their political élites are thinner, and their institutions less humane, as a consequence. The NEH summer funding to get away from academic routine gives these teacher-scholars a well-deserved opportunity to refresh their spirits, rethink their intellectual bearings and return to their home institutions better equipped to provide the moral foundations for the next generation. Hence, I do believe that it is incumbent upon American society to celebrate these educators for their contribution to the general welfare. I was, therefore, glad to have had the opportunity to be able to organize a summer seminar on the Industrial Revolution.

THE INDUSTRIAL REVOLUTION

The Industrial Revolution has probably fascinated more historians than any other topic in human history.[1] It is one of the most momentous developments in the history of civilization, one which had an impact on virtually all aspects of human experience, and on all segments of society (Hartwell 1969, pp. 1–30, especially p. 3). It changed the very basis of human existence, from how long we live, to how we experience our family lives, and how we determine our political system. It penetrated every nook and cranny of our daily lives. In short, the processes unleashed by the Industrial Revolution are crucial to understanding the social, political, and economic forces that shaped the modern world. Yet, in spite of the immense outpouring of literature on the topic, there is much confusion regarding appropriate conceptualizations, particularly at the undergraduate level. This volume should help undergraduates gain a deeper understanding of the complexities of change, and to think of the Industrial Revolution as a multidimensional pan-European process with deep roots in the past.

The Industrial Revolution might be defined as the immense expansion in economic activity that began in the middle of the eighteenth century and has lasted with temporary interruptions into our own day.[2] The European economy had been growing for a millenium prior to the eighteenth century, even if growth was both slow and intermittent (Jones 1988, p. 13). Upswings were followed by centuries of reversals, even stagnation. Yet, progress was being made, even in per capita terms, but it was hardly noticeable to successive generations, and it was confined to a small segment of the population. Change was at a glacial pace.

The expansion during the Roman Empire was followed by the decline and stagnation of the Dark Ages. The boom of the High Middle Ages fizzled out with the coming of the plague in the fourteenth century, and the concomitant end to population growth. The Commercial Revolution was overtaken by the crisis of the seventeenth century. In short, economic expansions were temporary: European societies frequently faced the threat of subsistence crisis (Mokyr 1985). Growth was constrained by the availability of food, as well as by recurring epidemics. Hence, the acceleration in the growth of output after 1750 was hardly unique. There were similar episodes in the past, even if they were less powerful, and less well documented.

The economic expansion of the 1750s built upon former achievements. The major difference between the Industrial Revolution and earlier economic and demographic expansions was that the forces of growth, fueled by technological change, by capital accumulation, and by myriad other improvements, including institutional change, ultimately won over the forces of stagnation. The earlier constraints were no longer binding. In other words, the European societies were sufficiently advanced, and grew sufficiently quickly, to overcome the negative forces associated with an acceleration in population growth that had been a brake in prior centuries. This was the case even as an increasing share of the labor force was detached from the land. Neither the availability of food, nor the threat of epidemics posed insurmountable challenges as they did in earlier centuries. The minimum biological needs of a growing population were maintained even if the biological standard of living deteriorated in the short run. Although the Malthusian threat of increasing pauperization was in widespread evidence, the threat was ultimately overcome, and intensive growth remained a permanent feature of the European economies.

The mainstream view of the 1960s was that the Industrial Revolution began in England (Deane 1969; Pollard 1981). The weakness of this paradigm is that there were other regions the size of England and even states, such as the Kingdom of Saxony, which had as large a share of Gross National Product (GNP) originating in the industrial sector. Another problem with this position is that it places excessive value on industrial production, and not enough on services. It also overlooks the fact that the Netherlands had a higher per capita income than Britain until the very end of the eighteenth century (Maddison 1991, p. 31).

Thus, the countries on the continent were seen as following in Britain's footsteps. The kernel of this notion is that improvements in cotton spinning and weaving technology were the essence of the Industrial Revolution. Its weakness is that it emphasizes excessively the few industries in which Britain was, indeed, an unquestioned leader, but it does not acknowledge sufficiently the large number of continental achievements. Britain was not more advanced than other countries in a large number of branches, from needle to knife to glass production.

In fact, in most minds the Industrial Revolution is practically synonymous with the technological changes of the eighteenth century: "the technological changes that we denote as the 'Industrial Revolution' implied a far more drastic break with the past than anything since the invention of the wheel" (Landes 1969, p. 42). In this view the mechanization of spinning and weaving, particularly of cotton, improvements in the steam engine, and the development of iron puddling, all British achievements, signaled the beginning of the Industrial Revolution. This argument does not acknowledge sufficiently the precursors of the great technological breakthroughs of the second half of the eighteenth century. Mechanization had, in fact, been a part of economic life for centuries prior to 1750 (Cipolla 1980, p. 168). Examples abound: thousands of water-driven machines had provided an inanimate source of power since the Middle Ages. The Domesday survey of 1066 documented 6,000 water mills in operation in Great Britain. The discovery of the spinning wheel in 1530 increased labor productivity manifold. Steam engines had been operating in mines since 1712. These are just a few examples to argue that the innovations of the eighteenth century took place in a civilization that was technologically and scientifically already advanced, and that sophistication was by no means confined to the British Isles.

The proponents of British technological superiority also fail to give proper credit to the numerous improvements in other spheres of the economy, such as the financial sector, which also increased productivity. The significance of the increased use of paper money, just to name one example, can be easily overlooked. In a similar vein, improvements in public sanitation were important in guarding against epidemics. There were also advances in the definition of property rights, such as the development of patent laws. In other words, practically all aspects of the society and economy were improving and helping to shift the production function outward. To accentuate improvements in physical technology without giving proper emphasis to the other improvements is misleading.

Some historians have argued that the spread of factories was one of the major causes of the Industrial Revolution. The change in industrial organization enabled entrepreneurs to benefit from economies of scale and also enabled the new large-sized machines to be put into operation. Hence, this emphasis complements the view that equates the Industrial Revolution with technological change.

Although it is unquestionable that mass production was becoming more prominent during the second half of the eighteenth century, the most important problem with conceiving of the Industrial Revolution as a transition to factory production is that "factories" predate the Industrial Revolution. Medieval silk filiatures bore similarities to their eighteenth-century counterparts producing cotton yarn. In addition, "it is unreasonable to exclude from the factory sector ironworks, copper-smelters, chemical works, engineering shops," inasmuch as these were often large establishments even before the classical factory age (Crouzet 1985, p. 8). Huge iron combines (or multiplant firms) had already come into existence in the early seventeenth century, and many large preindustrial enterprises, such as bleacheries, dye works, glass works, blast furnaces, paper works, and textile printing firms employed hundreds, often thousands, of workers. All used some machines in the process of production. In short, mechanized large-scale production was not an invention of the Industrial Revolution.

The discontinuous nature of the Industrial Revolution has also been emphasized. If mechanization and changes in industrial organization were unique developments in the eighteenth century, and if technological change proceeded abruptly during the second half of the eighteenth century, then the processes of growth represented a distinct break with the past. In the 1950s and 1960s scholars adopted such metaphors as "take off" and "great spurt" to describe the beginning of the process (Gerschenkron 1962, 1970). One of the weaknesses of this position is that it compares the processes and rates of change during the Industrial Revolution with the half century just preceding it. Those were years of relative stagnation, so that the growth of the economy after the 1760s does appear discontinuous. However, the upswing phase of a business cycle always looks impressive if compared to the trough just preceding it. In order to make a balanced judgment of the intensity of the upswing one needs to compare it to the previous boom phase of the cycle, and for this reason it is important to compare the upswing of the late eighteenth century to the upswing of the late sixteenth century, the previous time during which the European economies were expanding rapidly.

RECONCEPTUALIZING THE INDUSTRIAL REVOLUTION

Against the backdrop of these mainstream views economic historians developed an alternate set of positions which constitute a paradigm switch for the conceptualization of the Industrial Revolution. The mainstream consensus view of the 1970s began to fragment with Nick Crafts's and Knick Harley's iconoclastic essays of the late 1970s and early 1980s. They demonstrated convincingly that the rate of growth of British industry was overestimated by the first generation of quantifiers of the 1950s and 1960s.[3] Instead of growing at a rate well in excess of 3 percent per annum during the closing decades of the century, the new estimates put the growth of industrial product closer to 2 percent per annum (Hoffmann 1955; Deane and Cole 1962). On a per capita basis the revised estimates of GNP growth are even more striking: in the range of 0.5–1.0 percent per annum, practically halving the previously obtained results. In spite of the fact that the economy grew more slowly than hitherto suspected, there is general agreement that technological change and capital accumulation increased sufficiently rapidly not only to outpace population growth, but to overcome diminishing returns to labor at the same time. In a historical context that was hardly a trivial achievement.

Historians also agree that there was a "germinal" modern sector alongside a traditional sector in Britain, and the two coexisted for a long time. There is also consensus that the growth rate of per capita output accelerated in the 1780s and again after the Napoleonic Wars. Yet, it is crucial to the understanding of the Industrial Revolution that "mechanization in early nineteenth-century Britain was a complex and uneven process; large parts of the country and many sectors of the economy were changing slowly, and even in the most rapidly transforming areas there were many surviving legacies. The amount of craft and small-scale industry was high and still expanding" (Berg 1980, p. 29). The pace of transformation in the aggregate required much longer than the use of the word "revolution" normally connotes. Thus, the emphasis on the developments in the cotton textile sector is misleading. Old technologies and traditional modes of organization did persist, and the production of a large number of products was not mechanized even by the end of the classical phase of the Industrial Revolution in the 1830s. Hosiery production, clothing, leather trades, coach making, construction, food production, and scores of others were using traditional methods well into the century.

Some historians conclude from this that the Industrial Revolution is, therefore, essentially a "misnomer" (Cameron 1982, pp. 377–84). If, however, one takes a longer view of the processes of change, say measured on a scale calibrated in centuries, then the metaphor becomes much more appropriate. After all, the structural shift experienced around the globe during the last two centuries from agriculture into industry and services was surely unprecedented in its intensity and speed. Provided one emphasizes the importance of the antecedents of the upswing, as well as the persistence of both the traditional sectors, and of traditional modes of production in the economy well into the next century, one can obtain a balanced perspective on the processes of change.

The new research on the Industrial Revolution also emphasizes that its origins are sought in the eighteenth century in vain (Kisch 1981, p. 61, 64). Instead, its roots are to be found in the long-run continuity of economic processes, and in the accomplishments of prior centuries (Cipolla 1970; Jones 1981; Komlos 1989b, pp. 191–206; North 1981, p. 162). "Ordinarily we believe that growth won only once, in the 'industrial revolution.'" asserts Eric Jones, but we fail to appreciate the extent to which "the pressure for growth was there all the time" (Jones 1988, p. 1, 6). From this vantage point, economic growth becomes a typical component of human experience, and the absence of growth atypical. Indeed, the recognition that western Europe in the eighteenth century was wealthy even by today's standards, and that the economies were already complex, with widespread specialization, implies that intensive growth, even if slow and intermittent, must have been going on for a long time prior to 1760.

Europe was much more advanced, more industrialized and more urbanized by 1750 than at any time earlier. Even during the course of the crisis-torn seventeenth century, urban population increased by some 25 percent.[4] On the eve of the Industrial Revolution, western Europe was already capable of sustaining an urban population of nine million, 10 percent of the total (de Vries 1984, p. 30, 39). The urban share of the population had roughly doubled since the beginning of the previous upswing in the 1500s. Towns incorporate more social overhead capital (infrastructure) than villages, and this fact is indicative of the broad level of wealth amassed by the beginning of the Industrial Revolution. Transportation facilities and technologies were much improved over the centuries, bringing down the cost of moving goods across short and long distances. The decline in transport costs was an inducement to trade, to spatial mobility of labor, to shifts out of the primary sector, and to the division of labor within industry. By the 1760s, the division of labor in the production of such varied products as pins, toys, and pottery "had reached such complexity . . . as to permit reductions in cost of staggering proportions."[5]

By the dawn of the century that was to witness the beginning of the greatest upswing in economic activity in recorded history, only 40 percent of England's national product originated in the agricultural sector, a share that Hungary did not reach until the twentieth century.[6] In England improvements in river navigation by private companies during the century prior to 1750 doubled the navigable waterways.[7] The length of turnpikes also increased markedly. Mines in the early seventeenth century used wooden railways, suction pumps, and water-driven bellows; forge hammers and stampmills were part of the sophisticated technologies in use. By the first days of the eighteenth century, copper, tin, and lead were smelted in reverberatory furnaces using coke as fuel, preparing the way for their adoption in the iron industry (Hammersley 1991, pp. 155–74). Darby's invention of iron smelting with coke in 1709 paved the way to the adoption of this technology later on in the century. Coal was widely used in a number of industrial applications requiring heat.[8]

In other words, the Industrial Revolution was preceded by a "quiet revolution" in many European economies. It did not create modern industry; it did not bring about industrialization; rather, it was a continuation of the processes of development, and built upon the staggering achievements of earlier centuries. All three major inventions of the Industrial Revolution were extensions of existing technologies. They were not independent breakthroughs. Watt's engine was an improvement of Newcomen and Savery's design. Hargreaves's hand-operated spinning wheel, and Arkwright's waterpowered version, were adaptions of earlier patents along similar principles, and emulated technologies successfully employed in the silk industry.

AN EVOLUTIONARY PROCESS

The innovators of the Industrial Revolution continued a tradition that had deep roots in the culture of early modern Europe. In the wake of the Scientific Revolution, ordinary people assimilated a worldview that was becoming more rational and secular. With the role of magic receding, attitudes were more materialistic and calculating. People could reason logically in conducting experiments with industrial technology, thereby amassing practical experience and know-how.

Herbert Kisch's regional studies of industrialization support the evolutionary perspective. He showed how far advanced German industry was in the eighteenth century, and he argued against the notion that the Industrial Revolution could be equated with a few innovations in the textile sector. He concluded that German economic historians have "failed to appreciate the achievements" of the industrial enclaves in the Rhineland, Saxony, and Silesia.[9] The argument is relevant to many other regions of Europe as well. The upswing of the 1770s and 1780s was very widespread. It is, therefore, misguided to seek the "causes" of the Industrial Revolution in the eighteenth century. It grew out of earlier achievements.

Technological change might have been the most impressive single aspect of these achievements, but the widespread nature of the efforts to improve the human lot is just as noteworthy. From agriculture to public health and to financial services, the emphasis was on doing things more efficiently. Moreover, neither invention nor innovation was confined to the major breakthroughs that have come to symbolize the birth of the industrial age. For that reason the "leading sector" model of the Industrial Revolution, according to which growth first accelerated in cotton textile production, and then spread to other sectors of the economy, is not the best way to conceptualize the actual processes of change. Prior and parallel achievements in other processes, important in their own right, as well as the widespread nature of the expansion, are implicitly undervalued in that view. From the very beginning, the Industrial Revolution encompassed a large palate of technologies and branches of industry. Practically everything produced was involved even if change took place in small ways.

Contrary to popular belief, machines were in widespread use in all industries even before the adoption of the spinning jenny. The linen mills in Scotland after 1729 "were equipped with machines for breaking and scutching flax" (Crouzet 1985, p. 28). The "first modern British textile factory" was a large water-powered silk throwing mill put into operation in Derby in 1721 (Crouzet 1985, p. 29). These improvements were perhaps not the types of breakthroughs that captured the imagination, but there were enough of them that taken together their contribution must have been considerable.

Furthermore, the technological "marvels" of the eighteenth century initially found limited application, even within England. Economic growth had become a permanent feature of European experience even before these technologies contributed significantly to labor productivity. Moreover, productivity could be increased through many other means, not only through the introduction of new techniques. Smith's example of the gains in efficiency brought about by the division of labor in a pin factory is part of the folklore of economics. Less well appreciated, however, is that such gains occurred at the same time in a large number of other branches.

To be sure, without technological change it would have been enormously difficult to maintain the momentum of the upswing in face of the capital-diluting effect of population growth; as a consequence, the process of expansion eventually might very well have been halted, as it was in the sixteenth century. Yet, we should not focus on the cotton textile sector. Moreover, it is important to note that technological change of the eighteenth century was not unique. Throughout its existence, the human species has left an impressive archeological and historical record of the desire to improve its material condition with the use of productivity-enhancing devices. Thus, the innovative processes of the eighteenth century were an outgrowth of, and a continuation of, earlier achievements, even if the rate of technological change after 1760 was in itself unprecedented (Sullivan 1989, p. 424–52).

CONTRIBUTORY FACTORS

Technological change was one of the several necessary causes, but not a sufficient cause of the Industrial Revolution. Although it is true that technological creativity is innate in human beings, its acceleration was aided by urbanization, which facilitated a creative response to the challenges of the increasing population pressure Europeans faced after 1750. The unprecedentedly large urban sector was important, because "technological innovation proves to have been of distinctly urban origin" (Bairoch 1991, pp. 159–76, esp. p. 165). Thus, in order for technological change to have accelerated, it was beneficial that many people were living in urban areas—already 25 percent of the population in England—where inventive activity was more likely to occur than in rural ones.

It should be should noted that the Industrial Revolution was essentially a regional phenomenon.[10] According to Francois Crouzet, the "industrial revolution was not made in England but in a few small districts of England—south Lancashire, some sectors of the East Midlands and Yorkshire, Birmingham, and the Black Country" (Crouzet 1985, p. 158; see also Tilly's Introduction in Kisch 1981, p. 16). East Anglia or Cornwall did not industrialize. Thus, we should not analyze the process at the level of the nation state.[11]

Another issue worth considering is that capital formation did not play as important a role during the early phase of the Industrial Revolution as the economic historians of the 1950s thought (Lewis 1954, p. 139–91, especially p. 155). It did not need to increase so dramatically for the Industrial Revolution to become reality.[12] The rate of saving in England increased from 5.7 percent of national income in 1760 to 7.9 percent in 1801, as a consequence, rather than as a cause, of the increased rate of output growth (Crafts 1985, p. 74).

Historians did not fully appreciate that productivity can increase not only through the accumulation of physical capital, or technological progress, but also through a number of other means. Institutional change, learning-by-doing, accumulation of human capital, decreasing mortality rates, increased financial sophistication, and positive externalities generated by the increasing population densities can all contribute to increasing labor productivity. In addition, fixed capital formation was not only financed from new savings, but also from existing circulating capital that was freed up through improvements in transportation and communication. The new methods of production increased the speed of throughput, thereby saving capital invested in inventories. Thus, during the classical phase of the Industrial Revolution (1760–1830), the stock of reproduceable fixed capital per capita increased by only 0.2 percent per annum (Feinstein 1978, p. 42, 84). Still, in historic terms, just being able to keep pace with rapid population growth was, in itself, a noteworthy achievement. The cost of installing the new machinery, moreover, was insignificant relative both to the cost of structures, a fair proportion of which was already in place, and to inventories and other circulating funds, which had been required earlier as well. Thus, the new requirements of fixed capital did not put an unusually large demand on savings, at least until the investment in railroads required bulky capital expenditures. The early machines were, as a rule, not very expensive. Many of the early designs could be constructed by skilled carpenters. There is no convincing evidence that industrialization on the continent was constrained by capital shortage either.[13]

The newly invented machines with which the Industrial Revolution is identified composed a small percentage of the capital stock. Watt's steam engine, for instance, spread slowly. Merely 5 percent of

British domestic fixed capital was composed of machinery in 1750, and according to Deane and Cole, machinery was 2.5 percent of national capital in 1800, and 4 percent in 1832 (Feinstein 1978, p. 88; Deane and Cole 1962, p. 142). Initially, the application of the new steam engines was limited to the cotton textile sector. Even half a century after the beginning of the Industrial Revolution, Britain's industry was primarily powered the same way it had been for hundreds of years, that is, by exploiting the potential energy of falling water (Reynolds 1983). As late as 1850 one-third of the power used in woolen textile manufacturing came from water power (Landes 1969, p. 104). Regardless of which aspect of the process one considers, capital formation, industrial organization, or mechanization, one finds that the transformation was less revolutionary than hitherto thought, and instead there was "gradual metamorphosis and considerable elements of continuity with the past" (Berg et al., 1983, p. 6).

Even in England the "modern sector employed fewer than 20 percent of all workers as late as 1841" (Jones 1988, p. 14). In fact, Jones concludes that "few aspects of economic life were thoroughly altered by 1850." It is telling that among the four largest employers in mid-nineteenth century England, a hundred years after the "revolution" got under way, three were not the ones we usually think of: agriculture, domestic service, and construction.

CONCLUSION

One can think of the Industrial Revolution as the culmination of an evolutionary process. The socioeconomic transformation of the late eighteenth century was a continuation of the expansion in economic activity of the sixteenth century. In the preindustrial world rapid population growth for an extended period meant that the procurement of food became ever more problematic and eventually led to a subsistence crisis of various proportions. At such times nature struck back with force, choosing poor harvests, inclement weather, or plagues as weapons of choice. Yet, by the nineteenth century the Malthusian threat had practically vanished from Europe for the first time: with the major obvious exception of the Irish potato famine. With the permanent dissolution of the Malthusian constraint, the population of Europe and of its overseas offshoots could multiply manifold without bringing about a major widespread subsistence crisis.

In addition, knowledge of disease control was sufficiently advanced by 1760 to prevent major outbreaks of the communicable diseases that had killed so many in prior centuries. The institution of quarantines and the development of a vaccine against smallpox are just two measures that counteracted the devastating effects of epidemic outbreaks (Riley 1987). The consequence of better distribution of nutrients, of better agricultural productivity, and of better control over the disease environment meant that the European population could continue to reproduce itself even in face of an extremely steep rise in its numbers.

Admittedly, even in the eighteenth century, as during prior episodes of rapid population growth (Appleby 1978, p. 95; Abel 1974), the threat of a Malthusian subsistence crisis of food shortages was still evident, as the last vestige of the Malthusian demographic regime. There is perhaps no better indication of the dangers posed by rapid population growth to the biological system than the fact that the physical stature of Europeans diminished.[14]

This biological adaptation to the Malthusian threat meant that people required fewer calories per capita in order to function at a given level of productivity.[15] Diets also changed to be more in tune with the higher relative prices of nutrients. By the 1760s people ate less, and meat and dairy products practically disappeared from the plate of the lower classes. However, a full blown existence crisis did not actually materialize (Abel 1966; Slicher van Bath 1963, p. 225; Komlos 1990, pp. 69–91). The economy was developed enough and productivity was growing sufficiently to give the population enough time to adapt to the new circumstances. Compared to the previous demographic upswing of the sixteenth century, production as well as trade in nutrients was much better developed by 1750. The New World provided nutrients in the form of sugar, dried cod, and flour, and most important, new products such as the potato which increased agricultural productivity greatly in the Old World (measured in calories per acre). In addition, regions of grain production in eastern Europe were integrated into the European trading network to a greater degree than ever before. Hence, western European town dwellers were able to procure nutrients on better terms of trade than in the sixteenth century. Moreover, transportation and storage facilities had improved sufficiently to distribute food locally to the indigent, so that subsistence crises did not return with the same vengeance as they had in the fourteenth, and again in the seventeenth centuries. Thus, more food was available per capita compared to similar phases of previous demographic expansions.

In sum, the Malthusian threat was overcome, and economic growth could become permanent (Komlos and Artzrouni 1990, pp. 269–87).

The positive forces for growth had been there all along. However, they were counterbalanced by the negative forces of malnutrition and disease. Once these countervailing forces weakened and eventually vanished, it became possible to escape from the food-controlled homeostatic condition that had prevailed since time immemorial; the process of economic development could proceed unhindered in the nineteenth century. Thus, nutrition played a crucial role in the Industrial Revolution.

The Industrial Revolution was an upswing in economic activity, in a succession of economic-demographic upswings. The eighteenth-century boom was special in that the marked acceleration in the rate of economic-demographic growth was not followed by major reversals that previously hindered further progress for centuries. However, the Industrial Revolution did not bring about an entirely new economic system. Most of the institutional and incentive structures of capitalism were already in place well before the eighteenth century (North 1990, p. 131). Capitalism was not an offspring of the Industrial Revolution: "What is called capitalism had long existed in western Europe. In one or another of its forms, it is as old as civilisation. . . . " (Clapham 1968, p. 2). Furthermore, property rights tended to be secure, and capital markets were highly integrated (Neal 1990).

The major difference between the Industrial Revolution and earlier episodes of expansion is that economic growth did not fizzle out eventually as it had done previously. The production function could continue shifting upward, through institutional and technological change, through capital accumulation, and other reasons, because population growth was no longer constrained by the availability of nutrients. Arguably, the upswing was much more intense than the prior ones. The performance appears somewhat disappointing only relative to expectations created by the use of the word "revolution," and by the records of economic performance achieved in many economies after World War II and in the East Asian economies more recently.

NOTES

1. See Toynbee's *Industrial Revolution* (Toynbee 1884, 1969); Landes (1998).

2. A thorough survey of the literature is found in Joel Mokyr, "Editor's Introduction: The New Economic History and the Industrial Revolution," in Joel Mokyr, ed. (1993) pp. 1–131.

3. See, for example, Crafts (1976; 1977; 1985); Harley (1982); pp. 267–89;

Also important in this regard was research on continental economies. For example, Richard Roehl (1976); O'Brien and Keyder (1978); Komlos (1983).

4. Here urban is defined as cities with at least 10,000 inhabitants. The generalization is not true for some regions, that is, Italy. Jan de Vries (1984), p. 30.

5. No wonder that Adam Smith was impressed by the gains in efficiency in the Birmingham and Sheffield cutlery trades (Pollard and Crossley 1969, p. 170).

6. According to Gregory King's calculation, as cited in Hartwell (1969), "Introduction," p. 25. See also Eric L. Jones, "Agriculture, 1700–80," in Floud and McCloskey (eds.), *The Economic History of Britain,* Vol I., p. 71.

7. T. S. Willan, *River Navigation in England* (London: F. Cass, 1964).

8. "Coal-fired salt pans were a commonplace before the end of the sixteenth century." E. Anthony Wrigley, "The Supply of Raw Materials in the Industrial Revolution," in Hartwell (ed.), *The Causes of the Industrial Revolution,* 1969 pp. 97–120, esp. p. 101.

9. Kisch (1981) pp. 41, 361; and see also Richard Tilly's introduction in Ibid., p. 17.

10. This is the view taken by Herbert Kisch, "The Textile industries in Silesia and the Rhineland: A comparative study in industrialization," *Journal of Economic History* 19 (1959): 541–64, and in Sidney Pollard (1981).

11. Wrigley is an exception in this regard, for he concludes that, "industrial growth was essentially a local rather than a national affair." Wrigley, "The Supply of Raw Materials," in Hartwell, ed. (1969) op. cit. p. 119.

12. "A dramatic change in the savings rate, such as W. W. Rostow posits for his 'takeoff', is certainly out of the question: there is no discernible institutional, political, economic, or social turning-point in the eighteenth century beyond which people quickly doubled their savings. On the other hand, there is no convincing evidence that the lack of savings held back growth." Hartwell, "Introduction," p. 18.

13. For an argument in the case of Germany see, Borchardt, *Perspectives on Modern German Economic History,* p. 18.

14. This sign of a Malthusian threat was evident to a small extent even in such a nutrition-rich environment as North America when population growth and urbanization proceeded at too quickly. John Komlos, "The Height and Weight of West Point Cadets, Dietary Change in Antebellum America," *Journal of Economic History* 47 (1987): 897–927.

15. John Komlos, *Nutrition and Economic Development in the Eighteenth Century Habsburg Monarchy: An Anthropometric History* (1989); A "decline in living standards in the towns of the early XIXth century . . . has been verified by anthropological research on the height of conscripts." Maurice Aymard, "The History of Nutrition and Economic History," *Journal of European Economic History* 2 (1973): 207–19, esp. p. 218.

BIBLIOGRAPHY

Abel, Wilhelm (1935, 1966). *Agrarkrisen und Agrarkonjunktur: Eine Geschichte der Lande und Ernehrungswirtschaft Mitteleuropas seit dem hohen Mittelalter.* Hamburg and Berlin: Paul Parey (reprint).
Abel, Wilhelm (1974). *Massenarmut und Hungerkrisen im Vorindustriellen Europa.* Hamburg and Berlin: Paul Parey.
Allen, G. C. (1946). *A short economic history of modern Japan 1867–1937.* London: Allen & Unwin.
Anderson, B. L. (1970). "Money and the Structure of Credit in the 18th Century." *Business History* XII.
Andreades, A. (1966). *A History of the Bank of England, 1640–1903.* New York: Augustus M. Kelly (reprint).
Appleby, Andrew (1978). *Famine in Tudor and Stuart England.* Stanford, CA: Stanford University Press.
Ashton, T. S. (1948). *The Industrial Revolution, 1760–1830.* London: Oxford University Press.
Asselain, Jean-Charles (1984). *Histoire Économique de la France du XVIIIe Siècle à nos Jours.* Paris: Editions du Seuil.
Avrich, Paul (1972). *Russian Rebels, 1600–1800.* New York: Norton.
Axtmann, Roland (1992). " 'Police' and the Formation of the Modern State: Legal and Ideological Assumptions on State Capacity in the Austrian Lands of the Habsburg Empire, 1500–1800." *German History*, 10.
Aymard, Maurice (1973). "The History of Nutrition and Economic History," *Journal of European Economic History* 2.
Bairoch, Paul (1991). "The City and Technological Innovation." In Higonnet et al., pp. 159–76.
Baykov, Alexander (1974). "The Economic Development of Russia." In Blackwell, ed., op.cit.
Beales, Derek (1987). *Joseph II,* vol. 1, *In the Shadow of Maria Theresa.* New York: Cambridge University Press.
Berg, Maxine (1980). *The Machinery Question and the Making of Political Economy 1815–1848.* Cambridge: Cambridge University Press.

Berg, Maxine, Pat Hudson, and Michael Sonenscher (1983). *Manufacture in Town and Country Before the Factory.*
Berghoff, H., and R. Möller (1994). "Tired Pioneers and Dynamic Newcomers." *Economic History Review,* 47.
Berlanstein, Lenard (1984). *The Working People of Paris 1871–1914.* Baltimore: Johns Hopkins University Press.
Bernard, Paul P. (1991). *From the Enlightenment to the Police State: The Public Life of Johann Anton Pergen.* Urbana and Chicago: University of Illinois Press.
Bernard, Paul P. (1994). "Poverty and Poor Relief in the Eighteenth Century." In Ingrao, ed., (1994) op. cit.
Blackwell, William L. (1968). *The Beginnings of Russian Industrialization, 1800–1860.* Princeton, NJ: Princeton University Press.
Blackwell, William L. ed. (1974). *Russian Economic Development from Peter the Great to Stalin.* New York: New Viewpoints.
Blackwell, William (1982). *The Industrialization of Russia: An Historical Perspective.* Arlington Heights, IL: Harlan Davidson.
Blanc, Simone (1974). *The Economic Policy of Peter the Great.* In Blackwell ed., (1974), op. cit.
Boller, Paul F., and Ronald Story (1992). *A More Perfect Union: Documents in U.S. History,* 3rd ed., vol. 1. Boston: Houghton Mifflin.
Borchardt, Knut (1972). "The Industrial Revolution in Germany, 1700–1914." In Cipolla, ed., *The Industrial Revolution,* op. cit.
Borchardt, Knut (1991). *Perspectives on Modern German Economic History and Policy.* New York: Cambridge University Press.
Brophy, James (1992). "The Political Calculus of Capital: Banking and the Business Class In Prussia, 1848–1856." *Central European History,* 25.
Brose, Eric Dorn (1993). *The Politics of Technological Change in Prussia: Out of the Shadow of Antiquity, 1809–1848.* Princeton, NJ: Princeton University Press.
Brown, Lawrence (1981). *Innovation Diffusion.* London: Methuen.
Buret, Eugène ([1840] 1979). *De la Misère des Classes Laborieuses en Angleterre et en France. De la Natur de la Misère, de son Existence, de ses Effets, de ses Causes, et de l'insuffisance des Remèdes qu'on lui a Opposés jusqu'ici; avec l'indication des Moyens Propres à en Affranchir les Sociétés.*" Paris: Paulin (photo reprint 1979 Paris: EDHIS).
Cain, P. J., and H. G. Hopkins (1986). "Gentlemanly Capitalism and British Expansion Overseas. I. The Old Colonial System, 1688–1850." *Economic History Review,* 2nd. ser. XXXIX:4, pp. 501–25.

Cameron, Rondo (1982). "The Industrial Revolution: A Misnomer." *The History Teacher,* 15.
Cameron, Rondo (1985). "A New View of European Industrialization." *Economic History Review,* 2nd ser., 38.
Cannadine, David (1983). "The Context, Performance and Meaning of Ritual: The British Monarchy and the 'Invention of Tradition.'" In Hobsbawm and Ranger, op. cit.
Cardwell, D. S. L. (1971). *From Watt to Clausius: The Rise of Thermodynamics in the Early Industrial Age.* Ithaca, NY: Cornell University Press.
Chevalier, Louis (1973). *Laboring Classes and Dangerous Classes in Paris During the First Half of the Nineteenth Century,* trans. Frank Jellinek. New York: Howard Fertig.
Cipolla, Carlo (1962, 1970). *The Economic History of World Population.* Baltimore: Penguin Books.
Cipolla, Carlo (1969). *Literacy and Development in the West.* Harmondsworth: Penguin Books.
Cipolla, Carlo, ed. (1973). *The Industrial Revolution.* vol. 3, The Fontana Economic History of Europe. Harmondsworth: Penguin.
Cipolla, Carlo (1980). *Before the Industrial Revolution: European Society and Economy 1000–1700.* New York: Norton.
Clapham, J. H. (1921, 1968). *The Economic Development of France and Germany 1815–1914.* Cambridge: Cambridge University Press.
Clough, Shepard B. (1939). *France: A History of National Economics, 1789–1939.* New York: Charles Scribner.
Clough, Shephard B. (1946). "Retardative Factors in French Economic Development in the Nineteenth and Twentieth Centuries," *Journal of Economic History.*
Cole, W. A. (1981). "Factors in Demand, 1700–80." In Floud and McCloskey, eds. op. cit.
Coleman, D. C. (1983). "Proto-industrialization: A Concept Too Many." *Economic History Review,* 2nd. ser. 36, pp. 435–48.
Coleman, William (1982). *Death is a Social Disease: Public Health and Political Economy in Early Industrial France.* Madison: University of Wisconsin Press.
Crafts, N. F. R. (1976). "English Economic Growth in the Eighteenth Century: A Re-examination of Deane and Cole's Estimates." *Economic History Review,* 29, 1977, pp. 226–35.
Crafts, N. F. R. (1977). "Industrial Revolution in Britain and France: Some Thoughts on the Question 'Why Was England First?'" *Economic History Review,* 30, 1977, pp. 429–41.

Crafts, N. F. R. (1985). *British Economic Growth During the Industrial Revolution.* Oxford: Clarendon Press.
Crafts, N. F. R., and C. K. Harley (1992). "Output and Growth and the British Industrial Revolution: A Restatement of the Crafts-Harley View." *Economic History Review,* 4.
Crouzet, Francois (1985). *The First Industrialists: The Problem of Origins.* Cambridge: Cambridge University Press.
Crouzet, Francois (1990). *Britain Ascendant: Comparative Studies in Franco-British Economic History,* trans. Martin Thorn. Cambridge: Cambridge University Press.
Daniel, Wallace (1995). "Entrepreneurship and the Russian Textile Industry: From Peter the Great to Catherine the Great." *The Russian Review,* vol. 54, January.
Deane, Phyllis (1969) *The First Industrial Revolution.* Cambridge: Cambridge University Press.
Deane, Phyllis, and W. A. Cole (1962). *British Economic Growth 1688–1959.* Cambridge: Cambridge University Press.
Dennis, M. A. (1997). "Historiography of Science: An American Perspective." In *Science in the Twentieth Century,* eds. John Krige and Dominique Pestre. New York: Harwood.
de Vries, Jan (1984). *European Urbanization 1500–1800.* Cambridge, MA: Harvard University Press.
Dumke, Rolf (1991). "Tariffs and Market Structures." In W. R. Lee, op. cit.
Dunn, Richard S. (1973). *Sugar and Slaves: The Rise of the Planter Class in the English West Indies, 1624–1713.* New York: Norton.
Dunoyer, Charles (1842). "Des Objections qu'on a Soulevées dans ces Deniers Temps Contre de la Concurrence." *Extrait du Journal des Economistes,* (BN Rp. 2175).
Dyer, Christopher (1989). *Standards of Living in the Later Middle Ages: Social Change in England c. 1200–1520.* Cambridge: Cambridge University Press.
Engelhardt, Ulrich (1981). "Zum Begriff der Glückseligkeit in der kameralistischen Staatslehre des 18. Jahrhunderts (J.H.G.v. Justi)." *Zeitschrift für historische Forschung,* 8.
Engelsing, Rolf (1973). *Analphabetentum und Lektüre: Zur Sozialgeschichte des Lesens in Deutschland zwischen feudaler und industrieller Gesellschaft.* Stuttgart: J. B. Metzlersche Verlagsbuchhandlung.
Evans, R. J. W. (1994). "Introduction: State and Society in Early Modern Austria." In Ingrao, ed. (1994), op. cit.
Falkus, Malcolm (1972). *The Industrialization of Russia, 1700–1914.* London: Macmillan.

Feinstein, Charles (1978). "Capital Formation in Great Britain." In Mathias and Postan, op. cit.
Feldenkirchen, Wilfried (1991). "Banking and Economic Growth." In W. R. Lee, op. cit.
Felix, David (1974). "Technological Dualism in Late Industrializers: On Theory, History, and Policy." *Journal of Economic History,* XXXIV:1, March.
Felix, David (1977). "The Technological Factor in Socio-Economic Dualism: Toward an Economy-of-Scale Paradigm for Development Theory." *Economic Development and Cultural Change,* 25 (supp.).
Floud, Roderick, and Donald McCloskey, eds. (1981). *The Economic History of Britain since 1700,* vol. 1: 1700–1860. Cambridge: Cambridge University Press.
Fremdling, Rainer (1991). "Foreign Competition and Technological Change." In W. R. Lee, ed. op. cit.
Gawthrop, Richard and Gerald Strauss (1984). "Protestantism and Literacy in Early Modern Germany." *Past and Present* 104.
Geertz, Clifford (1973). *The Interpretation of Cultures.* New York: Basic Books.
Gerschenkron, Alexander (1962). *Economic Backwardness in Historical Perspective: A Book of Essays.* Cambridge, MA: Harvard University Press.
Gerschenkron, Alexander (1963). "The Early Phases of Industrialization of Russia." In Rostow, ed. (1963), op.cit.
Gerschenkron, Alexander (1970). *Europe in the Russian Mirror: Four Lectures in Economic History.* London: Cambridge University Press.
Gillispie, Charles C. (1957a). "The Discovery of the Leblanc Process." *Isis,* 48.
Gillispie, Charles C. (1957b). "The Natural History of Industry." *Isis,* 48.
Gillispie, Charles C. (1980). *Science and Polity in France at the End of the Old Regime.* Princeton, NJ: Princeton University Press.
Glassl, Horst (1975). *Das österreichische Einrichtungswerk in Galizien (1772–1790).* Wiesbaden.
Good, David F. (1984). *The Economic Rise of the Habsburg Empire, 1750–1914.* Berkeley and Los Angeles: University of California Press.
Graff, Harvey (1987). *The Legacies of Literacy: Continuities and Contradictions in Western Culture and Society.* Bloomington: IN University Press.
Hall, A. Rupert (1974). "What did the Industrial Revolution in Britain

Owe to Science." In *Historical Perspectives: Studies in English Thought and Society in Honour of J. H. Plumb,* Neil McKendrick, ed. London: Europa.

Hammersley, G. (1991). "The Effect of Technical Change in the British Copper Industry Between the Sixteenth and the Eighteenth Centuries." *Journal of European Economic History,* 20.

Harley, Knick (1982). "British Industrialization Before 1841: Evidence of Slower Growth During the Industrial Revolution." *Journal of Economic History,* 42, pp. 267–289.

Harley, Knick (1993). "Reassessing the Industrial Revolution." In Mokyr, ed., 1993, op.cit.

Hartley, Jean F. (1983). "Ideology and Organizational Behavior." *International Studies of Man and Organizations,* 3.

Hartwell, R. Max (1961). "The Rising Standard of Living in England, 1800–1859." *Economic History Review,* 13.

Hartwell, R. Max (1969). "Introduction." In R. Max Hartwell, ed. *The Causes of the Industrial Revolution in England.* London: Methuen.

Heaton, Herbert (1937). "Financing the Industrial Revolution." *Bulletin of the Business Historical Society* XI, no. 2, February.

Heywood, Colin (1992). *The Development of the French Economy 1750–1914.* Cambridge: Cambridge University Press.

Hill, Christopher (1958). *Puritanism and Revolution.* London: Secker and Warburg.

Hill, Christopher (1984). *The World Turned Upside Down: Radical Ideas During the English Revolution.* Harmondsworth: Penguin.

Hobsbawm, Eric J., (1957). "The British Standard of Living, 1790–1859." *Economic History Review,* 10.

Hobsbawm, Eric J., and Terence Ranger (1983). *The Invention of Tradition.* Cambridge: Cambridge University Press.

Hoffman, Walther G. (1955). *British Industry 1700–1950.* Oxford: Basil Blackwell.

Holborn, Hajo (1969). *A History of Modern Germany, 1840–1945.* Princeton, NJ: Princeton University Press.

Horrell, Sara, and Jane Humphries (1992). "Old Questions, New Data and Alternative Perspectives: Families' Living Standards in the Industrial Revolution." *Journal of Economic History,* pp. 849–80.

Huck, Paul (1993). "Infant Mortality and the Standard of Living During the British Industrial Revolution." *Journal of Economic History,* pp. 528–50.

Ingrao, Charles (1994). *The Habsburg Empire, 1618–1815.* New York: Cambridge University Press.

Jennings, Francis (1976). *The Invasion of America: Indians, Colonialism and the Cant of Conquest.* New York: Norton.
Johnson, Paul, and Stephen Nicholas (1995). "Male and Female Living Standards in England and Wales, 1812–1857: Evidence from Criminal Height Records." *Economic History Review,* pp. 470–81.
Jones, Eric L. (1987). *The European Miracle: Environments, Economics and Geopolitics in the History of Europe and Asia,* 2nd ed. Cambridge: Cambridge University Press.
Jones, Eric L. (1988) *Growth Recurring: Economic Change in World History.* Oxford: Clarendon Press.
Jones, Robert (1976). "The Origin and Development of Media Exchange." *Journal of Political Economy* 84, August.
Jordan, Sonja (1967). *Die kaiserliche Wirtschaftspolitik im Banat im 18. Jahrhundert.* Munich: Oldenbourg.
Kahan, Arcadius (1974). "Continuity in Economic Activity and Policy During the Post-Petrine Period in Russia." In Blackwell, ed. op. cit.
Kahan, Arcadius (1985). *The Plow, the Hammer and the Knout: An Economic History of Eighteenth Century Russia.* Chicago: University of Chicago Press.
Kahan, Arcadius (1989). *Russian Economic History: The Nineteenth Century.* Chicago: University of Chicago Press.
Kann, Robert A. (1960). *A Study in Austrian Intellectual History.* New York: Praeger.
Kargon, Robert H. (1977). *Science in Victorian Manchester: Enterprise and Expertise.* Baltimore: Johns Hopkins University Press.
Kiesewetter, Hubert (1989). *Industrielle Revolution im Deutschland, 1815–1914.* Frankfurt: Suhrkamp.
Kiesewetter, Hubert (1991). "Competition for Wealth and Power: The Growing Rivalry Between Industrial Britain and Industrial Germany, 1815–1914." *Journal of European Economic History,* 20.
Kindleberger, Charles (1964). *Economic Growth in France and Britain, 1851–1950.* Cambridge, MA: Harvard University Press.
Kindleberger, Charles (1993). *A Financial History of Western Europe,* 2nd ed. New York: Oxford University Press.
Kisch, Herbert (1981). *Die Hausindustriellen Textilgewerbe am Niederrhein vor der Industriellen Revolution: Von der Urspringlichen zur Kapitalistischen Akkumulation.* Göttingen: Vandenhoeck and Ruprecht.
Kline, Ronald (1995). "Constructing 'Technology' as 'Applied Sci-

ence': Public Rhetoric of Scientists and Engineers in the United States, 1880–1945." *Isis,* 86.
Knodel, John (1967). "Law, Marriage and Illegitimacy in Nineteenth-Century Germany." *Population Studies,* 20.
Komlos, John (1983). *The Habsburg Monarchy as a Customs Union: Economic Development in Austria-Hungary in the Nineteenth Century.* Princeton, NJ: Princeton University Press.
Komlos, John (1989a). *Nutrition and Economic Development in the Eighteenth Century Habsburg Monarchy: An Anthropometric History.* Princeton, NJ: Princeton University Press.
Komlos, John (1989b). "Thinking About the Industrial Revolution." *Journal of European Economic History,* 18.
Komlos, John (1990). "Nutrition, Population Growth and the Industrial Revolution in England." *Social Science History,* 14.
Komlos, John (1993). "The Secular Trend in the Biological Standard of Living in the United Kingdom, 1730–1860." *Economic History Review,* pp. 115–44.
Komlos, John (1994). "The Nutritional Status of French Students." *Journal of Interdisciplinary History,* pp. 493–508.
Komlos, John (1995). "The Industrial Revolution as the Escape from the Malthusian Trap." Unpub. ms.
Komlos, John (1996). "The New World's Contribution to Food Consumption During the Industrial Revolution." Unpub. ms.
Komlos, John, and Marc Artzrouni (1990). "Mathematical Investigations of the Escape from the Malthusian Trap." *Mathematical Population Studies* 2.
Krieger, Leonard (1970). *Kings and Philosophers, 1689–1789.* New York: Norton.
Kühnel, Harry (1960). "Die soziale Betreuung des Personals der Linzer Wollzeugfabrik im Zeitalter des aufgeklärten Absolutismus. *Historisches Jahrbuch des Stadt Linz.*
Kussmaul, Ann (1990). *A General View of the Rural Economy of England 1538–1840.* Cambridge: Cambridge University Press.
Kuznets, Simon (1953). *Economic Change.* New York: Norton.
Lamberti, Marjorie (1989). *State, Society, and the Elementary School in Imperial Germany.* New York: Oxford University Press.
Landes, David S. (1969). *The Unbound Prometheus: Technological Change in Industrial Development in Western Europe from 1750 to the Present.* Cambridge: Cambridge University Press.
Landes, David S. (1998). *The Wealth and Poverty of Nations: Why are We so Rich and They so Poor?* New York: Norton.
Laski, Harold J. (1962). *The Rise of European Liberalism.* London: Unwin Books.

Laslett, Peter (1986). *The World We Have Lost,* 3rd ed. New York: Scribner.
Laudan, Rachel (1987). *From Mineralogy to Geology: The Foundations of a Science, 1650–1830.* Chicago: Chicago University Press.
Lee, W. R. (1977). *Population Growth, Economic Development and Social Change in Bavaria 1750–1850.* New York: Arno Press.
W. R. Lee, ed. (1991). *German Industry and Industrialization: Essays in German Economic and Business History in the Nineteenth Century.* London: Routledge.
Leuchtenmüller-Bolognese, Birgit (1981). "Bevölkerungspolitik zwischen Humanität, Realismus und Härte." In Herbert Matis, ed. *Von der Glückseligkeit des Staates: Staat, Wirtschaft und Gesellschaft in Österreich im Zeitalter des aufgeklärten Absolutismus.* Vienna.
Lévy-Leboyer, Maurice, and Francois Bourguignon (1990). *The French Economy in the Nineteenth Century: An Essay in Econometric Analysis,* trans. Jesse Bryant and Virginie Pérotin. Cambridge: Cambridge University Press.
Lewis, W. A. (1954). "Economic Development with Unlimited Supplies of Labour." *Manchester School,* 1954.
Licht, Walter (1995). *Industrializing America: The Nineteenth Century.* Baltimore: Johns Hopkins Press.
Lindert, Peter (1983). "English Living Standards, Population Growth and Wrigley-Schofield." *Explorations in Economic History,* pp. 131–55.
Lindert, Peter, and Jeffrey Williamson (1985). "The Standard of Living Debate and Optimal Economic Growth." In Joel Mokyr, ed., *Economics of the Industrial Revolution,* Totowa, NJ: Rowman and Allenheld.
Lockridge, Kenneth A. (1974). *Literacy in Colonial New England: An Enquiry into the Social Context of Literacy in the Early Modern West.* New York: Norton.
Lucier, Paul (1995). "Commercial Interests and Scientific Disinterestedness: Consulting Geologists in Antebellum America." *Isis,* 86
Lundgreen, Peter. (1975). "Industrialization and the Educational Formation of Manpower in Germany." *Journal of Social History* 9:64–80.
Maddison, Angus (1969). *Economic Growth in Japan and the USSR.* London: Allen & Unwin.
Maddison, Angus (1991). *Dynamic Forces in Capitalist Development: A Long-Run Comparative View.* Oxford: Oxford University Press.
Mathias, Peter (1969). *The First Industrial Nation, An Economic*

History of Britain, 1700–1914. New York: Charles Scribner's Sons.

Mathias, Peter, and M. M. Postan, eds. (1978). *The Cambridge Economic History of Europe* vol. 8, pt. 1, *The Industrial Economies: Capital, Labour and Enterprise.* Cambridge: Cambridge University Press.

Maynes, Mary Jo (1979). "The Virtues of Archaism: The Political Economy of Schooling in Europe, 1750–1850." *Comparative Studies in Society and History* 21.

Mayr, Otto (1976). "The Science-Technology Relationship as an Historiographic Problem." *Technology and Culture* 17.

McCaa, Robert (1995). "Spanish and Nahuatl Views on Smallpox and Demographic Catastrophe in Mexico." *Journal of Interdisciplinary History,* XXV:3, Winter, pp. 981–1008.

McCusker, John J., and Russell R. Menard (1985) *The Economy of British America, 1607–1789.* Chapel Hill: University of North Carolina Press.

McGrandle, Leith (1973). *The Cost of Living in Britain.* London: Wayland.

McKendrick, Neil (1973). "The Role of Science in the Industrial Revolution: A Study of Josiah Wedgwood as a Scientist and Industrial Chemist." In *Changing Perspectives in the History of Science: Essays in Honour of Joseph Needham,"* Mikulás Teich and Robert Young, eds. London: Heinemann.

Melton, James Van Horn (1994). "Introduction." In Ingrao, ed. (1994).

Mendels, Franklin (1972). "Proto-industrialization: The First Phase of the Industrial Revolution." *Journal of Economic History,* XXXII, pp. 241–61.

Mendenhall, William (1983). *Introduction to Probability and Statistics,* 6th ed. Boston: Duxbury Press.

Mitch, David (1992). *The Rise of Popular Literacy in Victorian England: The Influence of Private Choice and Public Policy.* Philadelphia: University of Pennsylvania Press.

Mitchell, B. R., and Deane, Phyllis (1971). *Abstract of British Historical Statistics.* Cambridge: Cambridge University Press.

Miyamoto, Mataji, Yotaro Sakudo, and Yasukichi Yasuba (1965). "Economic Development in Pre-Industrial Japan, 1859–1894." *Journal of Economic History,* XXV:4, pp. 541–564.

Mokyr, Joel (1977). "Demand vs. Supply in the Industrial Revolution." *Journal of Economic History,* 37, pp. 981–1008.

Mokyr, Joel, ed. (1985) *The Economics of the Industrial Revolution.* Totowa, NJ: Rowman and Allanheld.

Mokyr, Joel (1990). *The Lever of Riches: Technological Creativity and Economic Progress.* New York: Oxford University Press.

Mokyr, Joel, ed. (1993). *The British Industrial Revolution: An Economic Perspective.* Boulder, CO: Westview Press.

Mokyr, Joel (1994). "Technological Change, 1700–1830." In Roderick Floud and Donald McCloskey (1994), op.cit.

Mokyr, Joel, and Cormac O'Grada (1988). "Poor and Getting Poorer? Living Standards in Ireland Before the Famine." *Economic History Review,* pp. 209–35.

Morogues, Pierre Sébastien Bigot de (1832). *De la Misére des Ouvriers et de la Marche à Suivre pour y Remédier.* Paris: Dondey-Dupre.

Mueller, Christine L. (1994). "Enlightened Absolutism." *Austrian History Yearbook,* 25.

Musson, A. E. (1976). "Industrial Motive Power in the United Kingdom 1800–70." *Economic History Review,* 2nd ser. 29.

Musson, A. E. and Eric Robinson (1969). *Science and Technology in the Industrial Revolution.* Manchester: Manchester University Press.

Neal, Larry (1990). *The Rise of Financial Capitalism: International Capital Markets in the Age of Reason.* Cambridge: Cambridge University Press.

Nef, John U. (1977). "An Early Energy Crisis and Its Consequences." *Scientific American,* 237, November.

Nicholas, Stephen, and Peter Shergold (1987). "Human Capital and the Pre-Famine Irish Emigration to England." *Explorations in Economic History* 24.

North, Douglass C. (1966). *The Economic Growth of the United States, 1790–1860.* New York: Norton.

North, Douglass C. (1981). *Structure and Change in Economic History.* New York: Norton.

North, Douglass (1984). "Government and the Cost of Exchange in History." *Journal of Economic History,* June.

North, Douglass C. (1990). *Institutions, Institutional Change and Economic Performance.* Cambridge: Cambridge University Press.

O'Brien, Patrick (1982). "European Economic Development: The Contribution of the Periphery." *Economic History Review,* 2nd. ser. XXXV:1, February, pp. 1–18.

O'Brien, Patrick, and Caglar Keyder (1978). *Two Paths to the Twentieth Century: Economic Growth in Britain and France, 1780–1914.* London: Allen & Unwin.

O'Brien, Patrick, and Ronald Quinault, eds. (1993). *The Industrial Revolution and British Society.* Cambridge: Cambridge University Press.

Ohkawa, Kazushi, and Henry Rosovsky (1960). "The Role of Agriculture in Modern Japanese Economic Development." *Economic Development and Cultural Change,* IX:1, pt.2, October, pp. 43–67.

Olson, Richard (1990). *Science Deified and Science Defied: The Historical Significance of Science in Western Culture. Volume 2: From the Early Modern Age Through the Early Romantic Era, ca. 1640 to ca. 1820.* Berkeley: University of California Press.

Osterloh, Karl-Heinz (1970). *Joseph von Sonnenfels und die österreichische Reformbewegung im Zeitalter des aufgeklärten Absolutismus: Eine Studie zum Zusammenhang von Kameralwissenschaft und Verwaltungspraxis.* Lübeck and Hamburg: Matthiesen.

Pallot, Judith, and Denis J. B. Shaw (1990). *Landscape and Settlement in Romanov Russia.* Oxford: Clarendon Press.

Pipes, Richard (1992). *Russia Under the Old Regime.* New York: Collier Books.

Platonov, D. N. (1989). *Ivan Pososhkov.* Moscow: Ekonomika.

Pollard, Sidney (1981). *Peaceful Conquest: The Industrialization of Europe 1760–1979.* Oxford: Oxford University Press.

Pollard, Sidney, and David W. Crossley (1969). *The Wealth of Britain, 1085–1966.* New York: Schocken Books.

Pososhkov, Ivan (1987). *The Book of Poverty and Wealth.* Stanford, CA: Stanford University Press.

Postan, M. M. (1944). "The Rise of a Monetary Economy." *Economic History Review* 14.

Price, Roger (1975). *The Economic Modernization of France.* London: Croom Helm.

Ranis Gustav (1973). "Industrial Sector Labor Absorption." *Economic Development and Cultural Change,* XXI:3, April, pp. 387–408.

Ratcliffe, Barrie (1994). "Manufacturing in the Metropolis: The Dynamism and Dynamics of Parisian Industry at the Mid-Nineteenth Century." *Journal of European Economic History,* 23, Fall.

Reddy, William M. (1984). *The Rise of Market Culture: The Textile Trade and French Society, 1750–1900.* Cambridge: Cambridge University Press.

Reynaud, Jean (1832). "De la Nécessité d'une Représentation Spéciale pour les Prolétaires. *Revue Encyclopédique,* April.

Reynolds, Lloyd (1993). "The Spread of Economic Growth to the Third World, 1850–1980." *Journal of Economic Literature,* XXI, September, pp. 941–980.

Reynolds, Terry S. (1983). *Stronger than A Hundred Men: A History*

of the Vertical Water Wheel. Baltimore: Johns Hopkins Unversity Press.
Richardson, R. C., and G. M. Ridden, eds. (1986). *Freedom and the English Revolution*. Manchester: Manchester University Press.
Rider, Christine (1995). *An Introduction to Economic History*. Cincinnati, Ohio: South Western College Publishing.
Rieber, Alfred (1982). *Merchants and Entrepreneurs in Imperial Russia*. Chapel Hill: University of North Carolina Press.
Riley, James (1987). *The Eighteenth-Century Campaign to Avoid Disease*. London: Macmillan.
Roehl, Richard (1976). "French Industrialization: A Reconsideration." *Explorations in Economic History*, 13, pp. 233–281.
Roider, Karl A., Jr. (1994). "Reform and Diplomacy in the Eighteenth Century Habsburg Monarchy." In Ingrao, ed. (1994), op. cit.
Rosenberg, Nathan (1982). *Inside the Black Box*. Cambridge: Cambridge University Press.
Rosovsky, Henry, and K. Ohkawa (1961). "The Indigenous Components in the Modern Japanese Economy." *Economic Development and Cultural Change*, IX:4, April, pp. 476–501.
Rostow, Walter, W. (1960). *The Stages of Economic Growth: A Non-Communist Manifesto*. Cambridge, Cambridge University Press.
Rostow, Walter W. ed. (1963). *The Economics of Take-off into Sustained Growth*. London: St. Martin's Press.
Sandberg, Lars (1979). "The Case of the Impoverished Sophisticate: Human Capital and Swedish Economic Growth before World War I." *Journal of Economic History* 39.
Sandberg, Lars (1982). "Ignorance, Poverty and Economic Backwardness in the Early Stages of European Industrialization: Variations on Alexander Gerschenkron's Grand Theme." *Journal of European Economic History* 11.
Saxonhouse, Gary (1974). "A Tale of Japanese Technological Diffusion in the Meiji Period." *Journal of Economic History*, XXXIV:1, March, pp.149–165.
Schluenes, Karl (1979). "Enlightenment, Reform, Reaction: The Schooling Revolution in Prussia." *Central European History* 12.
Schofield, Richard (1973). "Dimensions of Illiteracy, 1750–1850." *Explorations in Economic History* 10.
Schofield, Robert E. (1957) "The Industrial Orientation of Science in the Lunar Society of Birmingham." *Isis*, 48.
Schofield, Robert E. (1963). *The Lunar Society of Birmingham: A Social History of Provincial Science and Industry in Eighteenth Century England*. Oxford: Oxford University Press.

Scholliers, Peter, ed. (1989). *Real Wages in Nineteenth and Twentieth-Century Europe.* New York: Berg.
Schultz, Theodore (1975). "The Value of the Ability to Deal with Disequilibria." *Journal of Economic Literature* 13.
Schwartz, L. D. (1985). "The Standard of Living in the Long Run: London, 1700–1860." *Economic History Review.*
Schwartz, L. D. (1992). *London in the Age of Industrialisation: Entrepreneurs, Labour Force and Living Conditions.* Cambridge: Cambridge University Press.
Sibum, Heinz Otto (1995). "Reworking the Mechanical Value of Heat: Instruments of Precision and Gestures of Accuracy in Early Victorian England." *Studies in History and Philosophy of Science,* 26.
Sismondi, Simonde de (1827). *Nouveaux Principes d'économie Politique.* Paris.
Slack, P. A. (1990). *The English Poor Law.* Basingstoke: Macmillan.
Slicher van Bath, B. H. (1963) *The Agrarian History of Western Europe, A.D. 500–1850.* London: Edward Arnold.
Smith, Thomas C. (1988). *Native Sources of Japanese Industrialization, 1750–1920.* Berkeley: University of California Press.
Solar, Peter M. (1995). "Poor Relief and English Economic Development Before the Industrial Revolution." *Economic History Review,* XLVII,1, pp.1–22.
Sonnenfels, Joseph von (1777). "Über das Wort Bevölkerung." In *Politische Abhandlungen,* Vienna: J. Edlen.
Spengler, Joseph J. (1942). *French Predecessors of Malthus: A Study in Eighteenth-Century Wage and Population Theory.* Durham, NC: Duke University Press.
Staudenmaier, John (1985). *Technology's Storytellers: Reweaving the Human Fabric.* Cambridge, MA: MIT Press.
Stewart, Larry (1986). "Public Lectures and Private Patronage in Newtonian England." *Isis,* 48
Stewart, Larry (1992). *The Rise of Public Science: Rhetoric, Technology, and Natural Philosophy in Newtonian England, 1660–1750.* Cambridge: Cambridge University Press.
Stone, Lawrence (1979). *The Family, Sex, and Marriage in England, 1500–1800.* New York: Harper & Row.
Stoneman, P. (1983). *The Economic Analysis of Technological Change.* Oxford: Oxford University Press.
Sullivan, Richard (1989). "England's 'Age of Invention': The Acceleration of Patents and Patentable Invention During the Industrial Revolution." *Explorations in Economic History,* 26.
Taeuber, Irene (1960). "Urbanization and Population Change in the

Development of Modern Japan." *Economic Development and Cultural Change,* IX:1, October, pp. 1–28.

Thackray, Arnold (1970). "Science and Technology in the Industrial Revolution." *History of Science,* 9.

Thomas, Brinley (1954). *Migration and Economic Growth.* Cambridge: Cambridge University Press.

Thomas, Brinley (1988). *The Industrial Revolution and the Atlantic Economy.* London: Routledge.

Thomas, Colin (1983–84). "The Anatomy of a Colonization Frontier—The Banat of Temesvar." *Austrian History Yearbook,* 19–20

Thomas, R. P., and D. N. McCloskey (1981). "Overseas Trade and Empire, 1700–1860." In Floud and McCloskey, eds. op.cit.

Tilly, Charles, Louise Tilly, and Richard Tilly (1991). "European Economic and Social History in the 1990s." *Journal of European Economic History* 20.

Tilly, Richard (1990). *Vom Zollverein zum Industriestaat: Die Wirtschaftlich-soziale Entwicklung Deutschlands 1835 bis 1914.* Munich: Deutscher Taschenbuch Verlag.

Tipton, Frank (1974). "The 'National Consensus' in German Economic History." *Central European History,* 7.

Toynbee, A. J. (1969 [1884]). *Industrial Revolution,* London: David and Charles Reprints.

Traugott, Mark, ed. and trans. (1993). *The French Worker: Autobiographies from the Early Industrial Era.* Berkeley: University of California Press.

Trevor-Roper, Hugh (1983). "The Invention of Tradition: The Highland Tradition of Scotland." In Hobsbawm and Ranger, op. cit.

Tsurumi, E. Patricia (1992). *Factory Girls: Women in the Thread Mills of Meiji Japan.* Princeton, NJ: Princeton University Press.

Tudesq, André-Jean ([1840–49] 1967). *Les Grands Notables en France.* Paris, 2 vols.

Tunzelmann, Nick von (1994): "Technology in the Early Nineteenth Century." In Floud and McCloskey (1994), op. cit

Usher, A.P. (1934). "The Origin of Banking." *Economic History Review* 4.

Villermé, Louis-Réné ([1840] 1989). *Tableau de l'état Physique et Moral des Ouvriers Employés dans les Manufactures de Coton, de Laine, et de Soie.* Paris: Renouard; reprinted 1989 by Jean-Pierre Chaline and Francis Démier, Etudes et Documentations Internationales.

Wangermann, Ernst (1973), *The Austrian Achievement, 1700–1800.* London: Thames and Hudson.

Ward, J. R. (1994). "The Industrial Revolution and British Impereri-alism." *Economic History Review,* XLVII, pp. 44–65.
Ward, W. Peter (1993). *Birth Weight and Economic Growth: Women's Living Standards in the Industrializing West.* Chicago: University of Chicago Press.
Westfall, Richard S. (1980). *Never at Rest: A Biography.* Cambridge: Cambridge University Press.
Williamson, Jeffrey (1985). *Did British Capitalism Breed Inequality?* London: Allen & Unwin.
Wolfe, Eric R. (1982). *Europe and the People without History.* Berkeley: University of California Press.
Wrightson, K. (1986). "The Social Order of Early Modern England: Three Approaches." In L. Bonfield, R. M. Smith and K. Wrightson eds. *The World We Have Gained: Histories of Population and Social Structure.* Oxford: Blackwell.
Wrigley, E. A., and R. S. Schofield (1993). *The Population History of England, 1541–1871: A Reconstruction.* Cambridge: Cambridge University Press.
Zahediah, Nuala (1994). "London and the Colonial Consumer in the Late Seventeenth Century." *Economic History Review,* XLVII, 2, pp. 239–61.

INDEX

absolutism, 8, 33
  in Austria, 34, 38
  in Russia, 129, 142
America, colonial, economy of, 71–71
Ampère, André Marie, 103
anthropometric history, 172–74
Arago, François, 103
Arkwright, Richard, 240
Atlantic economy, 63–65, 69, 78
Austria, 5, 33ff

Beacon, Francis, 92, 93
Banat of Temesvar, 40, 44, 45
banking, 27, 153
beggars, in Austria, 43
Berthollet, Claude, 100
Bismarck, Otto von, 149
bleaching, 90, 100–102, 114, 116
Bohemia, 42
Britain, Great, 59
  creation of 50ff
"Britishness," 50, 58, 59–60, 61–62, 66
Buret, Eugène, 182, 183, 184, 195–98
Business College, Russian, 130

cameralism, 36–37, 46–47
Cameron, Rondo, 26
capital deepening, 213
capitalism, 90, 154, 246
Carnot, Sadi, 103
Catherine II, 142
Catholicism, 19, 20, 21–22, 24
Celtic Fringe, 59
charcoal, 123
chemistry, 94, 97–102
child labor, 52, 194
child labor laws, 194, 195
civil society, lack of in Russia, 141–42
Civil Wars, English, 55, 57, 66

class 51, 186
  in Russia, 133, 143
coal, 115, 121
  in iron industry, 100, 116
College of Manufactures, Russian, 130, 135
College of Mines, Russian, 130, 135
colonization, 64, 72–75
  internal, in Austria, 44–46
commandité bank, German, 154
competition, 155
cotton textile industry, 112–14, 118, 122–23
Crafts, Nick, 170, 238
Cromwell, Oliver, 56

Dalton, John, 95, 104–5
debt, in Russia, 140
Desaguliers, John, 94, 104
Descartes, René, 92–93
development, economic, 203, 221, 226
dualism, 207–12, 215, 224, 238
  in Japan, 222
Dunoyer, Charles, 181, 188, 198–200

economic growth
  American, 28, 71
  British, 238
  Prussian, 28–31
economic history, study of, 158–59
economies of scale, 122–24, 213, 216, 237
education, 157–58
  compulsory, 28
  importance of, 18, 233–34
  technical, in Prussia, 19, 27–28
Elizabeth I, 52, 57, 66
enclosures, 53, 58

engineering, 91, 102–7
  in Britain, 104–5
  in France, 102–4
  in Germany, 103
entrepreneurship, 91, 157
  English and German, compared, 157–58
  Russian, 132, 136, 138
epidemics, 172

family, 50
finance, importance of, 236
finance direct investment, 225
France, 179ff
  development "lag," 167
freemen, in Russian labor force, 139
Friedrich Wilhelm, 156

Galicia, 36, 44, 45, 46
Gay-Lussac, Joseph, 103
geology, 103
George III, 64
Germany, 147–59
  literacy in, 17 ff
  unification of, 151, 156
Gerschenkron, Alexander, 28, 133, 148–49, 237
"Glorious Revolution," 66
growth theory
  neoclassical, 206–7
  Smithian, 74, 75, 76
guild, weakening of, 38
Gutenberg, Johann, 20
Gwynedd, fall of, 60

Habsburg Empire, 5, 45
Hargreaves, James, 240
Harley, Knick, 238
Hartwell, R. M., 166
health, 39, 172–74, 244
  and industrialization, in France, 191–200
Highland Clearances, 62
Hobsbawn, Eric, J., 166
Holy Roman Empire, 151

ideology, 50, 180, 200
illegitimacy, 39
income insecurity, 203
Industrial Revolution, 1–4, 89, 109ff, 158, 168, 179, 234–46

  in Britain, 49, 234–35, 238–40
  and capital formation, 123, 243–44
  colonial contribution to, 69ff
  failure of, in Russia, 129, 133–34
  and family structures, 50–52, 66
  in France, 179ff
  in Germany, 31, 148–58
  in Japan, 216–26
  and living standards, 165ff, 182–85, 190–93
  mechanization and, 112–14, 116, 117, 220, 241–44
  military influence on, 156
  perceptions of, 180–201
  recconceptualization of, 238
  regional differences, 150–52, 241, 242
  science in, 89
  significance of, 2–3, 65, 126, 234
  timing of, 33, 49, 58, 118–19, 214
industrialization, 204–5, 223
  characteristics of, 4, 205–6, 213, 219–20, 237
  and immorality, 182, 192–94
  problems with, 149, 174, 187, 213–14, 224
  rural, 52, 143
industry, Russian
  under Catherine II, 142–43
  government control of, 134–37, 142
  under Peter I, 130–32, 136, 139
  under Peter I's successors, 132, 137–41
  "privatization" of, 136
innovation, diffusion of, 98, 99, 109ff, 213
  in iron, 100, 114–16
  in paper making, 116
  in textiles, 100, 112–14
Ireland, 53, 63
iron industry, 100
  technological advances in, 100, 114–16

Jacquard loom, 116–17
Japan, 203ff
  cotton textiles in, 220
  industrialization of, 216–26
  infrastructure in, 219
  traditional industry, 221, 222
Joseph II, 33, 34, 38, 41, 45
Junker, 24, 149
Justi, Johann Heinrich von, 37

INDEX

Kahan, Arcadius, 133
Kaunitz, Wenzel von, 35
Kiesewetter, Hubert, 150, 156
Kisch, Herbert, 241

labor, Russian, 138–40
  unfree, in Russian industry, 138–39
laissez-faire, 156
Lavoisier, A., 93–94
liberalism, 180–82
literacy, 5, 17ff, 54–56
  in Baden, 22–23
  in Bavaria, 23–27
  demand for, 19–21
  and economic growth, 5, 26–27
  in Germany, 17–32
  and income, 28–31
  measurement of, 17–18, 25, 29
  and Pietism, 19, 21
  and Protestantism, 18–19
  in Prussia, 27–31
  and religious differences, 21–23
  and schooling, 21–22, 28–31
  signature, 17, 18, 24, 55
  supply of, 21–23
  in Vaucluse, 21–23
Lunar Society, 96–97
Luther, Martin, 19, 20
Lutheranism, 19
Lyon, industrial agitation in, 189

Malthus, Thomas, 24
Malthusian ceiling, 3, 71
Malthusian crisis, 76, 235, 244, 245–46
Malthusian trap (*see* Malthusian ceiling, Malthusian crisis)
Maria Theresa, 34, 35, 38, 40, 43, 44
marriage, 38
Meiji Restoration, 218–19
metal industry, Russian, 130, 131
Methodism, 61
middle class, in Russia, 143
migration, 18
Mokyr, Joel, 49, 58, 70, 165
monarchy, British, 60, 65
money, paper, 26, 236

National Endowment for the Humanities, 233
Navigation Act, 81
Newcomen engine, 119–20, 240

Newton, Isaac, 90, 93
New World, 69, 79–80
Nicholas I, 129

Ottoman Empire, 44

paper making, 116
Parliament, in Britain, 58
passport, internal, in Russia, 140
patents, 111, 124
peasant revolts, 20
pensions, in Austria, 41
Peter I, 129, 130–32, 136–38, 139
Philosophes, 99
philosophical societies, 95–96
Pietism, 19, 21
Poor Law, 52–54
populationism, 33–34, 36–37
population policies, 34, 36–38, 39–40
  limitations of, 45–46
Pososhkov, Ivan, 141–42
poverty, 41, 182ff
  causes of, 41–42, 183, 187
  relief of, 40–42, 52–54
Priestly, Joseph, 95
printing press, 20
Pripisnye (assigned peasants), 139
proletarian, 185–86
property rights, 237
  absence of in Russia, 135–47
  and liberty, 141
prostitution, 39–40
protectionism, 24, 214, 215
Protestantism, 56–57, 66
Prussia, 27–31, 35
Pugachev, Emelian, 140, 142
pyrometer, ceramic, 97–98

railroads, 116, 121, 125–26, 156
  in Japan, 221
  and literacy, 26
Reformation, 18, 56–57
  in Britain, 56, 61, 62, 66
  and literacy, 18–19
relative backwardness, 132–34
religion, 56
  in Britain, 56–57, 59, 60
"revisionists," 170
Rosenburg, Hans, 149
Ruhr, 151
Russia, 129–44

267

Saint-Simonian movement, 186, 189
Saxony, 151
Say, Jean Baptiste, 188
school, attendance laws, 22
school, funding of, 22
schooling, and literacy, 21–22
science, role of, 89ff
  in Britain, 94–98
  in France, 99–102
  lectures on, 95
Scientific Revolution, 55, 89, 92, 240
scientific societies, 95–96
Scotland, 53, 61–62
  civil war in, 57
Shogun, 217, 218–19
signature literacy, 17, 18, 24, 55
Silesia, 151
Sismondi, Simone de, 185, 187
slave labor, 72, 77
Smeaton, John, 105–6
Sonderweg, 148–50
Sonnenfels, Joseph von, 33, 36, 43
Spearman test, 29–31
spinning jenny, 112
standard of living, 37–38, 165, 182–85, 190–93
  in England, 166–67
  in France, 167
  measurement of, 168–74
  and real wage, 169–72
state policy making
  in Austria, 34–36, 46–47
  in Germany, 153–54
steam engine, 104, 107, 119–22
  in cotton industry, 121–22, 125
  development of, 119–20
  diffusion of, 107, 120–24
  high pressure, 121
  in iron industry, 123
Stone, Lawrence, 50
structural change, 158

Tatishchev, V. N., 135, 137
technical education, 19
technological change, 69, 90, 155, 136, 238–42
technological diffusion, 91
  influences on, 110–11, 214–15
technology, 91, 95, 98, 207, 209, 210, 212, 223
  in cotton industry, 100, 112–14, 122, 220
  in Germany, 155–56
  in iron industry, 114–16, 123
  in Japan, 220
  in linen industry, 241
  in Russia, 130
textile industry,
  in Britain, 112–14, 117–18, 122–23
  in Japan, 220
  in Russia, 131, 132
Tilly, Richard, 151, 158
Tokugawa era, 217–18
trade, 70, 72, 214, 225
  British, 18th century, 80–81
  colonial, 72, 77–78
  composition of, 72, 79
  Russian, 131, 132
  Russian, internal, 143
transportation, improved, 205, 240

underconsumption theory, 187
underdevelopment paradox, 207–8
unemployment, 187, 211, 212, 215
  technological, 204
universal banks, 27
urbanization, 58, 74, 239, 242
utilitarianism, 181

vagrancy, 43
Villermé, Louis Réné, 184, 185, 186, 189–95, 197

wage, subsistence, 53
wages
  in Britain, 169
  in France, 171, 186, 187, 191, 195
  in Russia, 140
Wales, 53, 60–61
waterpower, 117, 122, 125
Watt, James, 96, 101, 106–7, 120
wealth, 24–25, 186
Wedgwood, Josiah, 97–98
Werner, Abraham Gottlob, 103
women and children, status of, 51, 66
wool industry
  Austrian, 41
  Russian, 132, 136

Zaibatsu, 225
Zollverein, 24, 152, 154, 155, 156